IGNITE

THE

HUNGER

IN YOU

IGNITE

is proud to share our many other international best-selling compilation books in the Ignite Series. Our books have reached best-selling status in 26 countries and 187 categories. We know there is one that you will love.

———————

Ignite Your Life for Women

Ignite Your Female Leadership

Ignite Your Parenting

Ignite Your Life for Men

Ignite Your Life for Conscious Leaders

Ignite Your Adventurous Spirit

Ignite Your Health and Wellness

Ignite Female Change Makers

Ignite the Modern Goddess

Ignite Love

Ignite Happiness

Ignite Your Inner Spirit

Ignite The Entrepreneur

Ignite Possibilities

IGNITE
THE
HUNGER
IN YOU

HOW TO DEVELOP YOUR GREATNESS
AND IGNITE HUMANITY

FEATURING #1 MOTIVATIONAL SPEAKER

LES BROWN

The world's most renowned motivational speaker,
author, mentor, and inspirational advocate

FOREWORD BY

John-Leslie Brown

President of Les Brown Enterprises

INTRODUCTION BY

JB Owen

Founder and CEO of Ignite and JBO Global Inc.

PRESENTED BY

ASHLEY MONTGOMERY • ASHLEY PATTERSON • ATUL BHATARA • CHAD E. FOSTER
CURTIS GHEE • DIANA LOCKETT • ERASMO RIVERA • ERMOS EROTOCRITOU • FELECIA FROE, M.D.
GLENN LUNDY • HOLLY H. KALUA, RN • JACKI SEMERAU TAIT • JAMEELA ALLEN • JB OWEN
JENISE 'SANDY' TODD • JESSICA T. MOORE • JOCELYN MCCLURE • JO DEE BAER
KATHERINE VRASTAK • LES BROWN • MARCY CODY, RN • MAYNARD NEAL • NIK REYNO
PAMELA BISHOP • PAT LABEZ • PATRICIA BARNES • PEARLETTE CASSELLS • RACHEL HARVEY
DR. RAOLEE • RENEE L. CUNNINGHAM • SHASHONEE L. SALES • STACIE SHIFFLETT • STEPH ELLIOTT
SUSAN WELTON • SUZANNE A. NAKANO • DR. TYRA GOOD • DR. YASMINE SAAD

PUBLISHED BY IGNITE AND PRINTED BY JBO GLOBAL INC.

Publisher's Note: We are delighted to offer the fifteenth compilation, and first Platinum book, in the IGNITE series. Our mission is to produce inspiring, motivational, and authentic real-life stories that will Ignite your life. Each book contains unique stories told by exceptional authors. They are of the highest caliber to offer engaging, profound, and life-changing examples that will impact the reader. Our mandate is to build a conscious, positive, and supportive community through our books, speaking events, writing workshops, Ignite experiences, podcasts, immersions, a TV show, and our product marketplace. We always welcome new book ideas and new authors onto our platform. Should you desire to be published and featured in an Ignite book, please apply at www.igniteyou.life/apply or reach out to us at support@igniteyou.life.

Published and printed by JBO Global Inc.
5569-47th Street Red Deer, AB
Canada, T4N1S1 1-877-677-6115

Cover design by Dania Zafar and JB Owen
Book design by Dania Zafar
Designed in Canada, Printed in China
ISBN 978-1-7923-4177-9 (hardcover)
ISBN 978-1-7923-4176-2 (softcover)
ISBN: 978-1-7923-4178-6 (eBook)
First edition: October 2021

Ordering Information: Quantity sales. Special discounts are available on quantity purchases by corporations, associations, and others. For details, contact the publisher at the above address. Programs, products, or services provided by the authors are found by contacting them directly. Resources named in the book are found in the resources pages at the back of the book.

This book is dedicated to:

Les Brown's mother, Mamie Brown, for gifting the
world with Les' greatness.

JB Owen's mother, Valentine Owen, for igniting the
world with JB.

all the authors' mothers for bringing them into the world
so that they can inspire you.

your mother for the treasure of life that she gave you.

TESTIMONIALS FROM OUR AUTHORS

I attempted to self-publish a book that I began writing four years ago, which turned out to be a disaster. Then I met JB Owen and her awesome, high-energy Ignite team who helped me revitalize my book and placed me on the path to completion. In addition, I have also become an Ignite author through the book *Ignite the Hunger in You* with the great Les Brown. This entire high-level experience with Ignite has been empowering, educational, and simply fun!

— Curtis Ghee

I want to say that writing with Ignite was an amazing experience. Every time I felt stuck, JB and the team were always there to help out. This was my first book as a co-author and the experience was amazing. The training was very valuable and I got to meet incredible human beings. Working with Ignite, JB, and the support team has been an amazing experience, full of value and support. I am a first-time author and the experience has been awesome. I highly recommend Ignite. Thank you!

— Erasmo Rivera

JB and the entire team at Ignite have been nothing short of miraculous. They have managed to transform me into an actual author. My experience could not have been better and my very high expectations were greatly exceeded. The support I received and continue to receive is off the charts. I went from zero experience, to now working on my solo book with the expectation of writing multiple books in the near future. Words cannot express my gratitude for everything they have done for me.

— Ermos Erotocritou

JB Owen truly ignited the inner author in me! Teaming up with JB and her extraordinary editors not only made the seemingly impossible task of becoming a best-selling author a reality, they helped me realize that sharing my story can genuinely help to inspire others to make today, tomorrow's successful yesterday!

— Holly H. Kalua, RN

My favorite part about Ignite as a writer was working one-on-one with the editors. They take their time to understand why you wrote certain things and help you craft your story to perfection. I'm grateful. Thanks Ignite! XOXO

— Patricia Barnes

As an author, one of the things that's most important to me is that my voice is the one that's being heard through my writing. I'm very pleased with the work that the Ignite family did to assure that. Each phase was a joy to work through and I'm excited to share my story with the world. Many thanks to JB Owen and the entire Ignite team!

— Jocelyn McClure

I've had an adventurous and storied life to this point, at 67 years of age. Oftentimes, when senior adults 'tell their story,' it becomes a decade drone of a personal resume. My writing experience with Ignite allowed me to 'hone in' and go deep on what has made me who I am today — my two Ignite Moments bring them and me into a new light and life! Now, my story has true relational relatability.

— Jo Dee Baer

Ignite's editing team is amazing at their craft of editing/writing. Having great editors for both of my edits is a treasured gift I'm eternally grateful for. The Ignite team is really talented at finding the right words to say what I was needing help on. Their ability to help me get focused on my messaging was also appreciated. JB was amazing at putting her loving touches where I needed it the most. Helping me to find quotes that aligned with my messaging was so valuable. I could not have done it without the Ignite team. I'm forever grateful for this AMAZING opportunity to be in *Ignite the Hunger in You* with Les Brown. It's a dream come true.

— Katherine Vrastak

This is my fourth published book, but my experience with Ignite has taken my writing skills, confidence, and reach to a much higher level. The one-on-one and group editing sessions were amazing! The marketing resources are phenomenal and the book is something that I will leave as a legacy for generations to come. Les Brown and JB Owen are master storytellers. To have input from both of them to help craft my story has been an unforgettable and extremely empowering experience. I feel like I have grown as an author thanks to Ignite.

— Marcy Cody, RN

This experience has been life-changing. The entire team has been thorough and operates in a spirit of excellence. They were able to inspire and empower me to tap deep in my soul and allow me to shine. I enjoyed the tender care shown throughout the entire process. They have mastered the process of unlocking your potential and showing you how to be your best. Thank you all!

— Renee L. Cunningham

Writing my story has been an exceptionally fulfilling, adventurous, and exhilarating journey. After many years of having the aspiration of becoming a published author, Ignite has been a very instrumental force in making this a reality. Working with the dynamic JB Owen and her team of extremely accomplished managers, editors, strategists, and designers has been an unforgettable experience. Without their loving support coupled with their extraordinary professionalism, I could not have achieved this milestone. Thank you Ignite for being a team of superheroes (and super-sheroes)! May God bless you all!

— Jenise 'Sandy' Todd

My dreams have come true thanks to the Ignite team and their staff! My story will finally be told, and if it serves one person on their journey, then my cup is full. Thank you!

— Steph Elliott

At first I was extremely anxious about writing my story for others to see. Then I met many wonderful people along the way to help me and the Ignite team kept me on track. Now I cannot believe I am an author!! And looking forward to doing it again! Thank you to JB Owen, her team, and Les Brown.

— Susan Welton

Working with JB and the Ignite team was truly a liberating and holistic experience. Their expertise, patience, and guidance helped me to develop a deeper level of confidence in sharing my story through writing from a place of unapologetic joy and boldness. The Ignite Community created a space for us to connect to our #GOODWithin and form worldwide friendships that will continue to uplift each other and transform lives through the power of our stories.

— Dr. Tyra Good

It has been a joy working with Ignite! The entire process has been very professional including the writing guidelines, the editing sessions, and the weekly live zoom trainings with JB Owen and Les Brown. I have stepped well out of my comfort zone easily in this supportive and nurturing environment. Ignite's formula, combined with their capabilities and competencies, provides a unique opportunity to acquire valuable skills that create continued success as an author and as an entrepreneur on a mission! Thank you JB Owen and Ignite!

— Stacie Shifflett

I am proud to share that I am a third time author with Ignite and, each time, I continue to be in awe of the quality and attention to detail throughout each part of the writing process, from the weekly masterminds, to the writer's nests, and the skillfulness of each editing experience. The Ignite team works tirelessly to champion the authors and build confidence for first-time authors while allowing their voice, their story, and their authenticity to shine through. Each time I have contributed to a book, I have learned more about myself, my writing, and how to take the seat of the reader. When you join the Ignite 'family,' you join a powerful and committed community of conscious leaders and authors with a shared vision to Ignite possibilities in the world. JB Owen is a heart-centered leader, a motivational coach, and an inspiration for what is achievable in one's life and how community can truly make an impact in the world.

— Diana Lockett

Through your writing, you give voice to your journey and the gifts that you discovered along the way. These gifts light up the path for others to shine. I highly encourage you to write your story. Ignite Publishing, its founder JB Owen, and its amazing team make the process very smooth for you. They share their gifts with you to create a chain reaction of people lighting up the path for others. It is a beautiful journey to embark on.

— Dr. Yasmine Saad

Divine timing is so real! Whether you picked up this book by chance, bought it to support a friend, or felt encouraged to look into starting your journey as an author, THIS is your sign that Ignite Publishing is for you! JB Owen and her team pour so much love and value into their authors, you will find yourself overflowing with tools, ideas, and excitement to do above and beyond what you've considered for yourself before. There is so much power in each individual's story and the entire Ignite family will make sure your voice is heard to make the greatest impact on the reader. That's the definition of Greatness: to inspire the next person to inspire others and so on. So, take a deep breath. You'll be taken care of well here. Your story is meant to be shared to ignite the hunger in others. Take the leap and join the family!

— Nik Reyno

It was a pleasure working with JB, Peter and the TEAM. They were professional, detail-oriented, and ensured that our stories were captured in a way that depict who we are and our experiences. Their care for the author is unmatched. I highly recommend them.

— Pearlette Cassells

TABLE OF CONTENTS

PREFACE
Message from the Publisher

It is not every day that the number one motivational speaker on the planet and the leaders in empowerment publishing come together to make something cataclysmically inspiring for the world.

As we stepped into producing our fifteenth book, and the first book in our Platinum series, we knew we wanted something that would be impactful, heartfelt, and recognizable around the globe. It didn't take us long to settle on one of the most iconic and influential individuals in the area of self-development and personal growth — Les Brown. Les is a legend in his field, and at IGNITE when we do something, we want it to be the best. Not for us, but for our authors and for you, our readers. We wanted to create the most memorable experience possible and make sure the stories are of the highest caliber and with the most genuine intentions; something you know you will get when you partner with Les Brown.

Les' charismatic personality, along with his truly divine messages of hope, faith, and inspiration, were an ideal fit for the next IGNITE book. Our goal at IGNITE is to Ignite a billion lives with a billion words and we knew that Les shares the kind of words that definitely Ignite lives! His passion for people and his obsession to help others make him the kind of speaker, author, presenter, and mentor that you can't help but hang on to every word he says. Not just through storytelling, but by sharing lessons and offering hope, Les' style of teaching is to truly connect with the heart of the listener. The more and more Les and I worked together, we discovered our common love for speaking for the ear and writing for the heart. Our excitement ignited as we knew this book would transform people on the deepest level possible. We knew that we could make something life-changing for many and we committed ourselves to doing just that.

I believe that is what makes IGNITE like no other publishing house anywhere. We make sure our authors have the best experience possible writing their stories and sharing their 'Ignite Moments' in the richest and most compelling way, while at the same time, we strive to share life lessons and golden learning so that our readers feel the magic and enjoyment from every single story. We don't just put words on a page to be read, we transpose truth and vulnerability onto the page, infused with wisdom, inner knowing, and conscious awareness; the same way Les does it on stage. We reach deep within ourselves and give it all we have so that you go through the emotions right there with us along the way.

Our purpose is to make sure that when you read an IGNITE book, especially one centered around a living legend like Les, you feel a deeper sense of yourself. That something inside this book awakens you and inspires you. We want you to see yourself in the many stories and come to believe that if 'he can do it, I can do it,' and 'if she got there, then I can get there also.' That is the beauty behind each story, the fact that they reflect the human experience that we all have, and something we each can relate to. This commonality is what I believe brings us together and diminishes anything that separates us. The human condition of triumph, perseverance, determination, fortitude, and many more all live within each of us. It is these qualities that we can see in ourselves and in others that eliminates any barriers and allows us to see ourselves in the reflection of our neighbor, friend, co-worker, or someone all the way across the world.

Les often speaks of the unity and camaraderie necessary among us all. And, in his 50 plus years speaking to people, he has been an influential part of igniting lives and awakening the hunger that lies within millions. His magnificent obsession is to help others, a mirror to what we feel is our mission; Ignite Lives and Impact Humanity. So, when Les and I decided this book needed to be created, it was full-out and all-in.

There is a quote by Les Brown that says, "Reading about the lives of other achievers and their impact on our world inspires me to continue to help others realize their greatness." I am not sure when he said it or how long it has been around, but what I do know is that when I read it, I felt like it was said for this moment, and for this book. I believe that everything happens for the right and perfect reasons, and I can't help but feel that Les' quote was a beacon to shine the light on this beautiful project and what it will do for you and many others.

I know wholeheartedly that each story in this book was written to profoundly impact you. I also know that Les Brown's inspirational messages will speak directly to your heart and awaken something new inside of you. This book is filled with a kaleidoscope of love, hope, motivation, ideas, encouragement, and all the things you need to step into the greatness of your life. To quote Les, "We each have the talent to take us past the circumstances and challenges life brings to propel us into our greatness. Instead of giving into the challenges and difficulties in life and asking yourself, 'Why me?' embrace the enormous possibilities and proclaim, 'Why not me?'"

You have everything you need to be exactly who you want to be, and it is with great affection we present an awe-inspiring book designed to help you do just that. Step into your greatness and Ignite the Hunger in You!

Founder and CEO of Ignite,

JB Owen

WHAT IS AN IGNITE BOOK?

BY JB OWEN

Inside the pages of this book is a story that will undoubtedly spark a hunger inside of you. Your deepest desires, ambitions, wishes, ideas, and dreams are bound to be reflected in a story shared by one of our authors. We know this because IGNITE stories represent the powerful human emotions in all of us. They are universal and ingrained in each of us. They reflect what we all feel inside and touch upon the very essence of the things that make us human in our human experience.

The very word 'Ignite' signifies the goal of our books and describes the intention behind the stories that are shared inside. We see our books as gifts to the world. Every one we publish is done so with the idea of inspiring, uplifting, and igniting the reader to discover what is wanting to and waiting to unfold in their life. We believe our books are a bridge for all human connection, and that each story is a beacon for what is possible for every person on this planet.

As you begin reading the upcoming pages, you will find that every story starts with a *Power Quote*. It is a self-affirming, self-empowering, self-inspiring statement designed to Ignite you. It is designed to uplift you, push you forward, and encourage you to break outside your comfort zone. Power quotes are phrases that you can use when you need encouragement or a dose of purpose and direction. They are meaningful statements intended to provoke thought, awaken ideas, spark action, and evoke change. Every power quote is written to inspire you to become all that you can be.

Below the power quote, you will find each author's personal *Intention*. These are the personal insights and genuine wishes the author wants to share with you. They are the reasons they have written their story, filled with both insight and meaning. Each author has the desire to Ignite something special in you and they share that eloquently in their intention. They want you to know right from the beginning what they feel their story will do for you.

After the intention you dive right into the Ignite *Story*. It is a genuine account of how the author went through their life to emerge a greater expression of themself. Through their unique experiences and circumstances, the authors explain how their 'Ignite Moments' transformed them, awakened them, and set them on a new trajectory in life. They reveal their honest feelings and share their personal discoveries. They give you an insightful account into the moment that resulted in magnificent change and elevated their consciousness to where they are today.

We all have Ignite Moments that change us, define us, and set us forth on a wonderful new journey of inner exploration. These stories are derived from those very moments and are told in the most endearing and heartfelt way so that *you* become aware of your Ignite Moments. They show that *life-altering* situations are designed to impact us in a way that ultimately inspires us to love ourselves more and step into the joy of knowing ourselves more completely.

What is even more special and amazing about this book, *Ignite the Hunger In You*, is that each story is also infused with the magnificent and ever so powerful teachings of the inspirational master, Les Brown. All the authors have in some way been touched and transformed by Les' messages and impactful speeches. Les has in some way motivated them and encouraged them. His words, in their own special way, took them from where they were to where they aspired to be. From a quote, a video, or a speaking event, every author shares how Les Brown, in his endearing way, moved them closer to discovering their own inner greatness. For some it was at a pivotal time in their life, a dark moment, a tragedy, or that time where their back was up against the wall. For others it was on the brink of a new decision, a leap of faith, or taking that next brave step. Regardless of the circumstances, each story has a beautiful sharing of how Les Brown had a defining influence that helped them move forward. If you are a Les Brown fan, then you will thoroughly enjoy reading how his powerful and divine sharing has been the catalyst for monumental, life-altering change. If you are not a Les Brown fan yet, you are soon to become one.

Once you have completed reading each wonderful story, you will find a list of *Ignite Action Steps*. Each author shares powerful, doable actions that you can take to move you toward greater fulfillment and adopting new habits that will benefit you. Each action step is an effective idea, unique process, or powerful practice that has been successful in their lives. The hope is for you to implement them in your life and then use them daily to manifest positive change. Each Ignite Action Step is different and unique, just like you are, and each has proven to have amazing results when done diligently and consistently.

As you sit down to read this book, know that it is not required to read it in the traditional way, by starting at the beginning and reading through to the end. Many readers flip to a page at random and read from there, trusting that the page they landed on holds the exact story they need to read. Others glance over the table of contents, searching for the title that resonates with them. Some readers will go directly to a story recommended by a friend or find an author's photo that inspires them to want to know more. However you decide to read this book, we trust it will be right for you. We know that you may read it from cover to cover in one single sitting or pick it up and put it down a dozen times over a long period of time. The way you read an IGNITE book is as personal as every story in it, and we give you complete permission to devour it in whatever way fits you.

What we do ask is, if a story touches you or in some way inspires you, that you reach out and share that feeling with a friend. Let someone else know how the story impacted you and use it as a way to connect and express your feelings. Stories have brought us together since the beginning of time and we want our stories to do that for you and the ones you love. You may find a story that you know will touch the heart of someone else, so we encourage you to share the book with them, so they too can read the story and receive the gift from it. Lastly, if a story was exactly what you needed to read to help move you forward, tell the author. Your words would mean the world to them. Since our book is all about igniting humanity, we want to foster more of that among all of us. Feel free to share your sentiments with the authors by using their contact information at the end of each chapter. There isn't an IGNITE author who wouldn't love to hear from you and know how their story benefitted you.

We know that the phrase 'Ignite Moments' will now become a part of your vocabulary. You'll begin to think about your own impactful moments and the times in your life that ignited you in a new way. If sharing your story feels important or writing your Ignite Moment is percolating to the surface, please reach out to us. We believe every person has a story and everyone deserves to be seen, heard, and acknowledged for that story. If your words are longing to come forth, we want to support you in making it happen. Our desire is to Ignite a billion lives through a billion words, and we can only do that by sharing the stories of people like you! We would love to show you how your story can help another person in their story. Stories bring us together and every person's story deserves to be told.

As you turn the page, we want to welcome you to the IGNITE Family. We are excited for what is about to happen because we know the stories in this book are about to Ignite you. As you dive into the upcoming pages, a million different emotions will fill your heart and a kindred spirit will be established. We trust that this will be a book that both awakens and blesses you. May you be honored, loved, and supported from this page forward and all your Ignite Moments be ones of exceptional change. May they lift you up and Ignite a fire, a desire, and a beautiful hunger in you.

JOIN OUR COMMUNITY

As part of our ongoing commitment to Ignite a billion lives with a billion words, we want to give you unprecedented access to our full library of content. **Ignite Connect** is our online platform filled with resources, information, articles, and valuable content designed to enhance your writing and Ignite your life. This is where you can connect with our authors, master your story-writing skills, and learn more about what we do to support others in raising the consciousness of all humanity. Go to ***connect.igniteyou.life/sign_up*** to find out more and be a part of our exciting community.

John-Leslie Brown

Foreword by John-Leslie Brown

"Hunger cannot be inherited. Hunger cannot be learned.
For Hunger to exist, it must be ignited."

Certain moments create a common ground among us all. Similar to Ignite Moments, I like to call them '*where were you when*' moments. Where were you when we lost one of our beloved presidents? Where were you when a preacher who fought for equality was immortalized by the thief of greatness? For some, it was where were you when a politician from Chicago moved into our nation's capital with his beautiful children and beloved wife? Or when the Princess was taken too soon in Paris, or when a tsunami consumed a tiny island in the South Pacific? Where were you when the word 'pandemic' became the most Googled word on the planet, surpassing the words 'God' and 'money'? Moments like these have changed us all, individually and globally, and have become like permanent cornerstones in our lives.

As you read this book, *Ignite the Hunger in You,* I want you to ask yourself an important question: Where were you when you recognized that the most important person in your life, YOU, was truly hungry for more than just a moment? For me, it was Thursday, March 19, 2020, the day of the first lockdown orders in the United States. There was a shortage of food and water, and believe it or not, toilet paper became more valuable than a Fortune 500's corporate stock.

I had just negotiated a half a million dollar speaking contract for the family business. My father, Les Brown, and my sister, Dr. Ona Brown, returned from traveling in Dubai just one week prior. The airports resembled the 405 Freeway in Los Angeles during rush hour. As a family, we were grateful that they both made it back before the lockdown. We had no idea that the National Basketball Association™ and hockey leagues would cancel their scheduled playoff games and suspend the entire season. We had to watch as restaurants closed, flights canceled, and every neighborhood in the country instituted a curfew. Health-care providers were becoming heroes, and my hero, Les Brown, who I have the pleasure of calling Dad, was more poised than ever to keep the spirits high.

Despite our international tour being canceled and our domestic dates starting to disappear from the calendar like the moon in the morning, not once did I see Mamie Brown's baby boy panic. I was frightened. I was fearful that our family business was crumbling right before my eyes and that the empire that my father and I had built would forever be a memory.

It's hard to put it fully into words whenever you have a 'where were you when' moment in your life. I felt that way when I witnessed my dad's hunger to speak Ignite to a whole new level. Every day at noon, I walked upstairs to the third floor and got Dad set up to Livestream™. Every day at noon, he went live to inspire as many people as possible during one of the darkest chapters in human history. Every day, Les Brown's hunger was on full display as he focused on what he was born to do — speak, motivate, and inspire. I wish you would have seen it firsthand like I did. It's one thing when a prolific motivator shares certain valuable principles with an audience on a stage. It's a whole new paradigm when you get to witness that same motivator apply those principles directly into the lives of people via their phones, iPads™, and computers.

My dad was more focused than he was frightened. He was more steadfast than I had ever seen him in my entire life. I will never forget his tenacity. I became ashamed of myself. I didn't believe in our family business anymore. I didn't believe that the opportunities would ever return to our family. More importantly, I looked at my dad and his daily Livestream as a useless effort — a waste of time at best. Our former life of traveling and speaking was over in my mind, and I thought that he was truly wrong in thinking that we would get to the other side of this world lockdown. *Hunger* cannot be inherited. *Hunger* cannot be learned. For *Hunger* to exist, it must be ignited from within. Les Brown was ignited by the chaos, the panic, and the hopelessness. He was able to look past the current circumstances and become hungrier than ever to create his future reality.

It wasn't until December 24th of that same year that I was truly awakened, and the spark of inner hunger grew in me. One day before Christmas, my dad, whom I was living with at the time, called me into the dining room, and these words flew out of his mouth with the force of a Mack™ truck hitting a wall, "My son is a genius, and he won't help me. My son is a damn genius, and he won't help me. Get your things and get out of this house. I never want to talk to you or see you again. What's the point of having a genius of a son if he won't help to build our family business?"

His words changed my life forever. I thought to myself, "Why do you believe in me? Why do you have so much faith in my abilities when I don't? How is it that you believe in yourself the way you do? How do you have so much faith when the rest of the world doesn't? I just want you to be safe, and you're still trying to live your best life during a global crisis."

I spent the rest of the Christmas holiday toiling in victimhood and telling everyone that I could how I was wronged. I never thought there would be a part of me that would change, but it did. Dad, if you're reading this, thank you for igniting my hunger again.

In January 2021, I went into my GoDaddy™ account and found a birthday gift I purchased for him. What do you get a person who has everything? If he loves his job, you buy him a great domain. That domain was called hungry-tospeak.com. For the past 20 years, I have been listening to my father as he trained speakers and tried to recruit people to become speakers, and I never understood that passion. So, for his birthday, I threw him a surprise party and got him a domain that I just knew would excite him. It sat in my GoDaddy account for three years, and I decided to build a website and offer our coaching services online. I built the site, and next thing you know, we were working together again and happier than ever. We got to know people that we never met in person but had a deeper relationship with them than some of the people that we had known and spent time with for years. Our collective 'new hunger,' along with the ability to connect online, allowed my dad's message to reach more people than ever before and my desire to be the one to make it happen flourished. I had a new life-altering 'where were you when' moment that indeed ignited a hunger in me.

We never know the words, circumstances, or situations that will bring about the change that needs to happen in our lives. What we do know is that when those magical moments arrive, we need to be ready, willing, and excited to step into the person we were born to become. We need to rise to the occasion before us and say 'yes' to the greatness we all have within. I often say, "We must be more dedicated to our destiny than we are to our distractions."

This book is written by a family — not one with the same DNA as it pertains to genes or bloodlines — but a family with the same core values. People that haven't given up on life like I once had and who have found a way to thrive despite all odds. If we can share their stories with you, I guarantee you one thing: Your genius won't be wasted, and your hunger will be ignited. There are millions of books in the world. Most of them are written by one individual or expert. What makes this book special is that the co-authors of this book come in all shapes and sizes with all types of different stories; however, we all come from the Hungry To Speak family. They are hungry to share their Ignite Moments with you. Not so that you can praise them, but so that you can prioritize your genius and keep moving forward in your life despite the hard times in your past or the challenging times that may occur in the future.

My only question for you is, where are you going to be while reading this book? Not just physically but mentally and financially. Make a conscious note of where you are before you start reading this book because when you finish with the subsequent pages, I am certain that this will be a '*where were you when*' moment in your life. This page-turner is a part of history. Start reading, and within the first chapter, you'll see why. IF I didn't get thrown out of the family house, we would have never met the co-authors of this book. IF I didn't pack up all my things in my car, hungrytospeak.com would still be just another domain in GoDaddy sitting there. Because my dad forced my hunger out by igniting my spirit and mind to think of new creative ways to be of service, we ended up meeting and building genuine relationships with these authors and now with you!

When you're finished reading all the unique, personal, and entertaining stories in this book, you will have one important question: *What are you going to do now that you know what real hunger looks like?* Ignite the hunger within you and watch a world of darkness turn into a chandelier. Dr. Denis Waitley, the author of *The New Psychology of Winning*, had a father who used to tuck him in at night and act as if he was blowing out a candle with magic as his back gently flipped the switch on the wall. He then would tell a young Denis Waitley, "I'm blowing out your light now, and it will be dark for you. As far as you're concerned, it will be dark all over the world because the only world you will ever know is the one you will see through your own eyes." You have the opportunity to see the world not as Dr. Denis Waitley's dad suggested, but instead through the eyes of some other remarkable hunger-driven individuals. Don't miss your chance to light up your world. Get your highlighters ready. Put on your sunblock. Because your life will never be the same once you meet the phenomenal authors in this book and discover the '*where were you when*' Ignite Moments that have shaped them into the successful people they are today. I know their stories will be exactly what you need to discover and uncover your own.

This has been Mamie Brown's grandbaby boy, Les Brown's baby boy, and Honor Brown's pride and joy.

John Leslie Brown

itsnotoveruntilwewin
johnlesliebrown007
harvardeffect
johnlesliebrown

INTRODUCTION BY JB OWEN

WHAT DOES IT MEAN TO FEEL THE HUNGER INSIDE?

It is with great honor that I welcome you to this book, *Ignite The Hunger in You*. This is a unique book in that it speaks about hunger, not in the literal sense where one wants morsels of food or tidbits or something to eat, but instead hunger in the deeper sense, where there is an insatiable desire for nourishment and sustenance not filled with calories or vitamins, but loaded with an inner, richer hunger derived from the very essence of the soul. All humans have this innate inner hunger. For some, it is to *be* more, *become* more, *have* more, *do* more, *achieve* more, or *give* more. For others is to *feel* more, *love* more, *enjoy* more, and *understand* more. For most, it is a long-ing, combined with a wanting-ness toward something that is beyond where they are right now. It is the kind of hunger that can not be quenched with a supersized portion or a Happy Meal™. It is the kind of hunger that comes from within, where the thirst for more is combined with the nagging need to go after something, go get something, reach for something, and rise above something. There is a burning, yearning need to feast on the very banquet of life. This is the hunger to say 'no' and not accept the smallest portion but instead to say 'yes' and consume all that is offered. This internal, impassioned hunger for the greatest experience in life is the exact hunger we are speaking of; the hunger in you!

When it comes to igniting hunger, there is one man who is known for his enraptured passion to inspire others to find their own inner hunger; his name is Les Brown. If you don't know the famed Les Brown, you are about to. His notoriety spans the globe. From Detroit to Dubai, Indiana to Istanbul, Les has spoken on thousands of stages and to millions of people over the last 50 years. He is an icon in the personal-development industry and a legend when it comes to motivating people to go beyond what they believe. He fires up the hunger inside of people to go after their dreams, and that they do! He uses his infectious personality, rhythmic speeches, and unforgettable laugh to speak directly to the hearts of individuals around the globe.

With a career spanning five decades that has included stage, television, radio, print, and of course every social media platform possible, Les's voice has been heard motivating others in every corner of the planet. His message is hard to miss if you are looking to raise your consciousness, awaken your heart, build your faith, or find your greatness. He has touched the lives of many, and once you hear him, you will never forget him.

I first heard Les Brown about eight years ago. His words touched my heart in a way other speakers had not. The raw, real, reflective manner in which he shared stayed with me over the years. In the back of my mind, I had Les Brown cheering me on, urging me forward, and inspiring me to see myself in ways I could not yet see. Les has a way of sharing that makes you feel like he is talking directly to you. And, if you have spent any time with Les, you may come to believe that his messages are sent from the Master himself; gifted to share among the flock. Les has a passion and a conviction that is so rare and so emphatic that some feel it is divinely sent from heaven itself.

Both myself and the many other authors in this book have been touched by the words of Les Brown. In some profound way, something he said or some interaction that took place, sparked a pivotal moment to unfold. His voice was exactly what we needed to hear to move us forward. He, directly or indirectly, had an instrumental impact on our next step and in his own way, he was a part of our inner evolution. He was there, in person or in spirit, when we made the shift; when we took that heroic leap. He had a part in the process, knowingly or unknowingly, in us becoming a greater version of ourselves. And, it is because of him that we are here now sharing what unfolded with you. We want you to experience the power of that change, that was fueled by Les Brown, for yourself.

There are thousands of people that can attest to this experience and many more who will happily admit Les Brown changed their life. The stories in this book are just a small collection of those magical moments; those 'Ignite Moments' where Les Brown was the catalyst for cataclysmic change and transformation. They represent the many moments that define us and push us to become who we were born to be.

We all have Ignite Moments where something that happened to us profoundly alters the course of our life and ultimately leads to discovering a better version of ourselves. The stories in this book reflect the many facets of those moments. They are the good, the bad, the ugly, yet the necessary. They are those times when we had to birth ourselves into something new. All of the stories have the common denominator that Les was a part of that special Ignite learning. He perpetuated it, triggered it, and contributed to the enlightenment that we have gained because of it. Les planted the seed and then we tended to it until it blossomed into what Les calls a magnificent obsession; a hunger in you.

As you turn the pages, you are about to read the many, personal Ignite Moments that these authors had that created a hunger in them. They are the 'real-life, real-deal' events that brought them from where they were to where they are now. Each one has undergone a process, a journey. None of them started off perfect, nor met no obstacles along the way. To the contrary, many experienced setbacks, disappointments, and failures that required fortitude and perseverance to overcome. They humbly share those moments solely to inspire you. They want their stories to help you redefine your own story. No matter where you are in your life, you will be able to identify with the authors and see a reflection of yourself in them. Their heartfelt sharing is designed to Ignite a new passion, desire, ambition, idea, or hunger in you! A hunger to go after your dreams and say 'yes' to your wishes. A hunger to reach farther and climb higher. A hunger to give, grow, and enjoy all the grace life has to offer. A hunger to help, heal, feel the humor, and promote more hope in those you love, those around you, and those you can support.

The best part is, every aspect of this book is designed to Ignite the kind of hunger that creates good in the world, fosters camaraderie, and builds connections between people of any color, race, creed, and conviction. The authors want this. Les wants this and I want this. We want every person who has the ability to read these stories to feel the power that comes from within themselves, and experience the results that happen when you unleash the hunger in you; and fuel it with intention.

Your hunger, at this moment, might be like a tiny seed still germinating, a bobbing boat on a raging sea, or it may feel like a roaring lion liberated from his cage. Wherever it is, let the many stories you are about to read Ignite it even further. Utilize the ideas, take the suggestions, and implement the Action Steps into your own life to reach the pinnacle of your desires. Allow something one of the authors shared, or a quote from Les, be the exact thing you need to Ignite that dream. We all need inspiration and a bevy of support. Let each author's story and the words from Les be precisely that. Decide that you are ready to step into that next great version of you, and it is no coincidence that you are reading this book; at this exact time in your life. Your soul, your inner knowing, the very essence of you is ready to blossom.

I always say, "Anything and everything is possible." Les always says, "You have greatness in you." Both are true. Both pertain to you. You have the possibilities to experience your greatness when you fully Ignite that magnificent hunger in you. Reach inside and grab hold of it and let this book be everything you need to bring it forth. When we allow the hunger inside us to reign, we can create a beautiful world; for ourselves and others.

May this book, written with love from all of us, be exactly what you need to do just that.

May your hunger Ignite the world.

How do I Ignite the Hunger in me?

IGNITE would not have done its job if we had not taken the power of all these stories and used them to Ignite a hunger in you. Going beyond just a passive reading tool, our goal is to be the instigator for something new in your life. Be it new thinking, new ideas, new action, or a new direction, we want this book to be the impetus of something exciting percolating in you. Our desire is that by reading the many stories, you begin to see how your life can take on new meaning and direction. Of course we know that any form of change takes work, so we are delighted to provide a workbook section at the back of the book for you to begin your own journey of change and exploration.

Start first by reading the many stories provided throughout this book until you have your fill. Pore through them at the start of your day, or nestle in with a few at the end, right before going to sleep. Have it with you in your bag during a long commute, or place it beside your favorite spot to enjoy while admiring a majestic view. However you consume this book, do it in a way that allows your mind to truly absorb the teaching and benefit from the many life lessons our authors share.

While reading, we encourage you to pause often and take the time to allow the words to fully permeate and Ignite you. Read the Power Quotes and ponder the words. Infuse a bit of each quote into your day and embrace their intent with conviction. Then absorb the heartfelt gifts from each Intention. Feel the desire from the author to uplift, inspire, support, and nurture your precious spirit. Dive into the stories. Laugh, cry, and applaud the victories along with each of the authors as they genuinely and vulnerably share the times in their lives where they choose triumph over defeat. Pause after each story to see how the underlying message and golden nugget in the story can be applied to your life. Take a moment to see the lessons and gain insight from the personal transformation that has been shared.

Once you complete a story, read over the Action Steps to see how you can systematically apply them into your own life. Good habits done consistently lead to amazing results, so pick an Action Step that appeals to you and do it with determination. Les says, "I have learned that to get out of life what I expect, I must commit myself to beginning each day by concentrating on positive thoughts and focusing on my goals." Focus on what you want to achieve in your life by choosing one of the many Action Steps that will propel you closer to the outcome you are aiming for.

Once you have read enough stories and feel the hunger stirring inside of you, turn to the back of the book where we have provided a powerful section of self-discovery. This area is for you to uncover and discover what ignites you. What feeds your soul and what is your magnificent obsession? This is a special place in the book for you to dive deep into you and find that hunger that may be lying dormant and ready to spring forth. It is designed to give you the time and space you need to uncover what matters to you. It is where the hunger you have been craving to discover, will generously be revealed.

Self-reflection, self-discovery, and introspection all lead to the most profound learning because all the answers to your questions and the solutions to your quandaries lie within you. You have everything you need inside of you to become your greatest expression. You just have to take the time to listen to yourself and trust that inner knowing. Use the workbook exercises we have formulated and the space we are holding for you to reach that place and be delighted with the treasures you find.

Allow the fortitude and conviction you read in these stories to *Ignite a Hunger in You!* Let them inspire something that has never been realized before.

Awaken to what is *possible* and embrace your *greatness*. Find out what you long for and seize the hunger you have inside to go get it. There is so much about you the world is just waiting to see! There is so much you can achieve when you know what that is. Take the time to *know thyself* fully and Ignite the magnificent hunger you so triumphantly have within you.

Les promises, "Shoot for the moon. Even if you miss, you'll land among the stars." Your life depends on you believing in you. So believe that everything and anything *is* possible and there is greatness hungry to come forth in you!

Much Love,

JB Owen

LES BROWN

"Live life from the hunger of your heart. When you fill your heart with what you hunger for, your mind will find the way to achieve your desires."

Since I discovered my purpose in life, my desire has been to leave a legacy of greatness that others may be inspired by. I was fortunate to have positive guides and examples of greatness that led me to uncover different parts of myself at critical times in my life.

My intention is to pay it forward and help other people trust in their abilities in order to achieve a life that reflects their individual goals, dreams, and passions.

Understanding and walking into your own personal power are crucial elements to discovering your personal, emotional, and financial success. I hope that you will allow my story to inspire you to believe that there's nothing you can't accomplish once you put your mind, spirit, heart, and HUNGER into it!

THE BEAUTY IN ACCEPTING YOUR GREATNESS

If you've followed my career or heard me speak, then you know that I believe we are each put on earth on purpose and with a purpose. It's true, we are all designed to create something great and meaningful in life, and it's our jobs to fulfill our purpose.

That's why even if we've never met, I can still say without doubt that you have GREATNESS within you.

All of us do.

Unfortunately, the majority of us never discover our greatness. We become trapped inside of faulty thinking and hold on to a smaller vision of who we truly are. As I often say, you can't see the picture when you're inside the frame, and you can't read the label when you're locked inside the box. You will often need someone else to help you reach your next level because they can see what you're too close or not properly positioned to see.

I understand all too well what it means to have the cards stacked against you and to have to fight for your dreams. I also understand what it means to live a life where dreaming can feel like an intangible luxury.

Even though my adoptive mother filled our lives with love and kindness, I still grew up in a very tense and scary time where just being myself seemed to be a crime.

I was a young Black boy in the South during some of the most tumultuous times in the United States in terms of race relations. I share some of my harrowing experiences and encounters with object discrimination in my most recent book, *You've Got to be Hungry*. I am always shocked at the number of people who still can't comprehend that such a time existed in what many considered the most progressive and inclusive country in the world.

I truly believe that in life there will be events and situations that happen in your life either for you, to you, or through you.

Growing through those experiences was essential and it happened *for me.* As I look back, I see that in some respects, I couldn't afford to live a sheltered life of innocence because I needed to be able to learn how to handle difficult circumstances.

Hindsight is 20/20 Vision

I've heard it said that there are some things in life that you can't understand or even see in life looking forward, you can only get the full view by looking backward. In other words, hindsight is 20/20 vision.

If you know my story, then you know that nothing about the start of my life was glamorous. In fact, most people would look at my humble beginnings and never see any indication that I would one day be considered a world-renowned author and motivational speaker.

I was born with a twin brother in an abandoned building in a poor section of Miami, Florida. At the age of 6 weeks my brother, Wesley, and I were given up for adoption by our biological mother. Fortunately, along with my other adoptive siblings, we were taken in, loved, and provided for by an angel on earth. Even though we struggled, we really didn't know that we were poor until much later.

I am known for attributing my entire success, motivation, and inspiration for achieving more in life to my beautiful and irreplaceable adoptive mother, Ms. Mamie Brown. The strength, tenacity, and fortitude that she had as a single woman to take in children that were not her own and raise them with love, compassion, and morals is a unique gift that I treasure. Because of her example, I have a special place in my heart for and believe that we should all honor the men and women who so unselfishly support and raise children in need.

I have to admit that being adopted is not always an easy road to walk along. I remember the day that I learned that my brother and I were not Mamie's natural children. I was a teenager, and as much as I'd like to say that it was a simple truth to discover, in a way I was heartbroken.

I instantly gained a new set of doubts and fears about the unknown in my life — but on the other hand, my newfound knowledge made me love my Mama, Ms. Mamie Brown, even more.

I then realized the true meaning of sacrifice and that she didn't have to do any of the things that she did for us. She did not give birth to us, but she gave up her life to give us our lives. I decided right then to make my life's mission to help her however I could.

As honorable as this may seem, and for as much as Mama nurtured and cared for us, I still couldn't help but feel that a part of me was lost. I would often wonder what my biological parents looked like, where they were, and why they gave Wesley and I away.

Nevertheless, I never felt bitter about the choices my parents made. I honestly didn't know what to feel, but I revered their places in my life. In fact, I often talk about the fact that I'm here because of two women — the one I've never seen who gave me life, and the one who gave me love. I say that God took me out of my biological mother's womb and placed me in the heart of my adopted mother.

Nature and Nurture Combine!

As my life progressed, I began to gravitate more and more toward jobs and careers where I had to use my voice. I have always been drawn toward those who had the 'gift of gab' and were great orators.

It all started as a youth hearing well-known voices like Martin Luther King Jr., Malcolm X, Paul Harvey, Norman Vincent Peale, and even local leaders such as my favorite and most influential high school teacher, Mr. Leroy Washington.

I would listen to their words and think, "I want to do that. I want to have people listen to me this way." I've always loved telling and hearing stories and making people laugh. In addition, Mama was quite an amazing storyteller. I would spend hours and hours listening to her when she talked to me, or anyone for that matter. She had a natural wit and charm to her that was captivating, so I spent my life believing that I had gotten my oratorical skills from her and the other influencers.

I know in many ways that it's true, but imagine my surprise and elation to find out after 77 years of life that my dream careers of being a radio host, television host, motivational speaker, legislator, and trainer were a birthright passed down to me from my parents and grandparents.

Finding the Missing Pieces

They say coincidence is God's way of staying anonymous. I have seen evidence of this demonstrated over and over again in my life, but nothing could prepare me for what happened for me in the spring of 2021.

I used to watch and become emotional seeing the reunions on television and online of parents and children who found each other after separation. I secretly longed to have this be part of my story, and on occasion, I tried to find my parents. After trying for so long, I honestly quit looking for them. Despite my own advice, I gave up on trying to put together the piece of the puzzle that was missing for me; however, thankfully, my oldest son Calvin did not.

We talk daily, but I will never forget the day Calvin called me and said, "Dad, I found your family!"

Without even knowing the full details, I began to cry tears of joy. "Wow," I thought, "After all of this time, it's finally happening." Calvin had researched our lineage and received an alert that would forever change our stories.

I'll share more details in my upcoming book on being unstoppable — but the most mind-blowing discovery was that both my biological grandmother and biological mother were well-known MOTIVATIONAL SPEAKERS!

I know… I know!

It was too much for me to believe as well. After all of this time, it was revealed to me that speaking and using my voice for good is an innate skill that was passed down.

Talk about an IGNITE MOMENT!

I still get goosebumps thinking about the stories I've heard about my mother, father, and their families. My biological mother's name was Dorothy Bell. When I see pictures of her smile and her face, it's like looking in the mirror.

I have my father's eyes.

My grandmother, Mrs. Beulah Rucker, even has an educational facility and museum named after her in Gainesville, Georgia, and she's known for being a prolific speaker and philanthropist.

I always wondered where I got this gift from. My voice has taken me to so many amazing places, and with the knowledge of my family's history of using their voices for good, I see that everything in my life has been God's timing and God's plan.

I've had some incredible experiences in my life and I've been fortunate enough to help change and influence the lives, duration, and the trajectory of so many. It always warms my heart to know that my words and my ability to use them in a positive way has touched another soul.

I am satisfied in knowing that the gifts of my grandmother and both of my mothers reside in me. I have to say that I am incredibly blessed to have met and formed instant bonds with so many of my beautiful biological family members.

The Revelation

I realize that my being given up for adoption was something that happened for me. I would be hard-pressed to imagine that the Les Brown that you know now could have come into being had I been raised by my biological mother.

I needed Mamie Brown's influence, I needed to be born the way I was, in the place that I was. I needed to meet Mr. Washington, I needed all of it to get *hungry* and become the man that I am today.

I am now able to use what happened to me and translate it to an experience that allows me to transform and Ignite the lives of others. It is why I connected with JB and aligned with her hunger to Ignite humanity through powerful stories and personal transformation. Her passion ignited me and is what brought this book to fruition for the many authors, and now for you. We know this book will Ignite lives and create a hunger in many around the globe; allowing true change to flourish.

My life is in a space where everything that happens through me will bene-fit generations to come. I am living proof that no matter what you have gone through, no matter the storms you've endured, no matter what circumstances and trials have come... all of those experiences should and can be used for your good.

Just like me, you have a story to tell. It's a constantly changing and expansive story, and you have the ability to grow and thrive through every opportunity and encounter.

IGNITE ACTION STEPS

Since you are reading this and I'm able to connect with you right now, I want to ask you some of the same questions I ask my audiences, starting with:

If you had your life to live again, would you do anything differently?
And if so, what would that be?

I ask that question because one thing that life has taught me is that it's never too late for you to take control of your life, turn it around, and become the person that you were born to be.

There will always be examples of people who make it despite incredible odds. You can be one of them, and you can show others how to overcome to achieve their dreams as well.

It's a Long Shot, but Keep Going!

"Just when I thought I had a handle on things, God broke the handle."
-Unknown

Throughout my life I've been amazed at what I accomplished when I focus on my 'why' and my passion for living. Meeting my birth family created a whole new world for me. There is something else yearning within you to be discovered about yourself too.

I told you I'd ask you some questions, here are a few more:

What are you hungry to achieve and what's standing in your way?

The first time I spoke to an extremely large audience, there were over 80,000 people in the Georgia Dome. I was beyond nervous. It was so bad that I actually had to be coached on stage, but once I got there, I understood and completed the assignment.

I told that crowd just as I am telling you — I know your dreams, desires, and the life you deserve can seem beyond challenging to obtain. Yes, it may be a long shot, but it's a shot you have to take.

I had to take the long shots in life to make it. It may be a 'long shot' to get from here to your next destination, your greatest destination; the leap of faith you need may be tremendous and seemingly unattainable to you right now.

I get it, I understand how it feels to have no choice but to run fast and hard toward your dream. I am here as a living testimony and witness to tell you that yes, no matter how long that shot feels for you, no matter how wide the gap, or how high the height seems for you to overcome, you have to make the decision to take the shot to reach your destination.

You can do this!

I did it. So many others have too. You've got this. You've just got to be HUNGRY enough to want to win.

I've personally encouraged those who were hungry enough to go after their dreams and to be unstoppable despite the real, perceived, and often literally false obstacles that they face. When you begin to cultivate, train, and feed your hunger to achieve more, you too will win!

Les Brown — United States
Motivational speaker, author, mentor, and inspirational advocate
www.hungrytospeak.com
LesBrown.com
thelesbrown
LesBrown77
thelesbrown

JB OWEN

"Your past does not define you, instead it refines you."

Some stories are our favorites to tell, others are the ones we hide away. For many years I hid this story thinking that if others did not know, it would make it not be so. Except I knew it was true, and instead of sharing it, I kept it within me, reflecting against the kaleidoscope of my life, causing shards of darkness at its will. It was when I finally shared my story, first in a whisper, and then beneath the tears, to now, where I share it openly in the hopes it will help unfurl you. Once a raging river, it has settled into a reflective pond. It has softened, soothed, and eventually calmed. My story, once embraced, has ignited a hunger in me to help others know that your past does not define who you are, instead, it refines who you will become.

GET UP, TRANSFORM, AND IGNITE!

This story doesn't have a pretty beginning. I was 16 the first time my boyfriend showed any sign of aggression toward me. When it happened, I did nothing. I just froze. I stood there with a shocked, dumb look on my face. I didn't fight back, call him out, or walk away; I just stood there, surprised, taken aback, and in total astonishment of what he had done. He passed it off as if nothing happened. He acted as if doing that was normal. To him it was, to me it wasn't. Yet my inability to process his behavior left me subject to it happening again and again over the next three years. I was like a lamb, unaware I was going to slaughter, and my naivete took hold.

In the beginning of our relationship, I found him incredibly charming. It was that ever so soft, stolen kiss that he planted on the side of my neck during the school dance that had me like a bee to honey. I was popular in high school and ran with the cool kids, but I wasn't sought after by any of the dreamboat guys. I didn't have a big rack, a proclivity to tight jeans, and I didn't smoke, drink, or party hard like many of the other girls did. I was more into theater and loved art, drama, and home economics, where you got to make things and cook things. Most of my friends were either super athletic or super smart. I was the anomaly in my crowd, known for my bubbly personality, passion for student council, and the one who always spearheaded the activities at the school like travel club and winter carnival. I loved coordinating events and being on committees. I didn't have much time for boys until halfway through my junior year, when a certain young man, six months my senior, planted the light, feather touch of a kiss on the virgin nap of my neck as "Stairway to Heaven" played from the gymnasium speakers. I was instantly smitten.

Our courtship was quick. We started writing notes to each other in class, then eating lunch side by side in the cafeteria. Since I was already driving and had a car, I would pick him up in the morning and take him home every day after school. Those were our golden moments, that precious time when we lost ourselves in the young, budding romance of two teenage kids.

We had been dating just a few months; a lifetime for two teenagers when it first happened. We were grabbing our books out of the same locker. He had moved into my locker since it was in the more popular part of the school, close to the student council room. His locker was at the far end of the school where the 'skids' were known to hang out. Moving to my locker, in its prestigious spot, was a step up for him and he liked the status it brought. Before meeting me, he was relatively unknown in my peer group and he took to it quickly. As we both scrambled for our prospective books so as not to be late for class, he shoved me out of the way, a bit too hard and a bit too serious. Then he flung out an insult and stared me right in the eye, waiting to see what I would do. Looking back at that moment, I realize that had I reacted or done something, it would have set a very different ball into motion. Instead, I froze, went silent, and simply stared back with the pleading eyes of someone who wanted to believe that it didn't just happen. That denial cemented the permission he needed to know that I would endure whatever he dished out in the future.

The second time it happened, we were sitting in the drive-through at McDonald's™, disagreeing about the fact that he had ordered an unnecessary amount of food, including the supersized drink. Since I was paying, again, I was a bit annoyed at his freewheeling excess. I had a part-time job; he did not. I had parents who owned a few successful businesses, he did not. I was able to buy things that he could not. In fact, his stepfather was a heavy drinker who couldn't hold a job and his mom only did part-time janitorial work at the hospital. They were living on mere means and dating me provided certain financial perks that he was becoming increasingly accustomed to. That day, he was spending my hard-earned money as if it was his own. I was complaining as to why he couldn't just order the regular size. I was explaining how he never drank all of the supersized drink and most of it went to waste. As the food came through the window and we drove away, I kept talking about the waste and the expense. That is when he took the supersized cup and threw the entire thing right in my face, telling me to shut up! The lid burst off the cup and the soda inside splashed everywhere; in my face and my hair, all over the windshield and my car, the seat, and my lap. I just sat there stunned, dripping wet and in shock. I froze in utter disbelief. He drove directly to his house, not saying a word, then got out of the car and went inside as if nothing happened, leaving me at the curb in the passenger seat, sopping up the mess. I went home that night terrified at what I did, how I must have provoked him, triggered his embarrassment for not being able to pay, stung his ego, and pushed the point a bit too much. I internalized the entire event, made it my fault, and that solidified exactly how he treated me for the next three years.

In between the gooey high school puppy love, I put up with his constant mood swings, from charming, doting boyfriend, to belligerent, bossy, and bad-mouthing. One day he was a dream guy, the other a nightmare, and the entire time I was in high school, I was his keeper, his bank, and his kicking stick. I don't know why I did it; why I allowed the abuse. I guess it was the romance that came after, the making up, and all the promises I received. Part of it was to avoid the disappointment of our friends as we had become the 'it' couple of the school. Of course, no one knew he was treating me that way. It all happened in private, and my own embarrassment kept it that way so that I would not look like a failure, a bad girlfriend, or the inadequate one. I protected him, shook it off, and accepted the apologies when they came.

As graduation arrived, tension between us grew. I was accepted to a school 2,700 kilometers away; he was not. I had options, he did not. My parents were encouraging me to spread my wings, his parents demanded he start supporting them, all while reminding him he'd never amount to much. Excitedly, I turned 18 and graduated high school within a week of each other. It was a very big celebration to finish school and become an adult all within the same week. It was June, and with school over, many of our friends were prolonging the parties and endlessly kicking back before July began. I was not. I had started my own little business in the mall, subleasing some space, and was determined to work as much as I could before the fall when I'd be going off to college. He was resentful and caused many occasions to make me late for work, required me to leave early, and stirred up some drama that only I could sort out.

The weekend following graduation, I got a phone call from a girlfriend to come and get him. He had been out with her boyfriend, getting drunk and was making a ruckus. It wasn't the first time he was drunk and disorderly at a friend's house. He boasted about how much he could drink, and he was happy to show you just how much that was. When I pulled into my girlfriend's driveway, I could see him stumbling on the front lawn in a drunken stupor. It was the first time I actually realized how bad he was for me; how much he was ruining my life. I was annoyed and plainly showed it as I rolled down my window and told him to get in the car so I could take him home. He acted happy that I was there and encouraged me to come join them for a drink. I could see the pleading faces of my friends who just wanted me to take him home. I declined and ordered him to get in the car. I was tired, not just from working a long shift, but from having to constantly nurse him, save him, and remove him from situations that he insisted on escalating. I tried to be the calm one, he was not. I was often the practical one, he was not. I was the one that wanted to work toward having a future and all he wanted to do was constantly work on making me someone I was not.

Despite his drunk, amusing pleads to not be such a bore, I saw the subtle shift in his demeanor. I knew the insults were coming, so instinctively I rolled up my window to avoid his alcohol-filled breath and prove I was serious; I wanted to go home and he better get in the car. That is when like a viper he changed, and with all his might, he punched the car window right in front of my face. The glass didn't break but made one hell of a noise, slipped off the track, and fell cockeyed into the door. I froze. I was shocked, stunned, and I remember seeing the faces of all my friends, astonished that he had just punched exactly where my face was. Then, like he often did, he turned mean and started swearing at me; blaming me. I put my car in reverse and backed out of the driveway. I drove home shaking. I was both terrified and appalled by his behavior. It was the first time I had ever defied him and the first time anyone had seen him treat me that way.

Inside my heart I knew it was over and I was grateful that by the end of summer I wouldn't have to break up with him, allowing moving away to take its course. I had become accustomed to his hot and cold behavior, and I assumed, like all the other times, it would blow over. Soon enough he'd show up remorseful and apologetic. I'd do what I always did, listen. He'd be sorry for the uncontrollable rage he had pent up inside due to his alcoholic stepfather and dead-end life. I'd pump him up and suggest options. I was always trying to find the solution, he was not. I was forever giving my best, he was not. I was at the place where I felt ready to move on, but he certainly was not and did everything to hang on to me with all his might.

I went to bed with the belief that in a few days I would find him leaning against my car, holding flowers, or on my front step with his puppy-dog look. Sadly, that didn't happen. That evening at 2:47 AM, in the middle of the night, I was awoken by the light turning on in my bedroom. I remember the time exactly because as my eyes opened to the light, I saw my alarm clock on my night table. I flipped over in fear as I knew I was home alone. My parents were divorced. My mom had taken advantage of my school being over and my newly acquired 18-year-old status to go away on a week-long holiday with her boyfriend. My father lived out at the coast with his new wife and my sister was living in residence at university. The only person who could be turning on my light at that hour was an intruder. With my adrenaline skyrocketed, I spun around to find him standing there, in my bedroom doorway; more drunk than he was before. Needless to say, I was annoyed and angry that he had both woke me up and scared me half to death. But I was also acutely aware of the fact that he didn't have a key to get into my house and the drunk look on his face was no longer amusing but menacing. I tried to take control of the situation by sitting up and reaching for my house coat, talking to him rationally and sweetly. That's when the first hit came. He punched me without any provocation right in the face. I flew back on my bed and within seconds he was on top of me, hands around my neck and strangling me with so much fury that spittle was coming out of his mouth. He swore and called me names; all the while squeezing my airway with both hands. It was a fight for my life as I clawed and bucked with all my strength. I was able to knock him forward and squirm out from under him. On hands and knees, I crawled to the doorway where he kicked me in the side, stomach, and upper thigh. He was a big soccer player and knew exactly how and where to kick. I flew against the wall, denting the drywall. I used the doorjamb to help me stand only to be hit again. I fell into the hallway, not knowing where I was going, just trying to get out of there. He pulled me back by my hair, pushed me into the wall, and kneed me in the torso. I stood to catch my breath, only to receive another hit to the face.

I could go on, but frankly the rest is mostly a blur. I awoke hours later at the end of the hallway, a heap on the floor. My face was swollen, my nails broken with blood crusted on my fingertips. My ribs were broken, my throat was burning and hoarse, and one of my legs wouldn't move. I crawled on my belly to the kitchen to telephone for help and saw that the phone had been ripped out of the wall and only torn wires remained sticking out. Terror washed over me that he might still be in the house. I froze, completely silent, listening for any sound or indication that he was still there.

From the kitchen landing I could see the front door and noticed that it was unlocked. I knew I had locked it the night before so the fact it was unlocked meant he had unlocked it to leave. I crawled to my mom's room to use her phone only to find it ripped out of the wall also. There was no way to call for help. I was on my own, and as my senses returned, I was becoming increasingly aware of how hurt I really was. I pulled myself down to the basement, where we had a junk room filled with old, discarded stuff due for a garage sale. I tore through a green garbage bag where I knew an old phone was part of the things we were giving to charity. I pulled it out and plugged it into an outlet in the basement and called the one friend I knew I could trust, Rob.

Rob had been one of my best friends for quite some time. He was like a brother to me, and I had spent many dinners with him and his family and numerous weekends at his house just playing video games. The best part was Rob's dad was my doctor. He was the doctor that had delivered me when I was born and had been in my life ever since as a professional confidant and fatherly role model. I loved Rob's dad as he healed my pains when I was a kid, gave me that preferable lollipop after a visit, and had the most caring and gentle heart of any man I had ever known. Rob was one of three boys, so I got super spoiled and was like the missing daughter in their family. In my battered state I knew Rob would help, so I dialed his number.

Rob was there within 15 minutes, loading me into his car and taking me to the hospital. When we got to the emergency ward, his dad was immediately called. As the nurses assessed my injuries and Rob's dad drove from his private clinic to the hospital, my mind raced. What was I going to do? I had told Rob in the car what had happened, and he was furious. He told the nurses, who called the police. X-rays were taken of my leg and ribs. My fingers were bandaged, and salve was applied to the cuts and scratches on my neck and face. Rob's dad did everything to take care of me, and when the police entered the emergency room, he lovingly squeezed my hand to give me courage.

When the first officer asked me what happened, I froze. I went silent. I didn't know what to do. A week ago, I was a 17-year-old kid enjoying the fun and frolic of high school. Now I was in a hospital, assaulted, with officers in front of me and no parents to save me. The police shared that they had been to my house and noticed the forced entry in a broken basement window and the ruckus in the house; all they needed me to do was name the person who did it and they would arrest him. Again, I froze.

I don't know why, but I couldn't do it. I couldn't say it was him; the boy I had spent the last three years trying to love, trying to save, and wanting to heal. I just shook my head as tears streamed down my face, unable to say anything. Rob's dad let go of my hand and exited the room. Letting him down was the biggest humiliation I had ever felt. I didn't have the courage or the strength to be the one responsible for ruining another person's life by condemning them to jail and I knew he'd go to jail for what he did. I stayed silent and refused to tell my side of the story.

When I got out of the hospital, Rob's dad paid for me to fly to the West Coast to stay with my father. My mom was still away, I had no one to protect me, and getting out of town was the best thing to do. Rob drove me to the airport and within 10 days of turning 18, I left everything I knew behind and ran from my home, my job, and that relationship. I was wheeled on to the plane in a wheelchair and off the plane in a wheelchair into my father's car. Not much was said. I felt paralyzed when I saw my past and stayed silent. Deep inside me, I felt it was all my fault.

I know my story is not unique in that many women have endured both similar and much more horrific situations than mine. As I grew older, I became aware of just how many women face physical, emotional, and psychological abuse all at the hands of someone who says they love them. I was equally aware of the many indicators of abuse and violence that show up in a relationship. I wouldn't allow swearing around me as I never knew when it would escalate into something bigger. I became closed off to anyone who drank a lot and avoided guys who made any derogatory remarks even in a joking way. Sadly, I never truly dealt with what happened. My parents were supportive and at the same time happy that I had freed myself of him and was starting a new life, living in a new city, and moving on.

I lived that new life for the next 21 years. I married and had two beautiful children. I did what all people do in their 20s, 30s, and chasing 40. I made new friends, enjoyed a wonderful career, traveled extensively, and forgot mostly about him until one day, six months after my divorce and one week after my 40th birthday. It began with a 'hello' on Facebook™, followed by a shy and polite request to apologize for the deplorable behavior of a young and stupid 18-year-old boy. It was spurred on by a restitution initiative inspired by a healthy sobriety program, and it seemed honest, heartfelt, and after almost three decades, sincere. I responded. Once again, I didn't want to be the one to hinder a healthy recovery program, so I was open to listening and hearing him out. With a wounded heart from my divorce and feelings of loneliness, I allowed his apologies to turn into long conversations about God, religion, spirituality, the cosmos, sobriety, self-development, and soul mates. He spoke profoundly about this new life and peppered it with humility and gratitude. It was both interesting and fascinating to hear he was aspiring for more while I was the one picking up the pieces of my life.

It didn't take long until we agreed to meet, to heal the emotional pain that both of us had been carrying from the past. I flew to see him. He was there to pick me up at the airport and started crying the moment he saw me. I was instantly convinced he was a changed man. Like two kids back in high school, we rekindled our relationship quickly. I trusted that I was wiser, smarter, stronger, and certainly more assured of myself; fully knowing what I wanted and what I wasn't willing to tolerate. I felt completely capable of creating a better relationship this time. He was eight years sober, working his program, aware, reserved, and focused on bettering himself while making me the happiest woman ever. I felt he had become the man I always wanted him to be.

Sooner than I should have, I introduced him to my kids, had him visiting often, and within six months we both moved to a town where we could start our lives over and be together. It all seemed perfect. Like a fairy tale. Reunited after 22 years, rewriting the past, overcoming the hurdles, finding each other once again after being apart for so long. I bought into it all: hook, line, and sinker. The perfect Disney™ ending of two lost loves reunited was all I could think of, and within a year we were married and living the life we had always talked about when we were teenagers.

Fifteen short days after the wedding, he got mad about something, swore at me, and spitefully said he never should have married me. I froze; I was almost immobilized. I had sheltered myself for almost three decades from any hint of male abuse and like Jekyll and Hyde, he just flared up two weeks after saying, "I do." I was mortified, horrified, and catatonic at what was happening. Like a bad horror story, his charming behavior all unraveled faster than it started. Of course, the instant apology came and kept coming. Within the first year of our marriage, he relapsed three times. I helped him into rehab, committed to starting over countless times, did my best to heal him, love him, and fix all that was broken. I did everything to save him when it was in fact me that needed saving!

Earlier in the summer, we had rented a lake cottage as per his need for peace, quiet, and a desire to get out of town (which had become a place that just made him want to drink.) In the beginning it was a wonderful reprieve for him and the kids as they enjoyed the lake water, fishing, diving off the pier, and some semblance of a normal stepfather. As the months went on, he used the cottage to be alone, get away, and isolate himself. I kept trusting his time there would be helpful until the day I showed up unannounced and saw a heavily tattooed woman with half her head shaved smoking a joint through my kitchen window. I loudly knocked on the door then walked into *my* cabin and watched as she threw the joint out the window and buttoned up the front of her shirt. She was scraggy and young, and by the looks of the place, completely disconnected to civilized living. The cottage was a mess. Pizza boxes all over, wet towels on the floor, dirty ashtrays, beer cans, and used glasses laid everywhere. I didn't recognize the place and was aghast at what had become of it since my last visit. All I could do was ask her where he was, and she pointed to the bedroom. There I found him, facedown on a bed that had no sheets or blankets but a bare mattress. The room was strewn with clothes and a suitcase lay open on the floor with three empty bottles of vodka. Another empty bottle was on the nightstand, and another was on the floor, inches from his hand hanging over the bed, as if he was reaching for it. Seeing him there, passed out, surrounded by all the chaos he had created, I realized the drugs, the hookers, the theft, the lies, the abuse, and the erratic behavior was not going to stop. There was no fixing this and once again, he was destroying my life.

I shook him to wake him up and like a bear emerging from a winter slumber, he rose in a foul mood. I should have known better, but I didn't. I confronted the bottles, the broken promises, the lies, and the woman upstairs, and that's when it happened. He punched me right in the face. I fell back into the wall and identical to that night 22 years ago, he grabbed me by the throat and started squeezing. I pushed him back and lunged for the door to escape. He grabbed my hair and pulled me back only to shove me into the wall and knee me in the ribs and torso. I fell to the floor, and he kicked me in the side of the leg, just like the last time, but this time as I stumbled backward and he drew his fist back to strike, I screamed, "SSTTOOOOPP!" in a long drawn out command at the top of my lungs. He froze, stared at me, and blinked like a fish in a dirty tank. I said it again this time with every fiber of my being spewing from my lips in a knowing that I had finally reached my limit and I was done being treated that way.

I stood there looking him straight in the eye, ready for whatever he was going to do next. I had taken it before, but I was not going to take it anymore! After seconds of a standoff, I saw all his brutish, bullying drain from him. I literally saw the skin on his face sag, the arch of his shoulders slouch, and the clench in his fist subside. It was as if he'd become a deflated balloon or a hollow shell. Not saying a word, he turned and walked into the bedroom, slamming the door behind him.

I limped out of the cottage and drove myself directly to the police station. I sat with a police officer and shared what had happened. My bruises, scratches, and torn clothing were all photographed and recorded. I gave my statement and signed it; something I should have done when I was 18 years old. I knew deep down inside we had been brought back together not for me to heal him, but instead for me to heal myself. I needed to stand up, find my voice, and finally put an end to that kind of treatment. After all those years of ignoring it, I had to make right on something I should have done the very first time it happened. Later that day, he was arrested, charged with assault, and taken to jail.

That may seem like the rewarding end to my story, but in truth it was just the beginning. It marked the start of a journey I had to take toward my own self-discovery and inner awakening. It formed the very epicenter of the necessary healing that had to take place within me. At first, I could hardly breathe as I sank into the devastating aftermath of all that happened. I had to face the shame, overcome the blame, and feel the crippling reality of the decision I had made to reconnect with him. I sank as low as I could go, burrowed myself in the debilitating consequences of how foolish I was to trust him again. I raged with self-hatred for supporting him despite countless warnings from others and overriding my own intuition. My self-loathing became an agonizing storm that ravaged over my entire Being, sinking me into the darkest depths of my life. I remember sitting at my kitchen table, locked in fear, devastated by the effects it had on my children, coping with the trauma of the assault, and dealing with the humiliation I felt inside. I didn't know my next step or where to turn. Like a drowning victim, I grasped for anything that would counteract the anguish and pull me from the wreckage I had made of my life. That's when I heard a voice on YouTube™. It was a confident, caring yet emphatic voice that said, "If you fall down, make sure you fall on your back because if you can look up, you can get up!" Something in that voice and those words spoke to my soul: *you can get up, you can get up, you can get up!* I played it over and over again. I listened to that recording day and night, putting it on repeat and listening to it endlessly. It became my mantra, my lifeline, and it helped me know that no matter what had happened to me, I needed to look up so I could get up!

Of course, the man who said that was none other than Les Brown himself.

His inspiring words pushed me to not just take care of myself, but to persevere and prevail. I began to follow Les and listen to whatever I could from him. I immersed myself in his teachings and saturated my mind with his messages. Over the next five years I devoted myself to doing everything possible to heal my life, my kids' lives, and the lives of others who have felt despair and sadness grip their hearts, like it has mine. I started using my voice to make an impact and devoted my efforts to blossoming into the woman I knew I was meant to become. I immersed myself in healing and started defining my greatness. I read, listened, studied, trained, self-taught, self-explored, and propelled myself forward in every way I could. I stopped freezing in conflicts, stopped being silent when things were unjust, and stopped letting anything happen to me that wasn't designed and determined by the healthiest version of me. I let my wounds heal over and become the callouses I needed to step into a new arena of possibilities that I was determined to create for myself. Life became full and abundant. God gifted me as he eternally does. I was awakened and freed, unleashed to be fully me.

I now bask in my past and embrace all of that story. Despite its unsavory beginning, the magnitude of its impact is what propels me forward. It is the story I needed to have to stand before you as the woman I am today. I decided to stop letting my story define who I was and hold me back, instead I chose to use it to refine who I want to become and unconditionally love that person. I learned firsthand the importance of raising my self-worth and elevating the beliefs I had in myself. I became hungry to develop new skills and show as many people as I could how it was possible to do the same in their lives. I have enjoyed the powerful benefits of working on myself and found a winning attitude toward cultivating greatness and mastering personal strength inside of me. All of my story has inspired me to help others achieve the same greatness in their lives and made igniting people's stories my magnificent obsession.

Much of what I do today, publishing other people's stories, is because I have this story. I am a better woman and human being because I have all that in my past. It is what makes me connect with others and value the unique stories they have. My desire to help people share their powerful stories led me to reach out and connect with Les Brown to create a book of inspiring stories from the other people he has influenced like me. This is that book, and it was a proud day in my life when I spoke with Les and we agreed to partner on this compelling compilation together knowing the positive impact it will make. Les has now become an amazing friend, and I am delighted and blessed that he is a huge part of my life in so many ways.

The best part is the full circle my story has taken. While working on this project, Les shared a powerful YouTube recording that was made of him. As he began to play it, the goose bumps formed on my arms and neck. It was the same recording I had listened to during my most difficult time. It was the same profound words that told me I could 'get up' when I felt so lost! Instantly my eyes welled up with tears, thinking about that devastating day when I first heard his life-changing words. As the tears began to fall, I immediately stopped myself, asking, why am I crying? What do I have to be sad about? I should be celebrating! Look at where I am in my life!

What I quickly realized is, when I first heard Les speak, it was *not* my darkest day, it was one of the greatest days of my life because it was the day the angels delivered his message to me. His words became the catalyst for me to get up and find my greatness. They became the beacon for me to learn more, grow as a person, and aspire for a greater life. I saw that what I thought was my darkest day was in fact my awakening, my enlightenment, a gift, a treasure, and the best day because that day got me to where I am right now! We often think a storm only brings the rain, but the rain feeds the flowers, produces the rainbow, and washes away what is no longer needed. I had to smile and redefine that day not as the darkest day, but the day that led me to this moment. A day where I feel a great sense of appreciation for every step that brought me to this very spot. It took all those twists and turns to guide me here: working, training, partnering, and mentoring with the great Les Brown. We are sharing stories that will help millions of lives. We are impacting the next great round of world-renowned speakers and we are creating an international best-selling book that will touch the lives of hundreds of thousands of people. I was mistaken thinking that his message came to me to pull me out of the darkness, when in fact it arrived to guide me to the light. The light I hope will Ignite you.

It is my intention that my story and all the stories in this book will help shine the light on the fact that what we think is one thing is often something else. What seems like darkness is indeed the beginning of the truth and the light. We don't know where our story will lead us as it begins, but what we do know is that the story is the foundation of the wondrous experiences we are destined to have. I believe every story matters, no matter what form it takes, no matter how it begins.

When you embrace your story and use it to Ignite your future, you develop a hunger so deep nothing can stop you. That hunger magnifies even more when you accept your past and appreciate your story; however it unfolded. It is when we share our stories that we empower ourselves, give new meaning to our stories, and use them to help others who may be going through the same situation. Your story will touch a life and spark a soul in ways you may never know. You have the ability to use your story to Ignite a passion and develop a hunger in others, so share it. Tell your story. Learn from it then use it to propel those that need to hear it forward so that they can 'get up' from wherever they are. See the light that shines from your story and know that your past does not define you, but instead refines you for the greatness, the possibilities, and the magnificent obsession you are destined to have. Everything that happens, happens for your highest good. Everything you experience is all part of the kaleidoscope that creates you.

I look forward to hearing your story and seeing how it has ignited and defined the greatness that resides in you. You are a gift like no other. You have magnificence in you and your story is your power. Use it.

IGNITE ACTION STEPS

Take the time to write down the facts surrounding your darkest day. List all the things, events, and situations that led and contributed to the feelings that made it your darkest day. There may be a long list dating back many years, or a short, shocking collection of incidents that just unfolded. Whatever led to that being such a challenging day, jot it down and add it to the list.

Once you have recorded the accounts of that dark day, set the facts aside and ask yourself, using hindsight to look back, what you have learned from that experience. Analyze all the things that have come to you since it happened. Start to see the hidden blessings behind the facts and the gems that are sparkling in the distant future.

Everything that happens, happens for a reason. See how you can turn the darkness into light. Find ways to discover the hidden gifts, the treasures, the magic that that situation is trying to birth. There is a master plan behind all that happens, designed by the Master himself. Use that knowledge to see how the story of your darkest day is in fact the gateway to something grand.

JB Owen — Canada
Speaker, Author, Publisher, CEO of Ignite, JBO Global Inc. and Lotus Liners
www.jbowen.website
www.igniteyou.life
www.lotusliners.com
 jbowen   *thepinkbillionaire*   *pinkbillionaire*

RACHEL HARVEY

"Fear is a necessary bridge to progress."

Have you ever 'frozen' with fear? Where you can feel it thick in your throat? The voice in your mind whispering, "What are you thinking? You cannot do this!" But then you feel your heart saying, "Don't listen! We all have something special to bring to the world! Run through that wall, jump over the obstacle, move around the trap... *you were born for this."* **I learned that being brave does not mean the absence of fear. My hope is that you are ready to Ignite the hunger in you and claim the fearless progress you've been waiting for.**

A CHANCE TO BE FEARLESS

I will never forget my first day of horseback riding lessons. After years of reading books about famous horses like Black Beauty and Seabiscuit, and watching my favorite tween movie *Wild Hearts Can't Be Broken*, I *knew* horses were meant to be a part of my life. At the age of 11, my parents finally succumbed to my relentless begging for horseback riding lessons.

On a crisp day in October, we pulled into the farm for the first time. The sweet smell of hay filled my nose, the sound of horses munching was like a long-lost song to my soul, and the happy heads of the resident equines poking out of their stalls seemed like a fairy tale. *It was finally my time.*

My parents and I walked into the barn where I met Barb, my soon to be instructor. She gave my mom the mandatory liability waiver. My 11-year-old mind had never seen such a waiver before. My mom thought this was a beautiful opportunity for learning, and asked me to read over the paperwork.

One particular line JUMPED off the page at me… that the barn was not responsible in case of serious injury, or even *death*. You see, I had forgotten that *falling* was a part of riding. Suddenly, Christopher Reeves popped into my mind. I could feel the terror settle into a pit in the bottom of my stomach. I wanted the magical part of riding, the relationship that goes deeper than words, the breeze in my hair, the power and speed that comes with a magnificent partnership between girl and beast… but wasn't sure if I was willing to risk it *all* in order to attain these things.

I searched my heart deeply, asking myself, "How badly do you want this?" My hands were shaking, and my palms were sweaty. While the fear was *real,* I knew I would *never* forgive myself if I didn't at least *try.* I signed the form.

Over the coming weeks, I found that I had a bit of talent with horses. They seemed to be at ease in my presence, my form was decent when riding, and my instructor kept using the word 'natural.' I had no idea what this meant, but I *did* know that barn days were my *favorite* days. Each week was full of new challenges, new skills, new information, new horses. I was in my element.

I progressed right through the winter months. As the weather got colder, the horses became less predictable in their behavior. Lessons were full of more explosive antics, 'spooking' or scooting forward as the doors would open, and people would come and go. Bucking and bolting were commonplace. If you were really lucky, after the snow accumulated on the metal roof, it would come zooming off in large sheets, sounding like a 747 taking off over our heads. On those days, it was notorious for someone to come flying off their saddle.

Each week I was forced to confront that fear of falling. I saw many other riders fall and felt the mounting tension. I tried to stuff it deep inside of me, but it was there. Ever present.

On one particularly cold Saturday, we arrived at the barn to find all of my fellow classmates had canceled due to the cold. My trainer popped her head out of the house and told us that I would be allowed to walk or trot on my own, but there would be no formal lesson. I had to be careful not to push my horse to ensure the cold air was not too hard on its lungs.

"No problem," I called as I eagerly headed into my frosty oasis. The air was so cold I could feel my nose hairs freezing as I took a breath in, but *nothing* would keep me from my favorite day of the week.

As I headed toward the end of the aisle where our assigned horses were posted, my stomach dropped. Next to my name was written *Chance.* Chance was a rescue horse, but not the kind like Black Beauty that happily was reunited with his true love. Chance was *angry*. He was angry that humans had hurt him, that they had given up on him, and he was determined to seek revenge for his mistreatment. I often had to ask for an experienced barn worker when cleaning stalls to help me move safely around his space. He was known for 'whirling' in his stall, which, while adorable in a dog chasing its tail, is a whole other story with a 1,200-pound animal confined in a small space. I had been warned that he may rear if he felt unsafe and to watch out for the 'occasional' bite, so I took those warnings seriously.

As I stood there looking at the board, I couldn't help but wonder, "WHAT was my instructor thinking?!" I had only been riding for a few months. I didn't have the experience I needed. I had seen Chance take many *experienced* equestrians for quite the ride. And of *all days*, this HAS to be the assignment on the day I do not have my instructor to guide me.

I checked over my shoulder, wondering if there was a way out of this. Would they know if I rode a different horse? No one else was here for lessons so surely I could just select one of my favorites like Golda-Mae or Breezy. Deep down, I knew I did not have permission for another choice.

My hands were shaking and my palms were sweaty. The thought, "Should I just skip today, like all of the other classmates?" *definitely* crossed my mind. It *was* insanely cold. Borderline unsafe. BUT this was my *only opportunity* to ride for the week. Did I want fear to rob me of my favorite time? "What do I do," was LOUDLY on replay in my mind.

As I walked over to his stall, I couldn't decide which plan of action to take. My fear was real, but just as on my first day of riding, I knew I wouldn't forgive myself if I didn't at least *try*. I took his halter and lead in my left hand. As I stood outside of his stall, I took a deep steadying breath, trying to calm my hammering heart rate. I slid the latch open with my right hand, and slowly, ever so slowly, crept into his stall.

"Heyyy bud," I managed to squeak out. Horses have a natural tendency to sense the emotional 'temperature' of a person. I *knew* he could feel my nerves. I took another cleansing breath whispering, "Try Rachel. Just *try.*" I reached out my hand and stroked his dapple gray shoulder. Surprisingly, he didn't shy away from my touch, he just kept munching his hay. His soft coat under my fingertips reminded me this wasn't a monster. It was a living breathing animal that had been hurt. My touch could remind him that not all touch meant pain. I ran my hands down his neck, under his mane, cooing his name and steadying both of us.

I slowly bent down to his head, gently slipped the halter over his nose, across his ears, and clicked the clasp into place. He didn't whirl. He didn't bite. He didn't shrink away. "Ooookay," I said to myself, "I think I can do this."

I gently led him into the aisle and secured the cross ties on the halter, which held him in place while I saddled him up. I took extra care to brush him well; to find the spots that made him nervous and the spots that made him melt. I moved slowly, attentively, learning each part of him as we moved around one another. Once he was ready, I put on my helmet and walked him out to the ring.

In the arena, my nerves began to rear their heads again. "What if he bucks me off, what if I become like Christopher Reeves? What if he bolts? What if *I'm not ready?*" As I stood at the bottom of the mounting block, holding the reins in my trembling hands, my mind was singing a chorus of doubts.

I was considering *my most certain death*, when my dad walked up behind me and placed his giant hands on my shoulders. Immediately, his steady presence reminded me of reality — Chance was standing patiently for me and I was not in danger. *Yet.*

At that moment, my dad said something to me that I have carried with me *every day of my life.* He said, "Baby girl, being brave doesn't mean you're not scared, it means you *choose to do it anyway."*

He gave me permission to be afraid and a choice to make.

I realized fear was a necessary bridge to progress.

I inhaled a deep deep breath, then exhaled the shaking from my body. I chanted, "Being brave doesn't mean you're not scared," over and over in my mind. I climbed up on that mounting block with 'fake it 'til you make it' determination. I placed my left foot in the stirrup, and before I had the opportunity to think, I swung my right leg over and took my place in the saddle. As I was getting my foot in place, I remembered, "He can *feel* you now, you're connected." I took another breath, reached down, and gave his long thin neck a stroke.

I gently said, "We're okay bud, we're okay."

As he walked, I saw his ears twitching ahead of him, and back to me, ahead and back. He was listening. This was a good sign. I gave his shoulder another pat, I kept the reins ready, but gave him room to breathe. Suddenly, I felt his sides puff up, and then felt a *big exhale.* He was relaxing!!

I gently gave him a squeeze with my legs, *asking* him to move, not telling. He sprang forward into a quick trot, and I settled deep into my seat, grounding us both with a confidence I didn't quite trust. I tried to set a rhythm with my posting, up, down, up, down in the saddle, the words "steady, steady, steady," a constant metronome in my mind. His pace began to regulate, he let out another deep breath, and we began to move together. Alone in the arena, we did circles, we changed directions, we did serpentines. We *danced*.

It was a short ride to ensure he didn't stretch his lungs, and that he didn't begin to sweat. As I came to a halt in the middle of the arena, I hopped down. *Elated*. I had done it! Chance nuzzled my shoulder with his nose, appearing as relaxed as I felt. My worst fears had not come true.

I had looked fear in the face and proceeded anyway.

I may have been inexperienced, but I learned that day that I had more inside of me than I had realized up to that point. Chance became my favorite assignment week to week. He called me to a higher level of skill, and each week, the small group of us that worked with him reminded him that human hands meant *love*, not pain. I learned that being brave *did not mean* an absence of fear. I learned, too, that I was not the only one who felt afraid, and I was in awe of Chance's willingness to be fearless despite his past.

As I grew older, my experience with Chance, and that mantra my dad had given me (which I later learned he paraphrased from John Wayne) prepared me for many difficult horses. With each one, the demand on my horsemanship increased and so did my confidence. I did go on to eventually fall, and realized, *it wasn't that bad*. That fear could have cost me the very foundation of who I am today if I had let it stop me. Instead, learning that *fear*, when combined with my passions, meant that something great was on the way. This pattern is one I have leaned on through many seasons and challenges of my life.

At 19, when the love of my life and I found out our first child was on the way, although we were scared, we chose to proceed anyway. When it was time to finish my college education as a young mother, I felt the fear and enrolled anyway. Shortly after graduating and working as a Spanish teacher for a year, my life called me to pivot. I left my career of education to pursue entrepreneurship and helping others. We took a leap and opened our own brick-and-mortar which we ran for three years, before it was time for yet another pivot. While selling our business came with a slew of fears: "Will my people be in good hands? Will it continue to stand the test of time? Are we making the right decision?" that lesson with Chance was the very thing that has led me to move forward confidently, knowing my gifts were calling me to climb *higher*.

At 11 years old, I was fortunate enough to learn that fear is not a sign to run. It is a time to slow down. Bravery means to feel the fear, evaluate where the opportunity is on the other side of fear, and move forward. Fear is the very thing that causes me to be more attentive, to take a different approach, and *almost always* leads me to progress.

Now as a speaker and expert in fearlessness, when I feel the fear of using my voice in front of others, that fear alerts me to the excitement and satisfaction that is yet to come. It is like a blinking neon sign that says, "Go here!" It's not a sign to run, it's a sign that it is about to get *good.*

Eleanor Roosevelt once said, "You gain strength, courage, and confidence by every experience in which you really stop to look fear in the face… You must do the thing you think you cannot do."

If you make this a standard for your life, it is only a matter of time before you too are marching forward into a future you can hardly imagine at this time. I believe we are each gifted with particular skills and talents that this world needs. Perhaps it is a song only you can sing, a story only you can tell, a business only you can create, a book only you can write, a product only you have the idea for, a service your community desperately needs, or a mission that has been planted directly in *your heart.* I am here to tell you that your passion is not given to you solely as a hobby, but as an avenue to help you tap into your *purpose.* My love of horses taught me to read others without words, how to shift energy from pain to passion, and how to coach authentically and from the heart. While I thought all of that was in preparation for becoming a Spanish teacher, it turns out I was meant to go far beyond the walls of my local high school, and instead inspire others to live the unbridled life of their dreams.

The Bible says, "If you hone your gifts, they will bring you before greatness." I believe your gift wants to do the same for you. My friend, YOU have greatness far beyond what you can imagine. All of the experience and qualifications you will ever need will be revealed to you as you share with the world *your gifts.* In fact, I believe *you* were born for this… born for fearlessness.

IGNITE ACTION STEPS

When you find yourself shaking in your boots, hands trembling and palms sweaty, afraid to take the next step and wishing you could be fearless, remind yourself that there is no progress without fear. Create forward movement for yourself by stepping into that place where you are most afraid of going.

Notice your fear. When you hear yourself saying, "My biggest concern is…" Those are grown-up words for fear. Ask yourself these questions:
1. Is your fear real or imagined?
2. When you consider what you are afraid of, is that fear based on *your own experience* or someone else's?

3. What is one thing about you that will help you confront this fear?
4. Is this fear in regard to a passion or desire of your heart?
5. What opportunity lies on the other side of your fear?

Use the answers to these questions to help you figure out how to cross the bridge of fear into your progress. You will find that most of our fears are imagined, and once you clarify what you're afraid of, you can begin to envision *victory* over that fear.

Next, set a timer for three minutes. Close your eyes and visualize yourself staring that fear in the face and *breaking through* it. What does that breakthrough feel like? Record these feelings and use them as an action plan when fear presents itself.

My last suggestion is to surround yourself with voices that remind you to be *fearless*. This could be via podcasts, audiobooks, or social media platforms. I would personally like to thank Mr. Les Brown for being a constant voice in my ear for the last 19 years. For reminding me in my darkest moments, that my mission is to, "Live full and die empty." That the only way through fear is *forward*.

This is your time to charge through that fear. Let nothing hold you back, go grab the reins of your life, and feel the victory of living a *fearless* life! This world needs *you*. It is time to *Ignite* your life!

Rachel Harvey — United States
Transformational Speaker, Life Coach,
Certified Nutrition and Movement Coach
www.fearlessprogress.com
🅕 *Progress with Rachel*
🅞 *Progress.With.Rachel*

Glenn Lundy

Glenn Lundy

"Changing the way you start your day will breathe life into how you live."

I believe that you and I are children of God. The God of the Universe. The God who made everything. And I hope you know THAT God made YOU to be the absolute best version of yourself that you can be. Not average. Not a little above average, or a little below, but the absolute best. This is no easy feat, but what I've found is that if we focus first thing in the morning, and change the way we start our day, it makes the journey to greatness much more achievable. It took me a long time to realize this, but through research, study, and personal experience, I believe I have unlocked a *'cheat code'* that will lead to success for you.

You Take Yourself Wherever You Go

One poor decision after another.

This is how I spent so many years growing up, in and out of jail cells that reeked of rotting food, sweaty criminals, and alcohol seeping through people's pores. A resident of Flagstaff, Arizona, I was known well by three groups of people — the local police, the local bar, and anyone looking for a car. That was me in a nutshell: a criminal, a party animal, and a salesman.

It did not take long for my hard and fast lifestyle to catch up to me. Between chasing women, experimenting with drugs, and trying to manipulate the law in order to stay out of jail, my life was a constant whirlwind of lies and deception. To say it was less than ideal is an understatement. It was downright absurd on every level. I was burning bridges left and right and coming desperately close to spending my life either behind bars or buried underneath one.

At 27 I had lost my job. I had lost my relationship with my daughter's mother, and I had lost custody of my 6-year-old little girl. I had disconnected from friends and family members, and devastatingly I had lost the respect and pride of my father. One step shy of completely alone, a new girlfriend was the only thing left in life for me to cling to. Soon after that I was broke, destitute, and desperate. I did not have a clue what to do, or where to turn, and my new girlfriend was increasingly embarrassed to be seen in public with me.

One day I decided to run away from it all. I packed up my white Ford Mustang™ with my favorite Raiders™ football jersey, my poker chip sets, and a defiant attitude as I hit the road. I had no idea where I was going or how I was going to make it once I got there, but I knew I had to get out. I had police looking for me, parents dreading the next phone call they might receive, and a small-town reputation you would not wish on your worst enemy. And it was everyone else's fault. I gave everyone that ever loved me the middle finger and ran away scared to death of what lay ahead.

I made my way to Vegas for a bit. Then headed out to Long Beach, California. I hopped around in South Beach and San Diego, then found Scientology in Tustin, California. I spent my nights sleeping on stained, moldy couches, filthy floors, and body odor-infested buses. My days were filled playing poker with other people's money whenever I could get my hands on it. I never pursued honest work because I seemed to have this uncanny ability to play cards well enough (MOST of the time) to stay afloat. I learned all I could about Scientology during this season of my life, and when I decided I wanted to learn something different, many days were consumed with staring into the ocean and trying to figure out where everything had gone wrong.

I still spoke to my girlfriend occasionally, and my mom would get a customary 'I'm alive' phone call every so often, but for the most part I simply roamed around with no real direction until ultimately, I ended up homeless. I had run out of places to go, couches to occupy, and people to intrude on. The streets were the only place left for me.

It did not take many weeks in the streets before I decided I'd had enough of that life, and that existence. My guess is a lot of homeless people go through this. You just reach a point where you lose hope, you have tried everything possible to get off the streets, and now here you are... rock bottom with nowhere to turn.

Feeling completely invisible I went to the most beautiful place I knew, the cliffs and beaches of La Jolla, California. I sat and marveled at the beauty of the ocean, its power expressed through each sound of the waves slapping against the rocks. That day, I decided, would be my last day. It was time for me to end the struggle. I walked out on to the beach and into the ocean, and I didn't stop walking. I could feel the coolness of the wake begin to clip my ankles as I traveled into the early edges of the vast Pacific.

Then, in a breath, I sensed every individual hair on my arms standing up, hyperaware of every aspect of my being. I was overtaken by a feeling of insignificance, while simultaneously feeling more than human.

I literally began to feel God.

I kept walking. The waves began to climb up my body and crash against my waist. The fear and loneliness I had inside began to wash away. I went deeper. I thought about my parents, how much they had loved me, though I never really understood why. I thought about the people I had used and abused and taken advantage of. I thought about the drugs, the parties, and the late nights. I thought about every step I had taken and then realized one simple truth — in every experience I was the only common denominator. It was not the rest of the world's fault I was here; it was mine, and now I was going to be the one to do something about it.

I began to think about my daughter. I got angry. I could not believe I had let go of the most remarkable thing I had ever created.

I felt worthless... Worthless... I was worthless.

The water began to reach my chest. I started to notice my buoyancy as my feet began to bounce off the ocean floor and for a moment fear started to set in. I did not know how to swim very well...

The salt began to stain my lips. I started to paddle out toward the horizon and the fear went away. I was going to drown here and I was okay with that. It made so much sense. If I could remove ME from the equation then I could remove the hurt. I could stop others from having to live with me, think about me, fight with me, be disappointed in me. I could make it all go away. It was so simple! Just swim. Swim out. As far as possible until there was no way I could ever make it back. Then I would sink. Then I would not be able to breathe. Then I would die, and all the problems of my world would die with me.

I went under...

Time started to slow down and speed up all at once. The waves were coming in and smacking me in the face, I would bob under and then pop back up, paddling my feet and arms, helplessly gasping for air. I went under again...

That was it. I was done. My arms and legs were giving up on me, my lack of oxygen taking its toll, the salty ocean surf starting to sting my eyes and sour my lips. That was it. I went under.

Then my feet hit the ground.

Luckily, I survived that day. You see, I was washed ashore by the incoming tide. I was such a weak swimmer that I could not even make it out past the break. When I gathered myself, I could see I was just barely off the beach, so I allowed the tide to push me back in and I rolled up onto the sand. At that moment I realized I was not going to be able to take the easy way out. I was going to have to figure out a way to not only survive in this world, but to thrive in it.

And then it hit me: "You take yourself wherever you go." These were the words of an old mentor of mine. I lay on the beach bedraggled, breathing heavily, exhausted and mortified at what I had just attempted. The stars of the night sky above me were a reminder of just how small my problems actually were, and how tremendously vast the Universe and its opportunities are. And the mentor's words came again: "You take yourself wherever you go."

I knew he was right but didn't want to admit it at first. Over the course of my life the environments had changed, and the friends and family members I spent time with varied throughout the years. I changed jobs, I changed zip codes, I changed everything around me, and yet, the results continued to be the same. Jailed. Broken. Alone. Invisible.

"You take yourself wherever you go," summed up the entire experience of my life! I had been blaming everyone else around me all this time when the reality was I was the one creating the very results I despised! Me! I was the catalyst of all things negative in my life! It was as if the mud had been wiped away from my eyes. I was blind but now I could see.

Once I realized that, everything changed. I began to ask questions like, "If I am the catalyst of all things negative in my life, then does that mean I can be the catalyst of all things positive?" and "Am I really just made of flesh and bones? Or is there more to me?" These questions, and many more like them, began racing through my mind to the point where I had to scratch the itch. I had to learn more about myself. I needed to know who I was and what I was made of.

In hopes of finding the answers to these questions I got a job at the Orange

County Church of Scientology. There I spent six months learning about every-thing from how to communicate to how to really study and retain information, and also about this idea of a 'Thetan' or 'Soul.' This helped me realize that we are THREE dimensional creatures, not TWO. We are mind, body, and spirit, and discovering that was the catalyst I needed to transform my life from the inside out.

That journey led me to study Buddhism and Hinduism, and ultimately I found my spiritual enlightenment through Christianity and Jesus Christ (a story I am happy to share with you on another day). Each lesson I learned along the way and every step I took played a part in the spiritual understanding I have today.

Since then I have had many successes, continuously striving to be the abso-lute best version of myself that I can be. I am married to a beautiful woman and we have eight children. After almost a decade of guilt, shame, and worry, I have been blessed to reconnect with my oldest daughter. I live in Lexington, Kentucky, where I recently bought a house for my parents and was able to move them here to be around their grandkids. I have built businesses and made a name for myself online and in the automotive industry. I have developed relationships with some of the most influential people in the United States of America, and I have created an online group called #RiseandGrind that has grown to over 31,000 members and continues to climb. I share my story and speak on stages all around the country now, and most importantly, I have come to know and understand God on a level unprecedented in my previous life.

Along with all of that, I developed an insatiable curiosity for all things sur-rounding success. What makes successful humans tick? How are they 'winning' at this game of life? What are their habits? Their disciplines? How does their mind work? I wanted to discover who I was and what I was made of. I began to unlock what was most important to me by understanding what was most important to others and how they had discovered that in their life.

That curiosity led me to uncover the many limiting beliefs and biases I had acquired over the years. In doing so I was able to find some common practices used by many of the most successful people worldwide and I began to apply them in my life. Some worked, some didn't, but over time I was able to unlock the code to a profound morning routine that requires just five simple steps to create an extraordinary life; *The Morning 5*.

This practice awakens greatness in me and has me hungry for more. It shows me that by starting with a really solid foundation each day, you can take on anything. It is like putting on armor and having the tools to deal with all that life throws your way. I use this system every day so that I can walk with my head held high knowing that outside influences no longer shape me but that I am the catalyst of my destiny.

One of the most impactful mentors in my life is Les Brown. He says, "YOU decide what your limits are, and YOU decide your level of success. You are responsible for the time that you spend on this planet." And I believe that is a responsibility we should all take seriously.

Change the way you start the day and it will make a massive impact in your life. I believe that you are a child of God, the God of the Universe, the God that made everything. And that God made you to be the best version of yourself that you can possibly be. You are the catalyst for greatness and the life you desire. Together we can do this.

If nobody has told you this yet today, I believe in you.

IGNITE ACTION STEPS

Step 1 — Never push the 'Snooze' button.

There is a lot of science around step one. Simply do a Google™ search on "Sleep cycles" and you'll begin to see how the 'Snooze' button is really the devil selling you 10 minutes of extra sleep in exchange for hours of Starbucks™ sipping grogginess.

Step 2 — Do not touch your phone first thing in the morning.

Step two comes down to the simple truth that your mind goes into a massive consume mode just after waking, and the content consumed at that time will ultimately determine your energy, your frequency, and your overall perspective and outlook on the day. If you hop immediately on your phone, (which is filled with violence, politics, hate, problematic emails, etc.) you are exposing yourself to all of the evils of the world FIRST THING! Friends! Your mind is not ready for that yet! Let's put in some personal foundational work FIRST!

Step 3 — Write down your gratitude list AND your goals.

Step three is a little challenging at first, but you'll get the hang of it. Grab a journal or a notebook and simply write down 10 things you're thankful for. Lights, a roof over your head, a loving spouse or caring family member, etc. Then once you've reached a good solid 10, your body should be vibrating at an incredibly positive frequency. THIS is when you want to write your goals. Daily goals, weekly goals, monthly goals, long-term goals. I usually do about 10 in total. This will get your juices flowing and set the intention and tonality for your day.

Step 4 — Take care of the physical.

Step four doesn't have to be rocket science. You can walk, you can run, you can work out, I don't care what you do, just get MOVING! An object in motion tends to stay in motion, an object at rest tends to stay at rest, so start off your day getting your heart pumping and your blood flowing and you'll experience the physical benefits, as well as benefits of mind and spirit!

Step 5 — Send out an encouraging message.

Step five is the most important. Now that you've spent the morning getting tuned up and dialed in, it is time for you to release that energy into the world! Send a text, a Facebook™ message, or write a sticky note. It doesn't matter how you do it, just send a message that lifts someone else up! You will be amazed by the impact it has on others, AND on you!

It's really that simple.

All together you have a morning routine that will set you up to be formidable in every situation you come across throughout the day, and that my friend is the *The Morning 5* cheat code to lead you to one absolutely extraordinary life!

Glenn Lundy — United States
Speaker, Author
glennlundy.com
🔲 *OfficialGlennLundy*
🔲 *glenn_lundy*

PAT LABEZ

*"Get hungry for life and create an appetite that's
scrumptiously, contagiously fulfilling!"*

**This chapter comes with some trepidation as it's a part of me that few have
seen. Yes, like many, underneath the mask of smiles and joy was often an
anguished person, tormented by self-imposed expectations, afraid to speak
up because of fear, guilt, and shame. Perhaps you can relate to my feeling
of not fully understanding your own plight and an existence of quiet desperation. Sharing my story may shed hope, inspiration, and empowerment
to you. If any part of this shines a glimmer of light, oh, what a blessing!**

MOM, ARE YOU OKAY?

"Whoa, watch that curve!" The car swerved to the left… then to the right.
Those zigzag roads of Lake Arrowhead, California can be wonderful — and
treacherous — driving to the beautiful mountaintop, the clouds enveloping
anyone passing through. Thousands of visitors flock to the lake to enjoy the
many quaint shops, friendly townsfolk, water sports, ice skating, hiking, bird
watching, duck feeding, and simply relaxing; being one with nature. The scene
was heavenly. Yet, all I could think of was getting to heaven sooner than later.
There I was in my own darkness, strategically contemplating a sure demise.
If I could miss that turn at just the right time, I'd go past the metal guardrails,
down the ravine, and...

Why? It was supposed to be a joyous time: I had just given birth to a beautiful baby girl! At age 40, I had friends who wished for nothing more than becoming parents yet could not. I heard of their mad scramble to beat the biological clock, oocyte cryopreservation, heartbreaking miscarriages, in vitro fertilizations, and desperate adoptions overseas. And yet here I was — with the gift of a new, amazing innocent life to care for — feeling paralyzed.

I consider myself a late bloomer, proud that neither marriage nor children were critical to feel 'complete.' Seven years after tying the knot with Dave, a surprise blessing came. Deemed as a 'high-risk pregnancy,' my excitement was tempered, as pressure was put on us to consider abortion! I was told because of my age, "The normalcy of this child is questionable. Are you equipped to handle any special needs?" This added angst for an already nervous mother-to-be, but we chose life.

I was put on full bed rest in the last two months. "Your daughter is in the fourth percentile," we were told. I didn't really know what that meant, but the next few weeks were extremely difficult as I was ordered to lie down on my left side, only allowed to get up for bathroom runs. I read and learned to knit. As someone so independent, I resented being totally reliant on Dave. I gave up work. I gave up seeing friends. I gave up my favorite things. I gave up my identity. The psychological, physical, and mental adjustment to parenting was eating at me.

Thirty-four weeks later, "She's not breathing properly. We need to get her out!," exclaimed the doctor. All I remember was getting wheeled into the operating room for an emergency C-section as I was still waiting for Dave to return with a pastrami sandwich. "Wait!" I yelled. My head was spinning. I'm about to be a mother? I'm not ready! Where's Dave?" They found him with his pastrami sandwich, in time for him to wash his hands and welcome our little one, Amanda Joy. It was magical. Crazy, but magical, and a moment of joyful bliss and fulfillment.

Being premature, there were many health challenges for Amanda from the start. I'd watched her, perplexed. Is this my imagination? I asked anyway. We discovered that she would frequently stop breathing and had to be connected to a heart machine. "If she stops breathing for more than 12 seconds, call 911," we were told. I was wracked with feelings of ineptness, never really sure what was real and what was 'just my imagination.' I don't think we ever really slept that first year.

For months, she never stopped crying, but doctors couldn't tell us why, dismissing colic as a possibility. We did the best we could in monitoring her. It was a mystery… and misery. During that time, my tremendous guilt was exacerbated when 'breastfeeding for your child's sake' came to a sudden halt. Shattered glass piercing through my chest was all I could feel as I thought, "What's wrong with me?" Multiple stressors were at play here. Then one night, Dave got a glimpse of a story about mold. I always sensed some mustiness in our house when we moved in. Another visit to the doctor resulted in a diagnosis: allergy to mold. "You need to get out as soon as possible," the doctor said.

"Noooo! I'm tired! We just moved here! I can't take it anymore!"

As exhausted and stressed as we were, we knew we couldn't live with ourselves had we ignored the mold as the likely cause of our baby's constant crying and obvious discomfort. So we moved to a drier community. Within two weeks, she was fine. A few years later, we discovered that her brother had developed a mold mass in his lung the size of a golf ball and was coughing up blood. Had we not moved, perhaps the same thing could have happened to her. Real? Or was that just my imagination?

Motherhood was simply overwhelming. The first two years were a blur. I survived and put on a happy face whenever others were around but I was miserable and didn't really even know why. I felt drained, exhausted, incapable. I couldn't breathe. I even ignored the fact that I was functioning as a one-armed bandit when I became unable to move my left arm. I thought it was my imagination until I got brave enough to mention it to my doctor during a routine wellness check two years later. "Pat, you have adhesive capsulitis!" — a frozen shoulder. It was real. I wasn't losing my mind. It took two outpatient procedures to rectify the problem.

We yearned for some peace. The mountains always called for us and so we eventually found our way to Lake Arrowhead, just a couple of hours' drive from Los Angeles. Beautiful. And yet, I couldn't look past the darkness of life. Guilt-ridden, I accepted the notion that I was at fault; that something was wrong with me, and I was being a 'bad mom.' It was a vicious cycle. "You'll get over it," I was told. While everybody was going goo-goo and ga-ga with the baby, I dug myself deeper and deeper into the abyss. Darkness consumed me as I disconnected. You see, I had been battling those 'thoughts' in my head for some time. Keeping them at bay was always a challenge. But I never shared those fears. Real? Or just my imagination?

One day, I snapped. I don't even recall what triggered it. All I remember was all those times of contemplating 'the end' suddenly became so vivid. It was real... not imagination. "It is time," I said, frantically searching for the car keys. But Dave got a hold of them first. There was nowhere for me to go. I was screaming and became a mad woman. He reached out to his sister, Kate,

60 miles away. "Pat's going through postpartum depression, Dave," she said. "Get her to Camarillo... now! She needs to see my doctor!"

Somehow — I don't know how — we got through the insane hysteria. My uncontrollable sobbing finally subsided. Shame took over. Unable to think clearly and totally ashamed for having been 'out of control,' all I could focus on was Amanda, who was now getting into the 3-year-old tantrums, yelling and screaming.

"I can't deal with this. I can't take it anymore," I thought. Afraid of what I might do and feeling alone, I went into the closet and locked myself in. I laugh at it now but it was no laughing matter then. It got quiet and a faint, innocent, little voice outside the door lovingly spoke, "Mom, are you okay?" Yup, it was role reversal time. I opened the door and quietly hugged her. Stop the madness. Be a good role model. That's the least you can do. But that couldn't be me as I was, right then, at my wit's end without even knowing why or how I got there. Guilt-ridden, ashamed, exhausted, confused, I found myself desperately crying out to God.

What I didn't expect was for Him to answer. I didn't grow up in a religious family, but simply adopted the Golden Rule in my daily life. To my surprise, my chosen preschool for Amanda turned out to be a ministry of a Christian church. One Sunday morning, listening to Pastor Darryl, I found myself sobbing. It was as if the words being spoken were exclusively for me. Real? Or just my imagination?

I 'turned over the yoke' to God, hoping He would lift me and carry me through these dark days. And ever so slowly, between Pastor Darryl, Pastor Charlie, and the warm, welcoming new friendships I formed, I started to breathe again. At 43, I was baptized. "I can do all things through Christ who strengthens me" (Philippians 4:13) became my daily reminder. There was an indescribable inner peace within me that would keep me grounded in the midst of life's many following storms. It was, in fact, a rebirth of my soul. I stepped into the real; not an imagination.

I found solace at church, at work, and immersed myself in volunteering with many agencies, supporting their good work throughout Ventura County. A newfound purpose emerged from the rubble of my postpartum depression. With my mother's Alzheimer's disease and eventual passing, I committed myself to senior services. I loved the innovative programs developed at the assisted living community I worked at. I was overjoyed when a family member would thank us for making a difference in their loved one's life, to see a twinkle in their eyes again, to smile and laugh again, to feel alive again with their bodies withering… blessings. A busy purpose-driven life and serving others kept me together and I discovered again that 'when one door closes, another one opens.'

My next position in human resources and volunteer administration would prove to be equally satisfying. On my 50th birthday, southern California seemed to be on fire. Calling on volunteers to donate their time, talent, and resources to help assemble a dozen emergency shelters and to help total strangers was exhausting but so gratifying, as I witnessed the spirit of mankind rise to the occasion, overcoming differences, and getting down to the basics of survival. Regardless of social or economic status, when tragedy hits like a house fire, we're all equally waiting amid the ashes. It was real, not an imagination.

As I look back now and reflect on what I might have missed had I been successful that one fateful day on the mountain, I can barely contain the sadness. I think of that precious visit my 15-month-old Amanda got to experience with my 83-year-old mom. They embraced and quietly giggled as they played with flower leis and shared applesauce; spiritually connected and intertwining secrets on another level.

Shortly after that visit, on Thanksgiving Eve, as mom took her last breath in Hawaii, I later found out that at that very moment, 3,000 miles away in California, Amanda suddenly cried out loud, sobbing and seemingly in pain for no reason, looking up, reaching out, and eventually stopping on her own as she longingly stared above her crib. That was real, not imagination!

I think of all the beautiful experiences with family and friends; the holidays and special celebrations. I think of the blessing of being able to help so many people along this path I almost chose to deny myself from experiencing. As some anonymous visionary once said, "To the world, you may be one person; but to one person, you may be the world." This is real.

I think about my sister, Joy, who valiantly fought for her life and overcame the odds of cancer by surviving her prognosis of three months, then staying with us for over four years. She taught us so much about life: embracing the present, loving people, and enjoying exactly where you are. I'm comforted at the thought that perhaps, at some level, I was able to contribute to that, and the ripple effect I had on others. I never knew what a bucket list was until Joy shared hers. In the middle of a cold, blistering winter, we made it to the New Year's Eve festivities at Times Square, to see that ball drop at midnight, welcoming another year that she thought may very well be her last. Sheer happiness. That was real.

I smile thinking of Amanda's many precious dance programs with ballet, tap, lyrical, and hip-hop in California, Texas, and New York. Then chuckle at her guppy to barracuda swimming lessons, bicycle training, and of course, her culinary creations with 'the best cooker in the world,' her dad. I think of her being the youngest volunteer as she maintained the rescue mannequins and put together educational health and safety brochures for the American Red Cross™. I adored watching her be the beloved 'adopted granddaughter' of our long-term care residents where she learned to play bingo and set up for events. I see that brave third grader 'Miss Amanda' being the Sunday school teacher's aide and parents loving her caring for their young ones. And, finally, witnessing that fragile little baby grow up into the fine young woman that she is today; all priceless. Having accomplished so much in her young life while overcoming her own obstacles, she is now thriving and ready to tackle the world independently with all the dreams and hopes of a bright future.

I look back and wonder how things might have turned out, how her life might have been impacted, had I gone through with all those thoughts of going over the edge. I'm grateful that, by the grace of God, those moments of desperation were somehow erased; hope, service, and divine intervention took their place. It was obvious, when we give, so do we receive.

I now find myself living an amazingly fulfilling life. I share my Third Act Encore program to give hope, inspiration, and practical ideas and resources for older adults and their families for a more joyful, fulfilling life. Thirty years after walking away from something that gave me joy, I now find myself back in the middle of it all. Surprise, surprise! I don't think I even realized how my mindset had actually shifted as I just tried to 'find joy in the journey' and go with the flow. I've been asked, "Don't you ever sleep? Don't you ever stop? What now?" When most folks are slowing down, I find myself racing for time and embracing whatever I do have. You see, I'm one of the fortunate ones. At 60 I had a nagging brain tumor that miraculously disappeared. Regardless of how — through my nontraditional, noninvasive measures, lifestyle change, redirected focus, or divine intervention — it was gone. I've been given a second lease on life. This is real. Not my imagination.

If you are dealing with trauma or depression, no matter the cause, please reach out to someone. Be kind to yourself, be real with yourself, and remember that every 'mistake' is a valuable lesson. **Choose life. Choose *your life*.** Learn, forgive, and move on. We are here for a reason and let's enjoy the journey. We have the choice of creating our own 'heavenly' experiences on earth that allow our souls to soar beyond imagination. In spite of the challenges, uncertainty, heartaches, disappointments, and chaos, yes, there IS sunshine, joy, hope, and blessings we can find everyday. It takes dark times to see the light, but there are always those who can help open our eyes when we are too scared to do so ourselves. With all the zigzags, detours, potholes, and roadblocks of our journey, there are also many pathways to happiness that await.

The Dash is a poem that subtly reminds us of how short our time is on earth, represented only by the dash on our tombstone between the beginning — and the end. **Make *your* dash count.** Make it real. Everything is fleeting. Life is fleeting. Fill it full to the brim with everything you imagine your life to be. Whatever is going on, it shall pass. So when your loved one asks, "Are you okay?" You can happily declare, ***"Yes, I am okay!"*** As the great Les Brown says, "Life is the gift that keeps on giving. Appreciate that blessing for what it is."

IGNITE ACTION STEPS

- Acknowledge the need for balance of mind, body, and soul. Take 15 minutes each day for yourself and light a candle to welcome in *joy* and peace.
- Remember you are never alone. Seek and accept help without guilt or shame. Reach out to me or another practitioner that can support you.
- Consider clinical and or alternative therapeutic options. Seek organizations in your community and those that specialize in enhancing mental health and wellness.
- Whatever you perceive God to be, believe and have faith in the good that exists.
- Feed your soul by reading, attending, and connecting with those who feel the same positive change.

Pat Labez — United States
Author, Actor, Advocate
www.PatLabez.com
www.ThirdActEncore.com
patlabez

Chad E. Foster

"You become the story you tell yourself."

Sometimes the most beautiful gifts are disguised in ugly wrapping paper. My gift of blindness has made me happier than before because I choose to tell myself a better story — the facts are less significant than the stories we tell ourselves. It is my sincere hope that you will be inspired to reimagine your life's vision and discover unforeseen possibilities, feeling confident, hopeful, and empowered to take on life's challenges. To live your best life you must step outside your comfort zone. You never know what's possible until you try.

From Victim to Visionary

"Try to prepare for the day when Chad's eyesight is gone," the doctors told my parents. "In the meantime, enjoy life while you can."

I was 3 years old when the doctors at Duke University Medical Center diagnosed me with Retinitis Pigmentosa (RP), an incurable genetic disorder that gradually causes blindness.

Weighted down by a feeling of incredible helplessness, my parents cried the whole ride home that day. Although a small number of those with RP retain some eyesight their entire lives, my parents knew it was likely that I'd eventually go blind.

As a kid all I wanted to do was run and play, even though I had poor peripheral vision and difficulty seeing in dim light. I bumped into things all the time.

I broke my leg falling out of the bed of a pickup truck. I split my head open on a low-hanging metal pipe I didn't see under the low light of dusk. I was such a regular at the hospital that the staff questioned me and my parents out of fear I was being abused.

Some people might have been deterred by the threat of constant injury, but that just wasn't me. From an early age I rode my bike and played basketball, football, and soccer. I lifted weights and joined the high school wrestling team. I even learned to water ski and ride a motorcycle. I ignored the signs that the darkness was closing in on me. At 16, I got my driver's license and drove during daylight hours until my condition made driving impossible. Even after that, I tried to ignore my vision problems. One night I fell into a roadside ditch because I'd decided to walk alone to a local burger joint. I ended up hobbling on crutches for six weeks.

These were my years of dancing with denial, of misguided thinking. I refused to prepare for the day when I would go blind. I didn't learn braille and couldn't use a walking cane. When I enrolled at the University of Tennessee, I took biology courses in hopes of going into medicine — a seemingly unrealistic aspiration for someone with RP.

Then, one day while reading a class assignment, the pages blurred before me. It was as though a swarm of buzzing bees had invaded my field of vision. The cold reality hit me like a sledgehammer. This was it. I'd read my last word of print. Seen my last sunset. Played my last game of basketball. Life as I'd known it was coming to an end.

A boa constrictor of hopelessness wrapped itself around me and squeezed me tightly. It was hard to move. Hard to breathe. I'd aspired to help others in the medical field, but now I felt like a victim who couldn't even help himself. I had to mourn the death of my imagined future self. My high-flying hopes and dreams were gone, and in their place was the prospect of a life marked by disability, dependence, and low expectations.

I was living with friends in a party house near campus and we spent most days lounging, playing billiards, watching TV, and playing video games. One time, my older cousin Mark came to visit from Texas and we went out for beers. Mark was easy to look up to because he had his life together, and he was also a big guy — about 6'4" and 250 pounds. As we talked in my driveway, he motioned toward the house and asked me, "You know those guys in there?" I nodded as I felt the anxiety over where his question was going. "All those guys are losers and if you don't stop hanging out with them, you'll be a loser too." I felt the searing sting of shame as Mark's words pierced my tough exterior because I knew, deep inside, Mark was right.

My parents were building a new home around this time, and I noticed the floor plan included a 2,000-square-foot finished basement with a private ground floor entrance. We never discussed it, but I knew they'd planned it in case the world became too hard for their disabled son. I started thinking of that place as the 'Loser Basement.' I vowed to never spend a day in it as long as I lived.

I didn't know what I wanted to be because I wasn't sure what I could be. I switched my major from premed to business because it gave me more broad and diverse career options. Then I had to relearn how to learn. I recorded all my class lectures on audiotape and the university provided me with a notetaker to help me. None of my textbooks were available on audio, so my mother spent countless long nights reading them into a tape recorder until her voice wore down to a rasp. Her heroic support inspired me. I couldn't let her down by not studying. I made the dean's list for the first time and I made straight A's from that point onward. Turns out, I was a better blind student than a sighted student.

In order to live independently, I wanted to get a guide dog to serve as my trusted companion. I spent four weeks training at "Leader Dogs For The Blind" in Michigan, but I ended up acquiring a far more valuable lesson from my classmates. Many of them faced challenges more daunting than blindness. Some had serious cognitive impairments and some had their eyesight stolen by diabetes and were on dialysis. Two young women there were both deaf and blind from birth. I had taken so many things for granted.

We all take things for granted don't we?

The living courage exhibited by these brave people left me ashamed of my self-pity and victim attitude. I had a fit body, a sharp mind, and I'd enjoyed 21 years of eyesight. I had a loving family and an active dating life. What right did I have to complain? I returned to Knoxville with my new guide dog, Miles, and with a new profoundly appreciative perspective on life.

None of us control the cards we're dealt, but we all control how we play them. For the first time in my life, I could no longer pretend to be a sighted person. There is no way to hide who you are when you are parading around with a 100 pound German shepherd. But when I got beyond my victim mentality, I discovered blindness comes with benefits. With Miles by my side, I rarely waited for a table at dinner. When I went out at night with my friends, young ladies bought me drinks. My dog was such an attraction wherever we went that my friends suggested I change his name from Miles to Magnet. This was the start of me accepting myself as I am, and it compelled me to love myself — at first despite my imperfections but eventually *because* of them.

I wish I could say life from that point forward was easy, but it wasn't. I felt the sharp sting of discrimination when company recruiters visiting campus didn't even want to talk to me. But I landed two strong job offers before graduation and accepted the one from the Atlanta office of a major Fortune 500 consulting firm. I moved to Atlanta's northern suburbs, which is where I met my wife-to-be, Evie. She captured my heart on the spot because she was the one girl who noticed me first, not my dog.

Together we moved to the Washington, D.C. area, where I started consulting on the accessibility of technology. Within a year I was at the world's largest accessibility conference in Los Angeles where Grammy award winner Stevie Wonder and his entourage were checking out the technology on display. While everyone was asking him for autographs, my ability to build accessibility solutions gave me the confidence to pitch my services so he could use his software more effectively. The next thing I knew I was in Hollywood, at Roscoe's House of Chicken 'N Waffles, eating crispy fried chicken and maple drizzled waffles with Stevie Wonder. I spent that weekend at his North Hollywood studio assessing his modified yet finely-tuned setup. I was thrilled to be hanging out with such a living legend who had faced similar challenges as me.

I kept expanding my comfort zone. I taught myself how to engineer my screen-reading software so that I could do my job more effectively, and turned it into a profession. I worked with large enterprises and government agencies, even building software that Silicon Valley said was impossible. Eventually, I found my strength designing the financial models and pricing strategy for complex billion-dollar technology projects. With my dog and my determination, I traveled for work frequently by myself, sometimes overseas, adapting and cultivating confidence with each new country and experience.

Having won billions of dollars worth of contracts for my company, my bosses asked if there was something the company could do for me. For some crazy reason, I asked them to send me to Harvard Business School (HBS). For some crazier reason they said okay. I attended a one-year program with mostly remote classwork, along with three on-site sessions at the HBS Boston campus.

The HBS class taught by Bill George, former CEO of Medtronic and author of the business best seller *Discover Your True North*, was an unforgettable experience. He taught how we can 'mine our lives' — identifying those personal moments that deeply affect us and linking them to our career pursuits. By linking past events that affect us emotionally to our profession, we discover our purpose — allowing us to journey toward our 'True North.' As my class-mates grappled with their experiences, my 'True North' slammed me in the chest. For so long I dismissed others when they mentioned I'd inspired them when I was simply doing my job to the best of my ability or just striving for my next goal in life.

Each class at HBS elects a speaker for graduation, and I had such a strong feeling that I'd be selected that I flew to Texas to work with a public speaking consultant. Together we polished a short 12-minute talk, and when I was indeed elected as graduation speaker, I was ready. For the first time in my life I used the story of my journey to try to help and motivate others.

The explosive applause, the hoots and the hollering took me totally by surprise, and what happened next changed my life. A small crowd formed around me to share their words of congratulations. More than a few told me I should become a professional speaker. Then one classmate pulled me close. "I'm going through a tough time," he confided, referring to his recent divorce. "And boy, you really gave me a gift. Thank you." Another classmate grasped my hand and told me earnestly about the young daughter he'd lost to cancer. Something I'd said had given him hope that he might see her loss in a new light. He broke down sobbing in my arms, and I teared up as I held him.

The trip back home from Boston ignited something inside me. During the quiet late-night flight I reflected on the speech and how everyone reacted. For the first time, I felt like my blindness wasn't just for me, it was for others. Finally, a realization hit me: "This could make going blind worth it." Tears began streaming down my face as I sat on the plane. The earth-shattering realization pierced my steely armor like a hot knife through butter.

I'd been so focused on my career and family for so long that I'd never thought about the impact I might have on other people just by sharing my story. The brilliant moment of clarity was terrifying — at age 40 I'd need to be a beginner all over again. I was being presented another chance to step outside my comfort zone and share my story publicly and professionally. It was fraught with uncertainty but my North Star was knowing I'd never forgive myself if I didn't at least try.

For the next four months the speaking consultant and I did the humbling work of turning my 12-minute talk into a full-length keynote. Sometimes we'd spend three hours on the phone to grind out three minutes worth of content. I had to strike the right balance between serious stories of overcoming adversity and lighthearted humor that would activate an audience.

My first engagement after HBS was a 25-minute talk at a local nonprofit. As

I waited for my turn, I felt a nervousness that I hadn't anticipated. I'd practiced the speech dozens of times, but what if I forgot what to say next? I obviously can't read notes while speaking. It was a tightrope walk without a net. I felt nervous the entire time yet delivered the talk flawlessly and with impact.

I've since given hundreds of talks to business leaders on six continents and I'm used to the feeling of nervous excitement that precedes every talk. I feel a thrilling sense of pride by having faced this fear, stepping through it to move beyond myself and help others. I decided not to let my lack of eyesight limit my vision and I stepped outside my comfort zone. Within a year of making the decision I was able to secure a book deal with HarperCollins Leadership, and my memoir, *Blind Ambition*, was published.

My life is an experiment in living outside my comfort zone. Learning the limitations of my eyesight, going blind, relearning how to learn, entering job interviews with a guide dog, traveling domestically and internationally without sight — all these were uncomfortable. But as I ebbed outside my comfort zone I noticed it expanding. I also observed my confidence growing because I demonstrated that I was capable of more than I thought possible. We're all capable of more than we think is possible, and that includes you too.

In recent years I began downhill snow skiing. Yes, a blind guy decided it was a solid idea to ski the mountains of Aspen, Colorado! I get my instructions through an earpiece from a guide skiing behind me. Although it was way outside my comfort zone, it has become a recurring adventure. I like to push myself, so I crash a lot. During my first year I pushed so hard that I separated my shoulder in one crash. I guess some things never change. But now I regularly ski the advanced black diamond trails and even tackled a double black diamond last year. What I love about skiing is that you don't have to look too far to find your edge of discomfort, and that edge is where your internal growth takes place.

During the pandemic in 2020, my friend and mentor, Ben Gieseman, died of brain cancer at the age of 53. Ben's parting lesson to me is the reminder that our time on earth is precious and limited. This stark realization heightens my sense of urgency to keep growing, to continue improving, and to use my blindness as a gift to others; inviting everyone to see their possibilities and their blindspots. As Les Brown famously said, "The graveyard is the richest place on earth, because it is here that you will find all the hopes and dreams that were never fulfilled, the books that were never written, the songs that were never sung, the inventions that were never shared, the cures that were never discovered, all because someone was too afraid to take that first step, keep with the problem, or determined to carry out their dream."

Some of our gifts are disguised in terrible wrapping paper, but we all have an obligation to unwrap those gifts and share them with the world. Your gifts can make you a happier and better person. They can lead you to a more intentional and fulfilled life. Whatever circumstances you face, there is always a path forward, whether you can see it or not. There are so many gifts right in front of you, if you would only open your heart and your mind to receive them. Unwrap your gifts and step outside your comfort zone. This is where life begins.

IGNITE ACTION STEPS

1. Start a gratitude journal. Each night write down three things you're grateful for that day. Consciously capturing gratitude helps to make it a subconscious behavior.
2. Each week perform an action outside your comfort zone. This may be as simple as asking a coworker about a big project, or having lunch with a company executive.
3. Find more exercises from Blind Ambition at www.chadcfoster.com/ exercises.

Chad E. Foster — United States
Executive Dealmaker, Job Creator, Billion-dollar Generator, Author,
Motivational Speaker, Resilience Leader, Blind Black Diamond Skier
ChadEFoster.com
☐ FindChadEFoster
☐ FindChadEFoster

Renee L. Cunningham

Renee L. Cunningham

"You are a diamond, with brilliance shining through you and radiating everywhere you go. Shine, Baby, SHINE!"

My intention is to stir, shake, and dance you into your polished brilliance. Life might be hard now, but those trials are part of the polishing process. Know that as you walk through your life you will have moments that will cut and shape you to reveal the precious jewel that is buried inside. Your flaws are your glorious marks that distinguish you as you walk into a room, and your character, dimension, and weight are all beautiful attributes. My wish is you will let them be your guiding lights to your greatest potential.

The Polished Stones

It has been several years, but when we talk it seems like no time has passed at all. We speak on every subject, reminiscing about our shared past and letting laughter and love fill every corner of the conversation. She is me, and I am her.

She, my oldest goddaughter, 'my Pamela,' which I affectionately call her, is all grown up now with a son of her own. We met after I graduated from college and Pam was only 13. We both attended a local church where I taught praise dance. Our coming together was magical. Even today, Pamela introduces me saying, "This lady is everything I am, and everything I want to be. She taught me everything I know." When I hear her say this, it makes my heart just melt.

"Pam, do you remember your first impression of me?" I asked her.

"I loved you," she replied, recalling how we first connected on the praise dance team. Apparently, she really didn't want to be on the team, but I had insisted that I wanted her to be a part of it. Dance ended up giving her the confidence I knew it would. "You brought that out of me. I felt like I wasn't as skinny as the other girls," she said. I could relate, and I wanted her to step into the spotlight and shine her light. "I started to be a drama queen when I got with you. Honestly, I got my personality from you," she shared. Hearing this made me smile; I was glad I could help her find her voice and let it sing. She admits I am the reason she made it through high school, but all I did was help her see she could get herself through it and thrive.

I told her, "I wanted to help you and other young ladies discover their true potential and help them know that you can shine in any room that you enter." But I know the reason I connected with her goes beyond that. "Pamela, when I saw you, I saw myself," I said, "because I felt like I did not fit in during that same time in my life."

In Jackson Middle School I was in modern dance class with Sherri, Kam, and Tamika, and all the other girls that were skinnier than me. I was so unsure about how I looked and every week the girls did not like me for one reason or another. They isolated me for any minute action like rolling my eyes or for what I looked like with my Sasson™ jeans, or my hair pressed. It was a nightmare. I felt alone, and their actions cut deep. I ate alone at lunch, I walked home alone, and lived a sheltered life with very little socialization. I used to pray for friends. That was a pivotal point in my development. I spent all my eighth-grade year hating myself and looking forward to a new school. As the people around me shut me out, I became sure of one thing: I was NOT going to go to the same high school as them.

I took a special exam that would allow me to enter a premier 'magnet' school that focused on math, science, and applied technology (MSAT). I swore to myself I was going to have friends and be my authentic self. I declared, "I will not have any regrets ever in my life. I am not going to second guess what I want, I will just do it."

And I did!

Everything was going well. I became the Vice President of my junior class in high school and the plan was for all current council members to run for senior class in the same positions. But, I had this strange, sick feeling; a burst of energy telling me I should run against Johnetta for the spot of senior class president. I immediately rejected the idea. Johnetta and I were friends and both part of the MSAT program. We were excited to be nominated and had agreed on our election strategy. She would be President, and I would remain Vice President. Running against her was NOT what we agreed to. But I began to feel a grip in my stomach, like I was going down a roller coaster. I *had* to run for President.

Initially, no one knew I had put my name in for the running, but the secret was out when the time came for the candidates to speak at our campaign assembly. When the student body saw me step on stage, it caused a busy murmur and rumble throughout the audience. I was nervous but I started with my favorite scripture, "Brethren, I count not myself to have apprehended: but this one thing I do, forgetting those things which are behind, and reaching forth unto those things which are before, I press toward the mark for the prize of the high calling of God in Christ Jesus." (Philippians 3:13-14)

When I sat down after my election speech, I was shaking but I felt the weight of the assignment leave me. I did it. I accomplished it. I ran for President of my senior class. BUT I LOST. I was not embarrassed — I had listened to my gut, done what I knew I was supposed to, I had no regrets. Even though I didn't win the race, I won the battle inside of me.

Senior year went on, and I embraced the confidence and conviction in myself as I took on all kinds of activities. Yearbook, National Honor Society, dance… I was in *everything*. I was driving my own car (yes, I knew how to drive a stick shift), and I felt unstoppable. I graduated in the top 15 percent of my senior class. You see, this was the beginning of living and learning to trust that I had the guts to push the limits and let the fire inside of me come out. I did not realize it at that time but the flaws and challenges in my life would become the foundation of my teaching other young individuals how to Ignite the brilliance in them.

"No one can determine your destiny but you. Will it be easy? Of course not. Can you do it? Of course you can. But it requires patience and persistence. Seize any moment of crisis as your opportunity to start fresh and live your dreams." This is a quote by the famous motivational speaker Les Brown and it sparked the hunger inside of me since the first time I heard it. I knew I had done this, choosing my high school and insisting on my path throughout senior year.

Of course, as Les' quotes states, the time came again where I was required to tap into my inner fire, upgrade myself, and push my limits. It happened when I was in my early 30s, married, and pregnant with my second child on the way.

I had been living a good life, a branch manager in a financial institution, going on vacations, owning our own home, and attending church diligently. I was living the fairy tale I grew up aspiring to have.

It all came abundantly clear what I was missing, and I didn't even know it. One day, as I entered the church with my family, we greeted the congregation, most of whom I've known for over 14 years. Initially it appeared like a typical Sunday morning in the Sunday school class. Although, something was different that day. We were talking about all our special gifts and the speaker said, "You don't want to get to heaven and God points to a room full of beautifully wrapped gifts and says these were all yours but because you were too afraid to act on what I told you, they stayed here instead of you enjoying them on Earth as I planned."

That hit me like a ton of bricks. Had I missed the messages and denied myself all the gifts from God? My husband and I were so busy being busy, and the rules and routine of our lives were not fulfilling us or feeding our souls. The speaker went on to describe the joy, peace, happiness, a sense of belonging in *conjunction* with the homes, the vacations, the cars, the experiences in life that were in the room blessed by God. From that moment I began to wonder, "Is this place serving me? I am not growing spiritually in this ministry, nor am I going to have so much responsibility for the sake of duty or obligation. I don't want to get to heaven and not use all the gifts that God has offered me. I would be devastated if I saw a room full of gifts that I did not open. There has to be more to life than this..." At that moment I declared that I would leave this world using, enjoying, and sharing all those gifts and all the blessings for the glory of God.

Several weeks had passed, but the feeling didn't; the feeling that I had to push away from the emptiness inside me. One night at dinner, I asked my mother if she ever felt like she needed more in ministry and what did she do? She said yes and explained how she left our previous church because of the exact same feeling. It was during a time when there were not a lot of female ministers and she needed more spiritually. I explained that that was what I was feeling and that I wanted to meet with our current Pastor and explain it to him before I left. I didn't want him to feel like he had done anything wrong or that I was angry with him or the ministry; that wasn't the case at all. He had been an important and wonderful part of my family's life and we loved him. Not meeting him and having the chance to explain why I was leaving would not allow me to share how grateful I was for all he had taught us. But no matter how hard I tried to meet with him, every time something would come up — some urgent meeting or unforeseen mishap — and we never connected. But I knew I could not stay any longer. The roller-coaster feeling was back, I felt the sick grip in my stomach and a push in my back to leave.

Sitting on the pulpit, on what would be my last Sunday, my tears began to flow slowly as I looked over the congregation, my devoted friends and family. The spirit was high as usual at that point in the service. I wiped the tears and got up and said, "Praise God," as I usually did, and read the Sunday announcements.

The fear of leaving the church family that had embraced me for the last 14 years was terrifying, but I told the Lord, "I NEED MORE." Leaving this ministry would impact everything. My relationships would never be the same; my husband, my kids, and my mother would be affected, and all the ministries in the church would be impacted. I had input in all parts of the ministry from radio, finance, Sunday school, administration, and the youth department. My departure would impact many, but my decision was made.

The service ended. I walked out and I did not say goodbye to anyone. My emotions were too raw. The security guard in the parking lot heard me crying as I made my way to my car. Sitting there with tears streaming down my face, I suddenly heard a powerful resounding voice coming from my unborn son, "You are doing this for me." My divinely knowing child was speaking to me from inside my stomach. His kicking and squirming gave me the courage to move and the strength to move forward. If I was not doing it for me, I was definitely doing it for him and others like him who needed to see the example of living out your brilliance and feeding the hunger that will drive you to accomplish anything.

I learned that as you allow the polishing to refine you, the dark empty places in your life are familiar and comfortable, but in order for you to grow they must be cut away to reveal a brighter fresh layer. I had left, as I knew I had to… but what next? Where would I go?

Sitting in the driveway after a work appointment fell through, I began to pray, "GOD, I NEED MORE." I started to drive and found myself in front of a big white church. It was refreshing like a cool drink of water. I felt light and happiness from the moment I entered the sanctuary. It was like finding the perfect home, and at that moment I was sure I belonged. I'd found my new church and knew that I would shine there. Just by seeing the way the Pastor admired and adored his wife, I knew he would shine the same admiration upon me, my family, and the entire congregation. And it turns out God has a sense of humor. The first lady's name was Pearl, and she has been one of the most precious stones in my life. She was my polisher; in the same way I had been Pamela's polisher. The lessons she taught me about being soft as a lady, a loving mother, and having fun with my husband were priceless.

Now, I carry these lessons forward to those under my wing. Every Wednesday I look forward to my phone calls with Pamela. We live eight hours away from each other, but during our weekly calls it feels like we're sitting on the sofa together.

"You are the reason I know when I walk into a room I shine in any situation," Pamela tells me.

I kindly respond, "I saw the beauty in you and want you to be your authentic self, and to see you now walk in your true self is joyfully rewarding. You were the first, the one that showed me how to help others polish their stones; my first goddaughter. I want to make sure you know it."

She quickly sasses back, "I know, I wanted to make sure YOU knew it, God Ma!"

We smile and laugh. I'm so proud of her. I know it is because she is one of the many polished stones I have helped along the way to become their brilliant self. Now my work is to show others how they can polish their lives. We are all different shapes and display unique gifts and talents. We each have experienced challenges, but God has used me to polish, refine, and show others how to bring themselves to their full brilliance. We all are stones that just need polishing so that we can shine.

Growing up, I did not know that I was being polished like a precious stone covered by life's dirt and these interactions were developing my attitude. My trials were setting the stage for me to choose what makes me happy and to realize I could not worry about who likes me or who doesn't. Even when they cut deep.

If you allow life's circumstances to polish you, you will live life to your optimal potential. Don't allow yourself to play small so others can feel big. You have all you need inside of you, and I encourage you to shine. Embrace all of you, body, mind, and soul to soar into the fullest of your life. Trust that if you make a step in your brilliance that the road will rise to meet you as you walk into your light. Dance when you hear the music in your heart and leave your glitter dust on all you encounter. You are the Polished Stone.

And Baby, you will SHINE.

IGNITE ACTION STEPS

The polishing process will help you reveal the beautiful diamond in those around you. There are many ways to help them see the value within them.

Weight of the stone: Encourage curiosity. Fill your heart, and help them fill theirs, with everything you are curious about and explore every opportunity. Try journaling, coloring, painting, dancing, or playing a musical instrument. There is no limit to how far that curiosity can go and how bright it can make someone shine.

Dimensions of the stone: There are many facets of your personality, and they get shaped over time. When a stone is developing, it must have a safe place to explore and sparkle, where its giving heart is protected from those who would use them. Communicate in love and listen with empathy to provide a sense of security and an environment free of judgment.

Character of the stone: Character is built through perseverance; it is not forced. You don't make a diamond shine, you let it catch the light. The stones you polish see you, just as you see them, so SHOW instead of TELL! They will seek wise consultation and their community will be developed.

You will be called to do the exceptional. Walk into it, embrace your flaws, crying, laughing, and following your heart to a beautiful place full of renewal and brilliance.

Renee L. Cunningham — United States
Speaker, Author, CEO of The Polished Experience, and Legacy Protector
www.thereneexperience.com
renee@thereneexperience.com
 Renee Cunningham
 legacy_credit_queen

CURTIS GHEE

"Your purpose has no expiration date."

I have a very strong desire to inspire and empower readers who secretly long to discover their true identity and what they were created to do. Through my story I hope to give someone the strength to find their freedom by unlocking their potential and busting out of their proverbial jail cell. It is time to break away from those lifelong limitations and destructive thought patterns that may keep you from the life you desire. Be courageous, free yourself to live your true potential, and share your purpose with the world.

UNCUFF YOUR POTENTIAL

I have never been arrested or even spent a moment behind bars. Throughout my life, I have had the privilege to come and go as I desired. I believed because I was *physically free* that I lived without restrictions. But on the contrary, my mind was locked up in a maximum security prison, often visited by my disappointed dreams, lost visions, failed ideas, and many wasted opportunities. Unfortunately, all of my high aspirations were vastly overshadowed by their cellmates: fear, doubt, regret, and feelings of inadequacy. At a point, I was lost, stuck, and drowning in a life of uncertainty.

I was born the youngest of five children in a two-parent household with my brother and three sisters in the great city of Philadelphia. Despite its reputation for being a tough town, it was affectionately known as the City of Brotherly Love. It is famous for its delectable Philly cheese steak and delicious soft pretzels. It also houses the historic Liberty Bell, the iconic statue from the blockbuster movie *Rocky*, and the famous hall where the signing of the Constitution of the United States took place.

I grew up in the early '70s in a predominantly Black neighborhood that was probably considered low to middle class. I was a well-mannered young boy who performed adequately in school and was well-known in my community. I had a great relationship with my mother and siblings, but not so much with my father.

My dad was about 6'1", 230 pounds, and very intimidating. He was a hardworking man who often worked double shifts as a sergeant at one of the local prisons. Although he was never physically abusive, I was always nervous around him. Whenever I heard his keys jingling at the front door upon his arrival home, my heart would begin to race. At 6 years old I remember gnawing with my teeth, out of worry, on the end of the dining room table, leaving a groove in the compressed wood. Although my dad and I would later develop a great relationship once I became an adult, I believe the emotional abuse from my formative years created a lasting effect on me.

By the time I graduated high school at age 17, my parents had divorced, and it was just me and my mom left at home. I was a bright student, but to the surprise of many, I decided not to attend college. I had several opportunities to play football at a few of the state colleges that were offering athletic scholarships, but instead, I began working at a nursing home in a housekeeping position that started me off at minimum wage. Even though cleaning bathrooms and hauling trash was not what I had in mind fresh out of high school, it actually felt good to have my own job. I enjoyed the responsibility and was able to help my mom with the bills and buy myself a used car. It wasn't my dream job, but it was an honest way to earn a living until I figured out what I wanted for my life.

After working about 18 months, I began to get a little nervous because of the looming uncertainty of what my future held that hovered over me. I was often reminded by my older coworkers, many of them old enough to be my grandparents, not to get stuck working at the nursing home. It was as though I was this young inmate doing a short time in prison, who was being mentored by senior inmates who were working through a life sentence of their own without possibility of parole. The thought of spending the next 40 years of my life in a dead-end job was frightening to me. Unfortunately, at that point, I still had no clue of what I wanted to do and stayed where I was.

When I was about 19 years old, I heard one of the most impactful statements ever shared with me. Mrs. Peggy Mitchell, my best friend's mother, who is like a second mother to me, referred to me as being a 'jack-of-all-trades and a master of none' after I informed her I was going to go to the community college right after graduating with a certificate from a trade school. She seemed puzzled, wondering what happened to the trade school degree and why it was necessary to go to another school for something totally different. I was embarrassed by her question, because deep down I knew I could not give her an answer.

In addition to being undecided in my quest for direction, I also suffered from shyness and lacked self-confidence. I was afraid to take chances and whenever I did step out to take on an endeavor, most times I never finished what I started. I was self-sabotaging; creating self-imposed limitations. I heard the great author and speaker, Les Brown once say, "If you argue for your limitations, you get to keep them." He referred to people who say they want something but right afterward say, "But, I can't because…" and then give various excuses. That was my life. I allowed my "but" to get in the way of my destiny. In reality, I was aimlessly attempting to find my purpose while hiding behind academics in order to make myself look busy. Now, tirelessly working during the day and going to school at night, I was stuck in my personal jail cell with no release date in sight.

After two part-time semesters at the Philadelphia Community College, I had only six credits and was no closer to figuring out what I was created to do. Just 21 years old and looking for a fresh start, my cousin and I took the police officer's exam for the Philadelphia Police Department. Kevin was my first cousin, and his dad was one of my four uncles who were in the department. Therefore, we were encouraged to join the proud lineage of officers that were in our family. Neither my cousin nor I had a career so we became increasingly more excited to get the call to join the police academy.

There was a three-year delay in the hiring process due to budgetary issues so Kevin and I had to wait. Then on March 3, 1991, in Los Angeles, a motorist by the name of Rodney King was beaten mercilessly by officers of the Los Angeles Police Department during his arrest after a high-speed chase. That left both Kevin and I feeling angry and in disbelief. It was almost a deal breaker for us not to join, as two young African American men who had witnessed such an unwarranted use of force on a defenseless Black man. As a result, four officers were brought up on criminal charges, only to be acquitted a year later. Although this did upset me, I felt that more than ever more Black officers like us were needed as agents of change.

When I first became a police officer two years after that event, my cousin and I ended up working together. We were both instantly thrust into action in the mean streets of the 22nd Police District, located in the north central area of the city, where violence was deeply woven into the fabric of the community. From sunup to sundown, the streets were full of all sorts of drama, and it appeared as though the city was well on its way to surpassing the 423 murders from the previous year. Nevertheless, the comradery on the job was great. My cousin and I blended in nicely with the veteran officers as they graciously taught us the essentials of the job.

Like most cops, I wanted to go out and make a difference. I wanted to clean up the blight and the bad reputation that had been associated with the community for decades. Being a difference maker meant going out day after day locking up the bad guys. Without fail, in no time, we did just that. In such a high crime area there was no shortage of people to arrest: from drug dealers and drug users, to robbers, rapists, and murderers. For a relentless rookie officer, this was a great place to quickly learn and become like one of the elite officers I had grown to admire.

I had found a job that I loved but felt no closer to my purpose than I did when I was a kid in high school, or when I was mopping floors and dumping trash at the nursing home. Was I any different from the guys and girls I was arresting who clearly lived life without intent? What was my excuse? I had a good upbringing and a decent level of education. I felt like I should have been much further along in my life at that point, but I wasn't. Yes, I looked the part as though I had it all together, but I didn't. I wore that imperviable mask to hide behind my insecurities. My mind was no more liberated than any of the individuals that I was handcuffing and placing behind bars. Who was Curtis Ghee outside of the uniform, without the badge and gun? Despite the arrest powers given to me by the Commonwealth of Pennsylvania, in my personal life, I felt absolutely shackled and powerless!

Then one day it happened. It was a slightly warm Sunday afternoon, six years after joining the police force, when my partner and I were working the 3 PM -11 PM shift. At around 4:15 PM, we received an emergency call:

{Police Radio Dispatcher} "Cars stand by! Cars stand by! Person with a gun, report of a shooting! There is a male shot outside of the church at 19th and Susquehanna Avenue."

{Officer Ghee} "22-Tactical 1, be advised, we are on location now! We have a man down with a gunshot wound to his chest and the medics are working on him now!"

{Police Radio Dispatcher} "Okay 22-Tactical 1, keep us advised."

{Officer Ghee} "Radio, be advised, male was just pronounced dead at 4:38 PM by Medic 14."

That was the day that changed my career and ultimately my life. Up until then, I thought a good cop was one who made a bunch of arrests, but that tragedy and the subsequent court proceedings that followed changed my perspective on everything.

The young man who was murdered was a 20-year-old Temple University student who was an innocent bystander. He was unfortunately caught in a gunman's cross fire as he and a friend had just left church and went into a food take-out establishment. The gunman was known to be a terror in the community, but what I learned about him during the murder trial — the unfathomable trauma he suffered throughout his childhood — almost brought me to tears.

I remember sitting in the courtroom thinking: "What if I could have been in this young man's life as a role model and influenced him to be better? What if I would have shared with him my belief in the Gospel of Jesus Christ? What if I could have helped, supported, or shown a different way of living? Maybe he would not be in a situation that led to this heartbreaking dilemma."

However, that 24-year-old murder suspect was sentenced to spend the rest of his life in prison without a chance of parole. I watched as another young man was put in the graveyard and another one put beyond prison walls.

A few days after the emotional trial concluded, I sat down and emailed my pastor and informed her that I felt compelled to start a prison ministry. She was ecstatic about the idea, and along with two other ministers in our congregation, we started the ministry in the spring of 2004 at one of the all male facilities.

It was that tragedy that touched my heart and gave me a revelation of who I was and what I was called to do! I was no longer just a cop. I discovered that although I have the power to handcuff and arrest people, my true power was to influence people and help them to unlock their potential! I believe that if a person becomes aware of his or her purpose and God-given potential, this can change the trajectory of their life.

As my career progressed, I was assigned as the district's Community Relations Officer, where I acted as a liaison between the police department and community. This was very gratifying as I was able to forge great relationships, some lifelong, with residents and community leaders. My mantras were, "Everyone has a story to tell," meaning that we all have a backstory that played a role in the good as well as the bad in our lives. The other was, "It is not the hand of a man that causes him to steal, but it's the mind that controls the hand that makes him a thief." I strongly believe if a person's mind is freed, then their behavior can change for the better.

There now was a shift in my career. I began to understand that although locking people up was a necessary evil, it was not always the best solution.

The desire to make arrests was overshadowed by yearning to make a difference. I began to become well-known and highly respected in the community, throughout my department, and around the city. I was given various awards and even a prestigious City Citation. I also became sought after as a speaker to address school students from all grades including several local universities. I discovered that my purpose was not meant to be found outside of me, but instead within me. Just like any manufactured product, my purpose was programmed right into me from the beginning. I realized that I was trying to discover myself through education, but I would later learn that going to school was not for finding my purpose, but for *refining* it. It's like buying white shoe polish before purchasing the shoes, only to discover that deep down in your heart you really wanted black shoes. The polish is designed to enhance the shoes, not the other way around. My purpose was defined by who I knew myself to be, not by who I told myself I was.

Ironically, the second half of my career shifted again, this time from working with the people in the community to working solely with officers. After 13 years, I transitioned to the department's counseling unit as a peer counselor, assisting police in need of stress relief. I would soon see up close and personal some of the trauma and dysfunction in the lives of many of my fellow comrades. Oddly, just like the people they were arresting, they too were mentally and emotionally bound by their circumstances, and in some cases, in desperate need to be released from their own personal jail cells.

I saw the correlation between physical incarceration and mental limitations that hindered both freedom and personal self-worth. That inspired me to map out *The 5 Keys To Your Destiny*; a program designed to help people find their *Purpose, Passion, Potential, Perspective,* and *Planning* for personal success.

Now, my wife, Falesha and I operate a nonprofit organization, Uncuffed Potential, Inc. that teaches *The Keys* and addresses lifelong limitations and destructive thought patterns that prevent people from living the life they desire. It is these internal issues that create the external concerns that we see today around our nation, including the tumultuous relationship between police and citizens. I say, "Before you are a color, first you're human, and before we became police officers, we were human as well." Part of our mission is to help bridge the gap between the community and the police by showing each side that we all have a story to tell. I also am passionate about counseling those living with circumstantial limitations to find their ultimate purpose.

It took me many years to discover that my purpose was not outside of me, but it was locked up on the inside. Your purpose has no expiration date! It is not too late to find it. When you do, live it to the fullest so when you die, you've poured everything you had out into the world; spent and satisfied. There is greatness *inside* of you, and I encourage you to use the key of your imagination to unlock your potential and unveil your true identity so that you may begin to live the unhindered life you desire!

You are not inferior, but you are unique and full of potential. Reevaluate how you see yourself, Ignite your passion, and get hungry to go after whatever you want to achieve. I allowed fear and self-imposed limiting beliefs to arrest me and I sentenced myself to a life of mediocrity. This does not have to be your story. You too have the power to overcome, but you must first uncuff your potential by freeing your mind of negative thoughts and allowing yourself to visualize exactly who you aspire to be.

Ignite Action Steps

If you are uncertain of your purpose, please do not be hard on yourself nor ashamed. Remember, no manufacturer creates a product without revealing its purpose to its consumer. With that in mind, know that you are God's greatest creation, skillfully crafted and wired for success! Everything you need to succeed in life is already inside of you, *batteries included!*

Try incorporating these five keys to manifest more in your life and unlock your destiny.

Perspective: Expand your vision by reading something inspiring every day.

Passion: Discover those things you have always wanted to do and just do them.

Potential: It is not what you have used up but what you have left to give. Dig deep.

Purpose: Ask yourself: Who am I? Why am I here? What have I been called to do with my life? Once you know those answers, go out and live your life to the fullest.

Planning: If you want to be successful at anything, you must devise a plan to stay focused on your goals… Yes… You have to stay focused!

Curtis Ghee — United States
Speaker, Author, Coach, Law Enforcement Officer,
Chairman of Uncuffed Potential, Inc.
www.uncuffedpotential.com   uncuffedpotential@gmail.com
🅕 *Curtis Ghee*   🅛 *Curtis Ghee*

Pamela Bishop

PAMELA BISHOP

"It takes the pain of your struggle to cross the bridge to your greatness."

Destinations wink at you, but your journey leaves imprints of your purpose, greatness, and gratitude in your heart. Wink back! Take a chance on you! As you travel with me through my journey, my hope is for you to fall in love with that person God created for greatness: YOU! Don't get stuck at a destination, stay on your journey. The roads you travel will lead you to the very best version of yourself!

SIX OF EVERYTHING

After my first birthday my mother left for Chicago and never came back. She was pregnant at the time with my younger sister, Vicki. My 20-year-old dad, who lived with me in Louisville, Kentucky, realized that he could not care for me on his own and give me what I needed while working full-time at a local distillery. He decided the best choice at that time was to move me in with my grandparents.

Reminiscing about my earliest memories makes me smile. A closet of ruffled dresses and the most beautiful red shoes are pictures embedded in my mind. I remember eating at the finest restaurants enjoying pink Shirley Temples, lots of shrimp, and cherry pie. Hugs were freely given. My grandfather Poppy was the chef and storyteller of our home. Often, he sat me on his lap and sang to me, *"Que sera sera, whatever will be will be…"* He would then ask me, "What do you want to be when you grow up?" As he smiled at me, he said, "Honey, you will be something special someday!" I can still see the glisten in his eyes.

My grandmother, who I called 'Mommy,' adored me and invested in me until the day she died. She went without, giving me everything. She worked alongside my dad at the distillery and was very active in the union. She introduced me to my faith and taught me many life lessons. I felt like the luckiest little girl in the world. My joy only grew when my grandparents got a sudden call to pick up my 2-year-old sister, Vicki, in Chicago. I found my soul twin, and once we were together I couldn't remember a time I was without her.

Six years later I began to realize I didn't have a traditional family. My sister and I would talk about it at times. Sometimes I missed having a mother to bake cookies with and talk to. I found myself wondering why she never came back for me. What did I do to make her not want me? Where does she live, and do I have brothers and sisters? Do they even know about me? Those questions began to shape my journey of feeling less than invisible… and not enough.

Vicki and I spent lots of time performing songs and skits on our front porch, charging neighbors a penny for admission. I believe I was developing that young entrepreneurial spirit, but we also just loved to have fun.

I had big dreams and visions for myself. I wanted to 'be somebody' one day. I spent hours in my journal writing poems, my feelings, my life. One day a family friend picked up my book — my heart — and read my poems out loud in front of everyone, making fun of me. I felt so hurt and violated. I never remember owning fear until that day. That was the beginning of me shrinking, devaluing my worth, and keeping things to myself.

I married in my 20s and had a beautiful little girl. She was my pride and joy. I set out to give her the life I never had — life with a mother. My mission was to make sure my daughter felt her mother's love. But after six years my husband and I divorced, and I saw it as another failure: I was just not enough. I convinced myself to be tough, hide what I was missing, and mask my pain by excelling in business, receiving awards and accolades. I had a deep desire to be a part of something bigger than myself, refusing to shrink down anymore. My work became a safe place to shine without anyone knowing the truth about my insecurities and pain. In that role, I built a brick wall around my heart thinking it would protect me. Yet, I was desperately seeking approval from many and looking for love in all the wrong places.

Knowing I had to take care of things myself, I took a few different jobs. I was raising a little girl, my husband was gone, and I needed to get serious. One day the owner of the accessory store I worked in, Bob, showed me the business plan he had written for me. Bob saw my talent, tenacity, and desire. In his powerful charismatic way, he took the time to show me what was possible for my future. I remember looking up into his eyes filled with awe. I felt like he truly believed in me and that set me on a new trajectory. After listening to him, I looked up and said smiling, "I believe I can do it." As I drove off that day, I thought to myself, "What would it feel like to accomplish those BIG goals? It would be everything I wanted. A car, stability, financial freedom, and finding myself." I thought if I could do it, it would lessen the pain and give me an opportunity to grow and learn.

After a few years of working with Bob, he taught me the ropes and everything to do with sales and marketing. I made a cold call to a chain of stores that had recently piqued my interest. I introduced myself to the buyer of the department I was interested in, and we made plans to connect. She was excited to discuss the possibilities and put a plan in place. The following week we finalized the business proposal. Everything was complete with the exception of the initial order for each of the stores. I was gearing up to head home as she was going to a Reds™ game that evening. At that moment she realized she had one extra ticket and invited me. I love baseball so that was a yes! We had a blast!

The next day we met early to complete the purchase order and she was called to a meeting at the last minute. I began to second guess myself and was visualizing the plan falling apart. I pondered what I was going to tell Bob, my mentor, after I'd really built up the deal. I gathered my papers as she headed toward the door, believing the deal was over. Suddenly she looked back at me… and with total confidence ordered six of every piece of jewelry I had. "Call me in a week or so and we will discuss the holiday line," she said before leaving. I was beyond excited! I sold more that day than I did in the six months before. I had never experienced the emotion I was feeling; pride in myself. I felt as though I had cracked the code that day. That was a defining moment for me — I began to believe in me!

One year later, the scenario was repeated, but this time instead of meeting a buyer for a department store, I met a buyer for a national grocery chain. When I told Bob the potential it had, he said, "You will never sell them jewelry! They sell milk!" For the first time his doubt did not shatter my confidence. The day had come for my meeting, and I was a ball of nerves. I rehearsed my business plan over and over. I wanted her to see how my plan would complement and add value to the beauty counters. My persistence and belief in myself paid off again. She loved the line and ordered it all. Before I knew it our jewelry was in three states and dozens of stores.

The success began to take a toll because I was traveling extensively and constantly competing for validation. I would shroud my sense of unfulfillment as years went by, but old 'mind junk' was creeping back in: feeling inferior and not enough. Money never really motivated me as much as accomplishment. I knew I was made for more and longed to find my purpose.

Several years later I made the decision to resign. It was tough because I had grown to love Bob. His mentorship changed my life. I knew switching professions would challenge me again and give me a purpose in serving others. It took me six months to study and pass all my exams to become a stockbroker, and in my first year I received the Rookie of the Year award. For a moment, things felt better and I was on the right path to finding what I thought I was missing.

It was a hot summer day in late July, and I had started a new chapter in my life. I was painting a beautiful stone-washed wall in the entry of my new home and was relieved that my girlfriend had accepted the painting challenge with me. She was always telling jokes and rolling with laughter during our projects together.

I was on the tippy top of the ladder with my brush when I heard the phone. I rushed to get it and said an out of breath "Hello?" It was my dad, and he told me he was going into surgery early on Monday morning. "I have throat cancer, and they are doing invasive surgery. Don't worry, everything will be okay," he tried to assure me. My mind began to race as I remembered the loss I felt when my grandparents died. Then the agony when my sister, Vicki, died at 22, and I never had the opportunity to say goodbye. Now my dad was facing cancer! I knew the one thing I had to do. I immediately said, "Daddy, you are not going by yourself, I'm going with you."

After several treatments, the oncologist told me his time was short and I was to get things in order. I cried out to God, "How am I going to maintain my career and take care of my ailing dad?" In 24 hours, I knew that my career had come to a screeching halt. I made a drastic and life-changing decision to work in his car dealership business even though I knew and liked nothing about running a dealership. I didn't know a Chevy™ from a Ford™ and I had to ask the manager, "What's an SUV?"

Days began to get stressful, and Dad was getting weaker. I remember him holding my hand one afternoon and telling me he was not always the dad he needed to be; that he wished he could have been there more. I know how much my dad loved me. What was I going to do without him? HE WAS MY HERO! MY CONSTANT!

I called the doctor and demanded that he do something different to save him. I needed my dad, and he could not die! I was not making funeral arrangements. NO! NO! NO! I remember calling out to God, "Please don't take him!" As the tears rolled down my face, I prayed and begged Him to hear my cry. I kept speaking life over my dad, still trembling inside. These fragile moments will live in my heart forever. The doctor ordered a very aggressive treatment, saying, "He will live or die with this." It was a long journey, but God answered my prayers. In six months we were told the cancer was in remission. Today my dad is still cancer free at almost 84; playing golf and living life. What a hug and wink from God!

My dad's life was spared, but his business was still on my shoulders. I learned through trial and error for 20 years. It was the toughest challenge in my life, and I began to feel empty as my world turned gray. My life had become meaningless. How could I close the door on my dad's dream? I was battling the fire inside of me that reminded me of my purpose. Fear wrapped around me like a blanket. I felt lost and alone. Depression and anger set in like dark clouds rolling across the sky; a storm that had been building for years.

The sound of my alarm woke me on an early winter morning. As I jumped out of bed, I caught a glimpse through my glass doors of the beauty of the fallen snow. The pond was frozen, and the ice glistened. The lights on the bushes were glowing as the beginning of dawn appeared.

Then the reality hit me that I had to go to work. My heart cried and my eyes filled with tears; my body was tired and run-down. I walked across my cold floor as I stepped into the shower and felt the steam rolling across my body. I asked God desperately, "Help me please! I can't do this anymore! Do I stay or can I leave? I need an answer, NOW! I'm barely hanging on." I took a deep breath after the steam had stopped and turned on the shower. As the warm water covered my body, I felt frail and broken, telling myself my dreams were shattered. It's too late for me!

Moments later, as I stepped out of the shower into my bedroom, my eyes focused on my TV. The words I heard dropped right into my heart! My eyes never moved as I read and listened, "Don't get hung up on whether to stay or go! When it stops working, you know it's over. You are free."

That moment changed the trajectory of my life.

My dad and I closed the dealerships, along with his dream, a few months later. Emotions were high. It took as much to close the business as it did to open it! It was a bittersweet moment and the hardest decision I had ever made. I have no regrets staying 20 years. Without the pain and struggle of that journey, I would not have had the opportunity to get to know my dad as the great hero that he is; a man who gave me tools to use for the rest of my life. I learned how to communicate, how to forgive, how to have courage, and how to have grace. I began to understand how important it is to look into the heart of hurt to fully understand the *why* and what really matters in life: the journey.

I dedicated the next six years to wellness inside and out. I reduced my workload, stopped medicating, and walked away from unhealthy relationships. My life began to turn around. Before, my world was busy with noise. I had no idea what I liked or wanted. Once I silenced the noise, I could hear again. I began to make big changes and do the things that I love. Healing my soul and my body has made me feel whole.

My passion is now to help people find their purpose sooner than I did. It took me a lifetime to find my joy and my worth. Now I show people what worth and inner wealth mean. It is wrapped around forgiveness, looking at the value in every situation and finding the gifts beneath it all. So many times, when we get caught up in life we give up on ourselves and bitterness grows instead of allowing the love to blossom.

My new mentor, Les Brown, has shown me how to work on my fear and finally let go of it. He has given me hope and confidence in myself and my desire to inspire and support others in their healing journey. I feel motivated and surrounded by others who serve. I feel as though I am on the path that God wants me to be on. Watching Les battle his own cancer has shown me true tenacity. I am in awe of him, and he truly is a new HERO in my life.

Through gratitude and forgiveness, I am able to love people again. I am reminded that my purpose lies in helping others, and I'm now doing so using the simple steps I've learned in my journey of hope. Through this mission and vision, I have been given a new life. I've discovered that it takes a lifetime to become who you were created to be. Your experiences design your life, and it takes all of them to make the most beautiful tapestry of you.

It's through the journey you find yourself and the true meaning behind your existence. Try to look at all the positive things in your life. Fear always exists; recognize it, feel it, and conquer it. You will begin to master fear when you simply understand its presence and purpose. There are many destinations but we are never meant to stay, rather, we are to learn and grow from the journey. Your pain in the struggle will take you to your bridge of greatness. And it is worth it.

Ignite Action Steps

Have COURAGE

Courage will help you through your pain and help you forgive. Remember Les Brown's wise words: "If you can look up, then you can get up." Whenever you feel like you can't, know that you can! Every morning remind yourself that you are powerful and you deserve the best. Replay those words in your head whenever you feel like you need that extra encouragement.

Develop BOUNDARIES

Set your own boundaries or others' boundaries will own you. Your boundaries give you courage to say, "No." You have to discover what your boundaries are so you can avoid anger, disappointment, abuse, and hurt. When you establish positive boundaries, you get to decide what is the best fit for you in all that you do. No one can derail you when you define clear boundaries.

Practice FORGIVENESS

You CAN master forgiveness and feel the awesomeness of being free. Reflect where the person wronged you. Ponder these questions:
1. What have they gone through in their life?
2. Look at their past, where they came from, and what they were taught.
3. See the good they tried to create.
4. Love them for who they are; there is no perfection in person.
5. Decide how much forgiveness gives to you.

LOVE without conditions

This also means learning to love yourself, all of you. Get to know your authentic self, then embrace that person with your whole heart. Love does not have to be two-sided, you can love first, love full-out, love with forgiveness at the forefront, and love with nothing attached. Just love unconditionally both yourself and those around you.

I dedicate this story to my Daddy, my HERO!! He always believed in me! xo

Pamela Bishop — United States
Speaker, Author, CEO of Live Brave and Courageous
www.livebraveandcourageous.com
Wellness Matters Consultant coachingwithpam@gmail.com
Your Journey of Self Discovery www.onpurposewithpam.com
pamelabishop pamelagbishop

Steph Elliott

"Forgiveness is for YOU, not them!"

My intention is for YOU to Ignite your power to live free: free of your past, free of your limiting beliefs, and free to live your magical life purpose, whatever that may be. YOU deserve it. You deserve to find forgiveness as it is for YOU and not them. My hope for you is to learn to love yourself again. Love your mind, body, and spirit. The time is now for you to live your highest good and have abundance in all areas of your life. You are love, you are light, you are worthy. You deserve everything life has to offer.

Being 'Good'

"Hello, I'm Steph, and I'm the daughter of an addict."

My father's addiction was self-medicating through the pain and struggles he felt due to a mental illness; pain which was then fed to my mother and I. You see, I'm an only child and I tried my hardest to always be strong for my mom so that she never felt as if she was going through the abuse alone. My mom always supported me. She protected me and I protected her. She is strong, she is my inspiration, and I never wanted to see my mom hurt.

After years of verbal and mental abuse, my mom finally set herself free and divorced my father. I was 18 at the time and had already moved out of our childhood home. I escaped before my mom did.

For years I tried to maintain a relationship with my father but it was just too much. My heart couldn't take it and I couldn't bear to expose my own children to the same experiences I endured. So I made a decision in my late 20s to set a boundary — a HUGE boundary — one that removed my father from my life completely.

Sometimes it felt freeing and sometimes it felt like I simply gave up. Some people supported me and some didn't, but I told myself over and over, no one else's opinion matters. I needed to know that whatever transpired and whatever unfolded down the road would be okay. When I looked in the mirror the person staring back at me would not have any regret or resentment. And I did not. I was 'good' for years to come.

Until, I was out one evening with friends and ran into an old friend of my father's. This person told me that my father had passed away. I let a couple tears fall and felt a little numb. The last bit of hope I was holding onto — of having a father that was loving, kind, and supportive — was gone.

I walked outside to catch some fresh air and do what I knew I had to; what I always did: told everyone I was okay. My famous line was always, "I'm good."

As the months went by, I moved on. I was free, no more worries of what might come or what the next day would hold. No more worries of him show-ing up at my door in a rage of anger. No more late-night calls from the police or rushing to his aid at the hospital. Anytime my uncle would call with news about my father, he would start the conversation off with, "The writer's are busy writing again," to describe what drama my father had created and the trouble he was stirring. With my father gone, I knew that anytime my uncle's name popped up on my caller ID that the conversation would never start that way again. That gave me a sense of peace.

Or so I thought, but boy was I thrown for a loop.

My eldest daughter sat in school one day and received a message from a stranger through social media. "I'm trying to reach your mom, can you have her call me? It's about your grandfather." The stranger left her number. I'm not sure who was more shocked, me or my daughter. Again, I did what I had to do and called the number. This sweet soft voice on the other end told me that my father was here in town and she had been helping him out. I'm not sure what I even said next. I was in disbelief. My father was alive and in the same town I lived in!

The next few days were a blur. When I saw the person looking back at me in the mirror, suddenly I questioned just how 'good' was I? All of those feelings that I buried deep inside were resurfacing. I was angry. I was sad. I was hurt. I was shocked. I was disappointed in myself for not being 'good.' And, I was scared. Yet every day that went by, I smiled even when deep inside I felt lost. I didn't know what I'd do or where I'd go. I thought, "My God, Steph, you haven't seen or heard from your father in 10 years, why do you feel this way?" I entered a dark place but I kept it inside. I battled myself and beat myself up.

As I would drive through town, I kept an eye out fearing I would run into him, but I never did. As the months went by, I knew I needed to do something. But what, I simply couldn't figure out. I booked an appointment for an oracle card reading. In that reading, she told me that I needed to go see him and say the words I never was brave enough to say before. When she told me that she would go with me, it solidified exactly what I needed to do. I needed to speak my truth to him.

Over the next few weeks, while still turning inward, I worked on getting my thoughts and emotions aligned. The wall I had built around my heart, that affected every single relationship I have ever had, finally needed to have one brick removed at a time. While it would've been easier to seek professional help, a pastor, prayer, or even family, I still had this image to maintain: the image that I'm strong, I'm independent, I'm 'good.'

With determination and inner will, I made my mind up! I told myself over and over, "This is it Steph, you're going to do this." I was going to find my father in this town and approach him. I was going to be in control and I was going to say what I needed to say. No fights, no arguments, just finally having a peaceful conversation.

'Peaceful' and my father were like oil and water. I needed to convince myself that no matter the reaction, no matter the words that he said, no matter what, I was in control. "I can walk away. I can walk away peacefully. I am safe."

It was a cold February weekend when I decided to find him. I had not yet told a soul. One Saturday afternoon, a rare moment when my husband, myself, and all three children had an opportunity to go to lunch, we sat down and ordered our drinks. After the drinks arrived and as we looked over the menu, I shared that I had news. The kids were excited to hear what I was about to say. I told them, "Tomorrow, I am going to find my father and tell him that I forgive him." Their faces instantly revealed the shock they felt. Next came, "Mom, are you crazy?" "Mom, you're not going alone!" "Mom, are you really?" Yes, I really was. We chatted about my feelings of the unknown and how I wanted to finally set myself free. We discussed their feelings of concern and worry, but I reassured them as I went over my plan.

The following morning my daughter asked me to attend church with her. I've never been a consistent attendee at church but my daughter is. I immediately said yes; it just felt right. We decided that I would meet her at the church and afterward I would be off to find my father, alone but brave!

I arrived at the church to meet my daughter. As we walked in, the music of the band started and it felt more like a Saturday night than a Sunday morning. The guitars strumming, the drums beating, and the *oh so* beautiful voices singing songs of praise raised my vibration and caused me to shed tears of every emotion. We sat down and the pastor walked on to the stage. The moment he started speaking, it was like I was the only one in the church. He spoke directly to me. Every word, every Bible verse, the entire message was cutting through the crowd straight to my soul. He talked about evil and forgiveness and as I listened, I cried. That was exactly where I needed to be on that day. The Universe had my back and put me right there to validate that what I was about to do, after the church service ended, was exactly what I should do. The little voice in my head that was trying to feed me doubt was silenced.

Church ended then my daughter and I hugged and said our goodbyes. Off I drove to the local homeless shelter in town, as that is where I was told my father resided. I pulled into the parking lot, parked, took a deep breath (*inhale the peace, exhale the doubt*), got out of the car, and walked into the building. I asked for him by name and the response was, "I'm sorry ma'am, he moved out four days ago. We can't give you any information." I headed back to my car and with every step I took, I wondered if this was a sign. Doubt tiptoed in again. Should I not be doing this? Is this not the right time?

As I started my car, I had a little meeting with myself. "Steph, get it together. Do not let the resistance win. You got this!" As I drove away, I remembered that somewhere in my phone was the last number I had for him. If I was going to do this today, I needed to find that number and call him.

Within a few minutes, I located the last number I had for him. I used the five second countdown rule to avoid procrastinating. *5, 4, 3, 2, 1* and pressed the green button on my phone for the number to dial. I anxiously awaited, unsure if I had the right number and worried if I even had the *right* to reach out after so many years. I had cut him out of my life and there I was the one calling wanting something from him. I wondered if he would recognize my voice or if he would ignore the call.

The phone rang and he answered. All I could say was, "It's Stephanie," using the name he always called me, despite me hating it.

The phone was awkwardly silent.

I thought maybe we had been disconnected.

I waited.

He finally said, "Stephanie?" in surprise and bewilderment.

I nervously answered, "Yes, your daughter."

I asked him if he would share where he was living and said I'd like to stop by for a few minutes. Unsure and confused, he gave me his address and I told him that I was on my way. Like so many times before, there I was parking the car, taking another deep breath, and preparing mentally to see my father.

I stepped out of my car, put on my long winter coat, took *one more* deep breath, and said to myself, **"This is your time as forgiveness is for YOU, not him."** I purposely parked far enough away so he wouldn't know what kind of car I was driving. This was a precaution to keep myself safe. I had no way of knowing where his addiction had taken him and I wanted to maintain my safety and privacy.

I saw that to get to his apartment I would have to walk up a hill six blocks in the cold, blustery sunshine. I spent the first four blocks just focusing on my breathing and remembering WHY I was doing this; repeating in my head, "Forgiveness is for YOU, not him." As I approached the final two blocks, I saw my father for the first time in 10 years but he didn't see me. Now the nerves really set in. I repeated in my head, "You got this, you got this."

He spotted me just moments before we were in close proximity. I knew that I needed to jump right into the conversation so I didn't lose focus or chicken out. I stood firm and tall, right in front of my father, looked straight into his glazed over eyes, and said:

"I'm here today to tell you that I forgive you. When I leave and walk away today, I'm no longer carrying the weight of the hurt and pain you've caused over the last 36 years of my life. I'm leaving it all here on the sidewalk. I hope that this also frees you and that you can go on in the next chapter of your life with a fresh start for yourself. But I will not continue to carry YOUR weight around with me any longer."

His reaction was stoic and he simply said, "Okay." The dialogue continued for the next few minutes. He asked about my children and how they were doing. He asked about my husband. It was so cold and windy outside on that February day and while I don't enjoy the cold or the wind, this time the Universe knew it was just what I needed to keep the conversation to the point. With every gust of the blustery air, I was that much closer to the conversation ending. My father and I embraced in a hug, said goodbye, and I walked away.

It's not a coincidence that I walked uphill to do the hardest thing in my life

— forgive someone who was never sorry. But now that I did, I walked downhill back to my car, walking freer than I ever have in my life.

The next deep breath I took of that cold air was the deepest breath I had taken in almost a decade. I inhaled peace, clarity, and new beginnings. I exhaled stress, verbal abuse, and fear. I was safe. At that moment I was finally me again. The Steph Elliott that I was born to be. I had just broken free of the chains that held me back and it felt so damn good!

I hopped in the car to call my husband and let him know how it went. I knew he would be sitting at home on the edge of the chair waiting for his phone to ring. I called my mom and shared with her what I had just done. The rest of my ride home, I drove in silence. I was always afraid of the stillness before but this time it was different. I didn't have that voice in my head wondering what was next. Instead, for the first time, I felt free of the weight and I was excited about my future. I felt a stillness enveloped me and a refreshing energy renewed within. That allowed me to feel love: love for myself. Love for my family. I was proud of myself. I *deserved* to feel love. As Les Brown says, "People inspire you, or they drain you. Pick them wisely." I knew at that moment, I had made a choice. I was going to forgive and be free.

In the next days and weeks the healing journey continued just as it does today. I continued to discover me, the Steph that was happier, the Steph that stopped holding grudges. I learned to listen to my intuition and live by it. We are all born with intuition but through life events and society, it is often silenced. Through different modalities like journaling, meditation, and oracle cards, I ignited my inner spirit, the goddess within, and started listening to her. I finally knew how to truly love another, be patient, and feel my emotions but not hang on to them. I ignited within me compassion, a fire to be better and live my true purpose and not hide my feelings behind the trauma.

This one action I took, this choice of forgiveness, allowed me to be a better wife, mother, daughter, and friend. I no longer hold others accountable for someone else's actions. The wall around my heart which I thought would protect me now has all the bricks removed. I'm truly 'good.'

Whatever trauma may exist in your past, burying it behind a wall and letting it sit there year after year doesn't allow us to be free. That wall inside of us may block the pain and memories temporarily but it also blocks all the beautiful experiences of loving yourself unconditionally. Remember, forgiveness is for YOU, not them. Forgiveness frees YOU. It allows YOU to love YOU again, and YOU deserve that!

Ignite Action Steps

Journaling. Grab a notebook and your favorite pen. Start by writing down what you're thankful for today. Write "I am" statements. It's okay if you don't believe them in your heart today. This is a great step to reprogram your subconscious mind to start believing them. Remember this is YOUR journal. Don't worry about grammar or complete sentences, no one is judging you. Just write whatever comes to mind. The more you practice, the easier it becomes. Adding color to your journal is fun and allows you to activate your creativity. I'm not an artist, but simple things like writing words or your affirmations in color adds a spark.

Setting boundaries. Boundaries are beautiful. You are the key holder to your boundaries; don't let anyone else hold the key. Remember that "No" is a complete sentence. You never have to add an explanation or a reason. If there is something that doesn't feel good or if someone asks you to do a task or activity for them that doesn't serve you, respond with, "No."

Practice meditation. Start with a small window of time. Even just two minutes and go longer each week. There are many options on YouTube™ and apps like *Insight Timer*™ or *Calm*™. The more you practice, the longer your mediation will get. Focus on your breathing and when thoughts come into your mind, let them come in and go back out.

Be gentle with you. Give yourself grace. When you plant a seed in your fruit and vegetable garden, you don't have the fruit or veggie to eat the next day. It's the same with ourselves. When we plant the seeds for self-love, growth, and change, we don't have them the very next day.

It takes time, we take time. Trust the process. The Universe always has your back.

Steph Elliott — United States
Author, Coach
www.stephelliott.club
TheRealStephElliott
therealstephelliott

Jessica T. Moore

"Focus your attention on your intention, not the things that you can't change."

My hope is that when you read my chapter, you are inspired to look in the mirror, fix your invisible crown, and not allow your imperfections to stop you from becoming the best version of yourself. No matter what obstacles you face or how much instability you experience, you can move forward toward your dreams as long as you keep your attention on your intentions. You don't have to allow your circumstances to define your destiny. My perseverance and persistence have taken me further than I could ever imagine, and I believe that the same can happen for you because the things worth having are worth fighting for. The journey is far from easy, but I promise you got this!

Girl, Fix Your Crown!

"She turned her 'can'ts' into 'cans' and her dreams into plans."

These were the silver letters embossed across the top of my graduation cap; the crown I would wear as I received my first degree at 22 years old. Walking across the stage meant so much more than just getting a piece of paper. It was a symbol of my willingness to do the work, my focus on making an impact, and my ability to never talk down to myself. You see, a lot of times, people talk themselves right out of an opportunity. We get so caught up in the 'what-if's' and become paralyzed by fear. I refused to be a volunteer victim and allow my circumstances to define me. I knew that I could achieve whatever I set my mind to. When I heard the words, "Jessica Tierra Hardison," tears rolled down my face as I switched my tassel from one side to the other. I glanced over at my baby girl in the audience as she smiled from afar. I thought to myself, "I did it. I *really* did it." I beat the odds.

Statistics say that less than two percent of teen mothers obtain a college degree, with that number being even less for African American women. For years, I had been waking up at 4:30 AM to get my schoolwork done before my daughter woke up. Many nights I cried. I doubted myself, wondering if it was insane to believe that I could finish school in the four-year time frame that I had given myself. It seemed impossible. But now here I was, walking proudly as the queen from a long line of queens, taking my turn in the spotlight.

I was always destined to the legacy of being a great woman. After all, I came from them, grew up with them, and learned from them. My early childhood experiences were everything I could ever imagine, full of special moments that brought me great joy. I remember spending just about every day with my mom, Tara, my grandmother, Joyce, and my great-grandmother, Helen. Everywhere we went, my great-grandmother proudly told people we were four generations of excellence. My family taught me leadership, service, and creativity. My great-grandmother was a cake baker, and she loved to volunteer to help children in the school system. My grandmother was a pianist and singer. She served with a heart of selfless love, and her gracefulness could light up a room. My mother loved to beatbox and rap. She was the life of the party, and her energy was contagious. I played the clarinet and sang operetta in plays held at the Detroit Fox Theater; I was a Girl Scout; and I trained as a junior police officer. My mom was so proud of me, and she never hesitated to tell me every chance she got. She told me, "You are amazing, and one day your name will be in lights." She was honestly my best friend. We used to wear matching outfits and create songs together. There was never a dull moment, so growing up with my family was absolutely amazing! Every day was an adventure. It was a rare love that not everyone gets the opportunity to have. I will always be grateful for those moments.

Dr. Seuss said, "Sometimes you will never know the value of a moment until it becomes a memory." On my 13th birthday, my mom blew out my candles. When I asked her why, she said she just wanted to celebrate with me because I had reached a new milestone. Thirteen was a big deal for my mom; I was her only child. Little did I know, it would be the last time we celebrated together. Less than a month later my world turned upside down when my momma passed away unexpectedly. I was in shock; my head spinning in circles as my family reluctantly told me she was gone. I had lost my Queen, my best friend, the one who loved me unconditionally.

The following week, I sat on the couch dazed as I watched our home be packed up. It was a nightmare. At 13, there was so much that I still needed my mom to teach me. Then reality set in. She wouldn't see me graduate from middle school the following year. She wouldn't be there at my high school graduation either. From that day forward, things went downhill for me, as anger, depression, and stress took over my mind.

My mom's death was a shock to everyone in my family, and I saw it weigh heavily on my grandmother, who had taken me in. On the anniversary of my mom's birthday, my grandmother was diagnosed with pancreatic cancer. I watched as her life slowly faded and I helped to care for her until she ended up on life support. I still remember sitting in her hospital room as the staff told me to say my goodbyes. I looked her in the eyes with pain and tears rolling down my face while she held my hand. I couldn't do it. I couldn't watch her go. I told her I would be right back, and she squeezed my hand. I was so overwhelmed, and I needed to take a breather. I said, "Grandma Joycie, don't worry. I'll be right back." I let go of her hand, and before I could make it to the door, I fainted. The next thing I knew, I was in a hospital bed. The nurses took me to the emergency room and told me that I had a panic attack. I insisted that they let me go back to spend my last moments with my grandmother. The nurses all thought it was too much for me and best that I didn't go back that night. I was so heartbroken because I had made a promise to my grandma. The next day, she transitioned from this earth, and I never got a chance to see her. My heart continued to be crushed.

With my grandmother's passing, I was left without a stable home. I couldn't adjust to all of the changes in my life. I moved several times: going to four different high schools and living in four different states. Every time I would get settled in somewhere with some family member, friend, or neighbor, I would either have to leave or got kicked out. I grew tired of that process. No one wanted to take a teenager into their home. I so desperately wanted my life to go back to the way it was before my mom passed; the joy and laughter I had known. But that part of my life was over. I remember only getting to fill one trash bag with whatever personal possessions would fit; forced to leave everything else behind. Instability became my norm.

Most of the time, I was angry. I had gone into survival mode. As a teen, there were days when I didn't even know where I would lay my head that night. With so much negativity around me, I had to find time to quiet the noise, find my voice, and write in my diary about my intentions:

Dear future Self, by now, you're an adult. I want to tell you how
proud I am of you for achieving all of your dreams, going to college,
and making Mommy proud. By now, you have the beautiful family you
wanted. You're probably out traveling the world as you're reading this.
I know you have a big house, nice car, and you're inspiring others with
your story. You will be the reason other people don't have to go through
what you went through. You made it, and I'm so proud. You are amazing.
I'm going to wipe these tears from my eyes.

Reading, writing, and music were always my escape. I used to read about
people that had gone through hard times in life, and I would see how their lives
transformed. I told myself if I can just hang in there a couple of years, that would
be me one day. I cut pictures out of magazines and made vision boards all the time.
I frequently imagined the life my mom told me I could have. I would think about
the times I used to sit in her arms as I sang along with her to the famous song:

"Butterfly in the sky, I can go twice as high.

Take a look, it's in a book, a reading rainbow!

Friends to know, and ways to grow…"

I used to love it when my mom and grandmothers would read to me. They
told me that reading is dreaming with my eyes open. I kept reading, and I kept
dreaming.

Then, my dreams took a very different turn. I found out that I was pregnant
during my first year of college. At the time, I was only 18 years old. I was
scared and alone. People who I thought cared about me told me I would never
make it. That hurt so bad. As I went to all of my prenatal appointments alone,
I desperately wished that I could give my baby the life filled with love that I
had known as a child. I wanted to give my baby girl the life I dreamed up in
my diary, but it felt like just that… a dream.

Even though I was alone, my baby girl was all that I needed at that moment.
I would lay down in my dorm room on campus as I played lullaby songs through
headphones on my belly; just like my mom said she did with me. I did what
I knew best. I continued to write my goals and dreams. I kept my attention
focused on my intention. I had a quote saved as the background of my phone
that said, "The most successful people see adversity not as a stumbling block,
but as a stepping stone to greatness." I would look at that quote every day.

After I completed my freshman year in college, I prepared to give birth. The
doctor asked me if I was having contractions yet. I told her no. I started to get
anxious. I hadn't felt any contractions and it was time for my baby to come.
Then, I ended up having to check into the hospital because I was past due. I

was feeling so many emotions. "Am I seriously about to be a mom?" I thought to myself. Yet, there were no contractions. *What's going on?* The anticipation began to build up as the nurses put baby straps on me. To my surprise, I had been having contractions the entire time and didn't feel them! "This must be a real sign of my strength," I thought. The next day, my baby girl came with ease. No complications at all.

Raivyn gracefully entered the world. I looked her in the eyes and was blown away at how much she looked just like my mom. Her beautiful brown eyes looked at me for the first time, and I instantly fell in love. The feeling was so surreal. I finally had a mother-daughter bond again. All of a sudden, the fear and anger was gone. As she smiled at me, I cried tears of joy. Even though my mom and grandma weren't there in the flesh, I could feel their spirits in that hospital room. How could I not give my precious baby a life well-deserved? At that moment, my dreams and goals were nonnegotiable.

I may not have had the support that I needed at that time, but something in the back of my mind knew that regardless, everything was going to be okay. In life, you can either be the victim or the victor of your story. Having my daughter pushed me in ways that I never realized were necessary. It was time to Ignite the hunger in me.

My first step was finishing my bachelor's degree. I was determined not to give up on my dreams, even if it meant being a mom while being a student. I remember someone asking me, "Who do you know that finished school as a single parent?" That question stuck with me as I realized that I didn't know anyone who had done what I was trying to do. But I knew I couldn't be the first single parent to graduate from college, so I decided, "Well, maybe I need to get out and meet them." I went on a mission to find other single parents who had finished school to figure out how they managed to graduate. I found that many of these parents surrounded themselves with other parents to accomplish the common goal of getting through school. It wasn't just single moms, many married moms faced similar obstacles trying to balance family and school. I paid attention to what I was learning. Success always leaves clues. I began to host my own meetings with other moms, and we grew together and helped support one another until we graduated.

The things worth having are worth fighting for. The journey is far from easy. Now, when I look back and reflect on all of the things that were said to me and the opposition that I faced from people, I can't help but to have empathy for them. Hurt people hurt people. The things that were said to me were only a reflection of how those people felt about themselves.

Les Brown says, "If life knocks you down, try to land on your back. Because if you can look up, you can get up." When I had to stay up late nights and early mornings, I had to look up. When the obstacles I faced seemed so big that it felt almost impossible to go after my dreams, I had to look up. What I learned was that the only thing that could have held me back was myself. Giving birth to my daughter birthed a new beginning for me. I had created a goal for us and followed it through the good, the bad, and the ugly. I can't help but think, what if I would have given up? How would my life have turned out?

My story isn't unique; so many young ladies are going through similar situations. That is why I chose to live a life of service and help teens aging out of foster care. Although I've never been in foster care, I understand the journey of instability and what it's like to be instantly removed from your home. I also have a community called, *Own Your Story,* where women can come and learn how to break their silence and heal their childhood traumas. You see, we have to begin to stand on our stories, not in our stories. Just because it happens to you doesn't mean it has to become the reason why you don't go after your dream life.

I look at my life today, compared to my past, and it is barely recognizable. I am a proud wife to Aaron and mother of three amazing children: Raivyn, Taron, and Taj. My husband and I started our legacy business at 25 years old, a foster care and drug screening agency supporting children and families through wraparound services and contracts with the government. I am so grateful to my husband, who leads our company, *Atlanta Youth Services,* as I lead my women's group. I am thankful to have a spouse who loves and supports me the way Aaron does. I am also blessed to now be a mom of three very creative, energetic, and loving children. I love to sit down with them and show them pictures of my family and tell them stories of my childhood. My sons, who are still babies right now, smile bright and giggle when we have story nights. My daughter says, "You did all that? Can I do it too?"

My response is, "Anything is possible for you baby girl. You were born into a Queendom."

Despite my setbacks, I found out who I was in the darkness of my life. I could only imagine that while I was going through my trials, my mom, grandma, and great-grandma were yelling down from Heaven, "Girl, fix your crown!" The biggest lesson that I've learned is that life is 10 percent what happens to you and 90 percent what you do about it. I strive every day to go beyond my capabilities. When I reflect on life, I am proud of who I chose to become, and the choices I made to persevere and rise up. And that is all I want for others; to be able to look into a mirror and say, "Because of you, I didn't give up."

When you align yourself with your purpose, life takes on a whole new meaning. No matter what your life looks like, your current circumstances do not define how far you can go. Adjust your crown even if it feels off-kilter because you were born for this. It's your birthright to have and achieve anything that you want. Focus your attention on your intention, not the things that you can't change, but instead on the things you *will* change. Intention is how you can quiet the noise and find your own voice. It will be the spark that ignites the hunger in you. Your goals and dreams are ready and waiting for you. Step into your Queendom and shine!

IGNITE ACTION STEPS

Embrace Your Imperfections

When we begin to embrace our imperfections, we open the doors to allow others to come into our lives and help us to reach our next level of greatness. Take a personality test and get to know your strengths and opportunities for growth. Use that information to begin to understand what you're good at and what you can excel in.

Use Your Imagination

A person's ability to imagine can change their life. As a child, I learned how to imagine and dream big. Through the worst times in my life, I still used my imagination. The storm doesn't last forever. When you begin to see yourself beyond your current circumstances, you open the doors for transformation. Create a vision board to map out your future.

Build A Community

Les Brown has a saying, "Community is the new currency," and this is so true. Surrounding yourself with people who strive for greatness as a normal part of everyday life will help you focus your attention on your intention. Find those people who will support and help you to fulfill your dreams. The Own Your Story community, Les Brown community, and the Ignite community are a great place to start.

Jessica T. Moore — United States
Author, Entrepreneur, and Transformational Coach
jessicatmoore.com
🅵 *Jessica T. Moore* 🅾 *thejessicamooreshow*

Diana Lockett

Diana Lockett

*"There is a golden nugget waiting to be harvested
even in the darkest moments of your life."*

My yearning is that you will see parts of yourself through my words; the parts of you that have tried to hold on to life when it was slipping away and the parts of you that have shut down to life when it became unbearable. My hope is that you trust you are exactly where you are meant to be and open to receive all that life offers you: the grace and the grief, the light and the darkness, the joy and the pain. May you remember that, in all of it, there are nuggets of gold that, once harvested, will allow you to see the potential of your life that may not have been conceivable without these stepping stones. My wish is that you see the higher perspective of the possibilities in your life and the hunger that is inside of you waiting to be revealed.

Harvest the Gold in the Grief

I was awakened by a whisper coming from the end of my bed. I looked at my clock. It was 1:30 AM and I was startled out of a deep slumber on this cold and dark April morning. "Mom, when will life go back to normal?" This was one of three questions asked that night by my 14-year-old son. I took a big exhale. You see, for the two of us, life would never, again, be 'normal.'

In March 2020, my son, daughter, her boyfriend, and I were in Iceland. I remember the flight so clearly. It was a red-eye and, when everyone was asleep,

I looked out the window and was mesmerized by the beautiful dance of the Aurora Borealis, the northern lights. Their green, pink, and blue shimmer was a miraculous and privileged vision. I tried to wake up my son but he didn't budge. I thanked the Universe for gifting me with that shimmering sight and knew this would be an unforgettable trip. By the time we landed, we heard the news — a global pandemic had been declared and the world was going into a lockdown. That became the shortest long distance trip I had ever done. We booked our return flight home as soon as we could and ended up only spending a weekend in Iceland. It was a memorable weekend as we watched people transition from a carefree and friendly disposition to being cautious, keeping their distance, and closing their stores. I knew the world would never be the same. I never imagined how much that thought would be a foreshadow of my life.

We knew that, upon our return, we would have to quarantine, so we arranged for my husband to stay at his mother's house, so that he would be safe, while my daughter, her boyfriend, my son, and I stayed in our little home. We made it an adventure — trying new recipes, playing games, and staying sheltered in. I enjoyed this extended and uninterrupted time with my children. We all thought it would only last a few weeks to months at best and cherished each moment. What I didn't know was that it would be the last time my husband would stay in our home. Within a few weeks, our marriage ended and we stopped communicating completely. I didn't know how to manage given the current climate in the world so I got busy with work and my kids.

I had the responsibility of setting up my family for success during the lockdown to ensure that school was done and we had adequate work spaces in our little home. I even created online meeting schedules so we did not interrupt each other. We planned daily workouts and shared experiences. Every day, I showed up and did what I had to do. I pivoted my Yoga Teacher Training program and coaching to online and taught my young private Speech Pathology clients how to do speech therapy virtually, while I searched for meaningful and appropriate activities to support their communication. I had longed for this time at home, having been so busy for eight years. I felt a sense of gratitude. But, in my heart, something was missing; my husband. I longed for his safe arms in this time of uncertainty, his partnership, his friendship. Overnight, I became a single mom (for the second time in my life). I felt alone.

A few weeks went by and our newly separated family got into a routine. As I slowed down, I began to pay attention to the health of my senior cat. It was becoming evident that he was not doing well and was slipping away. Patches had been with me through some major transitions in my life. He was a model of resilience, having gone missing for three months and, eventually, finding his way home. On a rainy Tuesday morning, I made the short drive to the vet, snuggled him, and said goodbye as he took his last breath, my tears landing on his soft black and white fur. I would miss his presence, his weight on my belly as I slept, his little meows that, I swear, sounded like "Mom." I shed a few tears that day but got back to work quickly as I had a day packed with scheduled meetings.

Spring gave way to summer and, as the days became longer, we started to have some fun outside. Playing Nerf™ war, baseball, and lots of basketball. I noticed myself laughing playfully and relaxing into this gentle schedule. Although there was a lot of laughter in my home, at night, when I meditated, I would often experience a global collective fear and grief, and I knew to release those feelings through a moan, a sigh, a movement, or a yell. My kids were used to these unpredictable expressions. It was something I had done for years. I didn't anticipate how that collective pain would soon become an expression of my own deep personal anguish.

Early one Monday morning in June, I woke up to see several missed calls from my sister and niece. They lived near my father, who was in a nursing home six hours away from me. I had been monitoring the COVID-19 numbers in his nursing home and fully expected they were calling me to tell me he had tested positive for COVID-19. I was not prepared for my niece's words when I called back, "Opa died." I dropped the phone, let out a curling scream, and began to sob. I was supposed to see him at the end of March but couldn't go because of COVID-19. But this was unexpected. My son ran to me and immediately engulfed me in a full body embrace, the pressure of his body a temporary soothing to my nervous system as I found myself gasping to breathe. My father and I had a complicated relationship but I was proud of how we reconciled in the last 15 years, having opened my heart with grace, forgiveness, and love for him. I got busy, along with my three sisters, planning an unwelcome virtual memorial.

The next few months I found myself needing more and more time alone. I had less control over my tears and my grief started to overtake me. I would go to bed early, sleep in late, and walk for hours a day. Often, I would sit on the floor of my bedroom, demoralized, crying. My daughter, skillful in how to hold space for people, would often find me there and slide down the wall to join me on the floor. She never asked me, "What do you need?" or said, "It's going to be okay, Mom." She just sat with me in silence. She was my greatest support as everyone else was a ghost during the shutdown. She sat with me most of that summer until the time came for her to follow her heart and she moved 4,300 kilometers away.

She had wanted to live in the mountains for years and this was the perfect time for her to transition to create and live her dreams. I told her we would come visit every few months and, eventually, her brother and I would move there. We had a tearful goodbye. As I watched her vehicle and trailer drive away, I felt like a part of my heart left with her, which I expected. I was unprepared for the intensity of the wave of grief and darkness that soon engulfed me. I felt like I had just lost my only lifeline. I was desperately alone.

The darkness called me in, "Come and sit here in your body. Be in this space." I had been successfully living in the tower of my mind for so much of my life and now was the time to move into the home of my body and welcome its wisdom to deeply heal. I knew it was an option to numb, to distract, to push down all the big feelings. To reach only for the light. It was an option for some but not for me. I was a spiritual teacher and conscious leader and committed to a path of awakening to all of life, not just the parts that felt good. For 12 years I had been teaching others how to turn toward their pain and use the present moment to heal wounds. Now it was my turn. I had to slow down, bring compassion to my emotions and bodily sensations, and cultivate loving presence and safety for all of my experiences. I knew that suffering was a result of resisting pain so I had only one option left — to be fully present to my grief knowing that:

Pain + Presence is the recipe for Freedom.

Each morning, I slowly peeled back my heated blanket from the small sliver of bed that I continued to occupy, while the other side remained empty and lonely. I gently awoke with an intention to greet my grief with kindness and curiosity, "Good morning Grief, what do you need today?" Sometimes it wanted to walk or dance softly. Sometimes it wanted to stomp and push against a wall. Other days or minutes, it showed up as a moan with big, loud, and messy sobs. I learned to turn on the faucet of my grief in digestible degrees. I gave it the most loving attention and I treated it like a friend who needed my time, my patience, my nurturance. I knew much of this grief was recent, and an equal amount of it was old and unprocessed from a young girl who had lived a life of neglect, abuse, and heartbreak.

Slowly, as I attended to this deep sorrow inside me, I welcomed all the sensations that needed to be expressed or moved through my body, and I found myself allowing each emergent moment without trying to escape, fix, deny, condemn, or change it. I realized that so much of my suffering in the past was due to my resistance to my discomfort but, when I welcomed my pain and opened the portal to its truthful expression, I allowed myself the freedom to embrace my true emotional-energetic being. I released judgment of the grief and of the pain. I realized there are no 'bad' emotions, simply ones that I have been conditioned to judge as 'good' or 'bad.' I let go and I let go some more. I surrendered to the Universe and trusted that it had my back with each breath, movement, and sound.

Over time, months that felt like years, my grief started to transform. As I welcomed it fully with love, it softened. Soon, I became aware of something awakening in me, a deep hunger and yearning for life. With it came clarity and purpose. I started to map out a vision for my future, where I would live, and what my life would look like. I found the right coaches to help me through my transition, did deep trauma and shadow work, and redefined my business. I began to see the nuggets of gold in the darkness. And slowly, I began to harvest the wisdom of those nuggets: love, gratitude, humility, patience, and deep respect for this grief process.

It was a tough year. In four months, I lost my husband, my cat, my father, and, for a while, my daughter. In the next 10 months, I left my stable job of 32 years, sold my beloved home, and moved to an unfamiliar community, 4,300 kilometers away to start anew at the age of 56. Through it all, I remembered that my task is not just to survive; I am on this journey to thrive.

Today, I am living in the mountains, by the ocean, near my daughter, and with my son. I manifested a home beyond my expectations and a work/life balance that nurtures me. I continue to coach, to run Yoga Teacher Trainings, to speak, to write, and am serving children with communication disorders in orphanages in Africa. I am aware that grief is not a linear process, and all healing has its time. For now, I feel complete in my grief and, still, am not surprised when a song or a memory triggers some sadness and I let the tears trickle down my cheek. Then I smile, I made it. I made it through this most grief-filled time and am living a life that I get to create not in spite of my pain but because of my pain.

Les Brown says, "When life knocks you down, try to land on your back. Because if you can look up, you can get up. Let your reason get you back up." After this year of grief and growth, my reason was now sitting on the edge of my bed at 1:30 in the morning.

My son's voice reached out in the darkness, with his anxious blue eyes looking for answers, "When will life go back to normal?" I tenderly reflected on this past year, knowing he had gone through everything I had experienced. I gently reached for his hand, and said, "Things may go back to some level of normalcy for some people but we get to create our new normal. I don't know exactly what it will look like but I do know that we will be living the outdoor life that we have dreamed of for four years and we will embrace this adventure." I felt myself excitedly anticipating this new season of our lives, for him and for me.

His second query, "What is the meaning of life?" This, a wise question from a 14-year-old who, just a few hours earlier, was laughing as we watched an animated show together. My curly-haired sweet boy who used to childishly sleepwalk his way to my room before these deep worries filled his mind. I remembered that his entire family, life, and world, as he knew it, had changed. I took a deep breath, wondering if he was ready for the truth. Then, I trusted in his wisdom and replied, "The meaning of life is whatever you make of it." I let the answer settle on his heart and watched as his brow relaxed, seemingly content by my honest response.

His final question, filled with both hope and courage, "Why are we here?" I paused to look at his curious eyes and wondered what response he was seeking from me. His soft but firm gaze affirmed that he was referring to the big philosophical question: "What is our purpose?" As my eyes met his, I gave him a big hug, smiled proudly, and said, "We are here to love my son, we are here to love."

And, just like that, with the innocence and acceptance of an untethered Being, he was back in his room and called to me, like he does every night through the walls, "Thanks Mom, good night, I love you." "Goodnight Ben, I love you too," I replied with motherly tears of pride in my eyes.

It took me a while to go back to sleep that night. Life is curious. I had mine planned out and something completely different was birthed through me in the last 12 months. I was gratefully reminded of the blessing of life on that night by my son. I trust that I have been given a gift wrapped with deep meaning, beauty, and love. The gift of surrendered presence. The gift of being in my discomfort until it revealed my uncrushable strength. The gift of believing when I cannot see the way. The gift of transforming my life with a clarity that has allowed me to consciously choose where I live, love, work, and play. Through this year of grief and all that I've grown from experiencing, I have been blessed with so much gold as I allow my tender heart to be wrapped with the remembrance that we are here to love.

Where in your life are you able to harvest the gold in your moments of darkness? The gold that shows up as wisdom, trust, and self-compassion even in the midst of grief? How can you use your life experiences as stepping stones to your growth, your strength, and your full potential? What hunger lies inside you, veiled by unexpressed emotions, that has the potential to become your birthplace for transformation? Through it all, can you wrap your gold in your loving presence to allow your life to thrive with clarity, meaning, deep reverence and joy?

IGNITE ACTION STEPS

1. What is the golden nugget that is longing to be revealed in your darkness? What might happen if you asked yourself: "Why am I choosing to have this experience?" Make sure to see your obstacles as stepping stones longing for you to rise to higher perspectives.

2. You are not your feelings, you have feelings. And, there are no bad/good feelings, simply some that we have learned to welcome and others we have judged and resisted. Ask yourself: "What am I unwilling to feel?" Be curious about these as they show up in your life and focus on the sensations that are experienced in your body as you name the emotions and the sensations. Then breathe, sit with the sensations, and allow them to flow through you.

3. Cultivate a self-loving kindness practice. Include the parts of you that are the light and the parts of you that hold the darkness. Let it all be wrapped in your loving arms and expressed through your open heart. There is nothing that doesn't belong. You can practice saying, "You, too, belong here."

4. Practice gratitude for all your experiences, especially the ones that, on a human level, are incomprehensible. Practice saying, "Thank you for the gifts," or "Good morning, Grief."

5. It's okay to get help. There comes a time when the best choice you can make is to surrender to help. Connect to a therapist, coach, or friend.

Diana Lockett — Canada
Canada's Only Re-Alignment Coach
www.Dianalockett.com
🅕 *dm.lockett*
🅞 *dianalockettcoach*

Jocelyn McClure

"The brutal truth can and should be spoken wrapped in love."

Leaving yourself open to the brutal truth can help pave the way to some of the happiest times of your life. Have you ever had the thought: "Stop the world, God, I want to get off?" I have. As a matter of fact, that's a space I lived in for a huge chunk of my life. That is, until I was faced with the very real possibility of death. I don't want *you* to wait that long. I want you to LIVE life to the FULLEST and do it now! My hope is that through my story, you will dream again, and be moved to choose life, choose joy, and choose to leave your beautiful mark on this world.

Beautiful, Brutal Truth

It was almost midnight. Why in the world was my phone ringing? I didn't recognize the number, so there's no way I was answering it. Must be a wrong number or worse yet, some overzealous potential buyer calling about a listing, expecting to leave a message.

Was it ringing again? What in the world?

As I answered the phone, I heard the voice of a woman. I didn't recognize her voice, but she spoke as if she knew me. Wait a minute… what was she saying? Something about my brother. "I'm sorry, who is this?"

"Jocelyn, this is Sharon. I'm a friend of Jimmie's. I've been trying to reach you. I'm sorry to tell you that your brother has passed."

My mind started racing, my heart was beating out of my chest, and I couldn't believe what I was hearing.

"Oh, God no!!! Noooo!!!" I screamed. "What happened? Oh my God! Jesus! God, please no!"

Sharon said they didn't know exactly what happened. All they knew was that Jimmie was found halfway in his bathtub. He was fully clothed, and it appeared that he had been cleaning the tub. They didn't know if he slipped and hit his head or what, but he had been there for some time. My mind was still reeling... what day is it?

It was Friday. They say he may have been there since Tuesday. I could only imagine the scene. What tipped them off was the other tenants in the building where he lived had begun complaining to the landlord about not having any hot water. They went into his unit to see if there was an issue, and that's where they found him.

My brother was dead. My big brother, who was here when I got here, was gone. Now, it's just me. That new reality was tremendously hard to digest. Why, God, why? I couldn't fathom what it really meant; it was all too much. I was now the only person left of my original, core family. First my dad, then my baby brother, then my mom, and now, my big brother. I thought, "I HATE THIS LIFE! I HATE BEING ALIVE! Seriously, Lord... why am I still here? Stop the world, God, I want to get off."

Once the memorial service was over, I sat alone in my home and thought again: "Why am I still here? I'm tired of hurting; tired of burying family members. The only ones left are my children and I, and frankly, I don't want to bury anyone else I love. I'm tired, Lord. So very tired."

I'd begun to contemplate life without Jimmie, and I was frustrated, hurt, angry, and confused. I had weathered the storms of all of the losses I'd suffered previously and had come to a conclusion; I wanted to speak with my pastor. I called him and said that I needed to see him in person. I had never done that before, but this meeting was important.

He wasn't just my pastor; he was my friend. He must have thought I was joking because he said, "No, you don't. You don't need a meeting." I said in the most sincere tone I possess, "Yes, I do." He must have heard my sincerity because his tone changed from playful to concerned as he said, "Oh, you're really serious." I had never been more serious. We set the day and time, and I was already a bit relieved just at the thought of having scheduled our meeting.

Things went well when we met. He has a beautiful heart and a great sense of humor. He and his wife have been two of my best friends for many years.

It was comforting to be able to speak with someone who knew virtually all of the difficulties I had faced over the years. He was someone who possessed the ability to encourage and uplift me. Things went so well that before I left, we were both laughing uproariously. I felt better. Nothing had changed but getting my feelings off my chest, to someone I knew genuinely cared, was cathartic.

In time, looking at Jimmie's picture didn't make me cry anymore. I could look at his face and remember some silly thing or the other that made me chuckle. That holiday season was difficult though. Jimmie had been a fairly regular fixture during holiday time, especially in the last few years, and not having him around was challenging. But we made it through.

After the holiday season was done, sometime in January, I was talking to my aunt who lived in California. We had kept in touch over the years. It so happened that this time when I was talking to her, my cousin, Cheryl, was there. I hadn't spoken with her in years; hadn't seen her in decades! We are just about a year apart, and our connection was instant and impermeable. We spoke for a while and then made a commitment to remain in contact with each other. And that we did.

That year, we traveled together and had a blast! We found out how much alike we were, even down to some birthmarks we had! It was amazing. We had similar life stories and experiences. Though we hadn't been in contact for years, it seemed that our lives had run on parallel tracks.

She and her youngest daughter came for Thanksgiving the next year. She met my sons and some family friends, went to church with me, and was totally immersed in my life. It was as if we had grown up together. We were so grateful that we had reconnected. We both needed that connection in our lives, and God knew exactly what to do in order to make that happen.

Just when it seemed things were at least tolerable, July of the following year came. I was preparing for a yard sale I'd been threatening to have forever. It was really hot already, and it was just 7 AM. I'd only had a cup of coffee but as I was setting up, I felt this really uncomfortable feeling in what I thought was my stomach, or lung or… I didn't know. It just felt like the worst indigestion in the world. I thought that perhaps I'd overdone it just a tad and had maybe better settle down some. I considered going inside and asking my eldest son and daughter-in-law (who had just moved in the month before) to help me. I started feeling a little better, so I dismissed the thought and continued on preparing for the sale.

All of a sudden, there was a pain that rushed to the middle of my chest and just sat there like a giant gorilla. I started breathing slowly, intentionally taking deep breaths. That wasn't helping. I thought I'd better get in the house in case something really was wrong. My daughter-in-law heard me on the steps and asked me if I was okay. I didn't know. I asked her to get the Aspirin™ off of my nightstand and bring me some water.

Ultimately, she called an ambulance and what I suspected was happening was exactly what was happening. I was having a heart attack. I was rushed to the hospital, they performed a procedure to remove the clot, and I was sent home the next day. That's right… thirty-six hours after having a heart attack, I was back home in my bed. Talk about the wonders of modern medicine! Other issues were ignited with the advent of the heart attack, but I lived to tell the story and for that, I am truly grateful.

There's something else that happened after this ordeal. For the first time in my entire life, for as long as I could remember, I actually wanted to live. I mean I REALLY WANTED to LIVE! I couldn't remember the last time I ever actually felt that way.

The brutal truth was, up to that point, life to me felt like punishment. Most mornings I awoke disappointed that I actually woke up. I hadn't had a great relationship with my mom growing up, though God did allow us to grow beautifully close before her passing. I hadn't had a great marriage. I loved my kids but truthfully, I felt most of the time that they could live without me.

Yep. That's how I'd felt most of my life. I gave my life to the Lord when I was relatively young, so I was essentially living to live again. I didn't expect much out of this life and that's what I had received; my expectations.

There were things I wanted, but since I hadn't gotten them, I'd gotten to the place where being here just felt like torment most of the time. No one in my family knew, but God knew, and He wasn't willing to let me 'escape' this life without making me understand my presence HERE meant something to HIM. I knew it mattered to my family but had no idea it actually mattered to my heavenly Father. I mean, I knew *I* mattered to Him, I just didn't realize that my presence on earth meant something to Him. Talk about a revelation!

That's when my whole perspective changed.

I actually began looking forward to making the best of this life. I loved my family. I loved my friends. I loved my church family. I loved being a Realtor®, and now, I loved being alive; truly LIVING and not just existing. Wow, this really was new!

When I began to contemplate what LIVING really meant, I realized something especially important. I realized I didn't have a dream. I had dreamt of being a nurse when I was a child, but that dream was abandoned long ago. Now,

I needed a whole new dream. I remembered that at some point I'd heard my mentor, Les Brown, quote the marvelous pastor, Myles Monroe. He said that the richest place on earth was the cemetery because when we die, we take our gifts and talents with us. Well, guess what? I decided that I wasn't doing that. From that moment forward, I was determined to be a grave robber! While this year was spent recovering from the traumas of the last, little did I know that just beyond the horizon was a killer that would try and snuff me out.

In early 2020, after I felt stronger and more determined to actually start living, I caught COVID-19. I'm not sure where or from whom but I caught it. I survived, but there was a point in time when I wasn't certain I would. I knew others who had succumbed. This was a devastating time for many around the world as the pandemic wreaked havoc. In addition, later in the year it was discovered that I had cancer again. Again. Despite all of these occurrences, I was determined to live. As long as there was breath in my body, I was going to LIVE!

My cousin, Cheryl, rushed to be with me when she heard I needed surgery, which I had just after my birthday in October. She arrived just a few days before and went with me to the hospital. She stayed with me almost an entire month and left right before Thanksgiving. Our family reunion had been canceled earlier in the year, so that was our only time together, and I was tremendously grateful for her presence.

The holidays passed uneventfully, and in January I was invited to join a new social media app called Clubhouse. It was terrific and allowed for real-time, live conversations with a bunch of people at once — some you knew and some you didn't. I was putzing around on it one Saturday morning when I came across a room where Les Brown and his son John Leslie were speaking. They were about to close out, but I was on the virtual stage. They had asked the people in the room for an original quote. Before they left, I was moved to ask if I could share a quote of my own. They said yes, and I said, "You don't have to have lived a lifetime of greatness in order to produce greatness in your lifetime." The reaction was explosive! Les Brown told me to send it to his email. I was stunned but did as he requested.

Later that day, I got a call from a Las Vegas number that I did not recognize, so I didn't answer. When I finished with my clients, I noticed that I had a voicemail. As I listened, my eyes widened in stunned surprise and excitement. It was Les Brown himself! I could hardly believe it. I called him back immediately and left a message, then called Cheryl and told her.

I was beyond ecstatic because I had decided that one of the things I was going to do with this newly lived life of mine was become a public speaker. It had been a secret passion of mine for years. I loved helping people and talking to people. I was determined to marry the two and get into public speaking but had no idea how. Now, through the magic of social media, here was my opportunity. I was floored.

When I did finally speak with Les, it was, as he put it, "As if he'd known me all my life." The conversation was easy, funny, and engaging. It ended with my making a commitment to join his group, Hungry to Speak™.

And so, here we are. I've joined Hungry to Speak and I'm being featured in this book *Ignite the Hunger In You* that Les Brown and JB Owen have inspired. As you can see by the snippets you've read, my life has been, to quote Langston Hughes, "No crystal stair." Life can be challenging, of a certainty, but being brutally honest with *you* about *you* is key to finding your way through.

What I know is, had I not accepted the brutal truth that I was alive but wasn't living; and had I not been honest about the fact that I had forgotten how to dream, I never would have started dreaming again.

Once I began dreaming again, I opened myself to the possibility that my dreams could become a reality. Then it was just a matter of following the trail that God laid before me; the invite to Clubhouse, joining the Clubhouse room with Les and John Leslie, becoming a member of Hungry to Speak, meeting JB, the publisher of Ignite, and now being featured in a book that my favorite speaker in the whole world is a part of. It is obvious that God has a plan for my life and His intention is for me to embrace *this* life to the fullest.

Just recently I thought about something my mom used to say. Whenever someone would make a particularly illuminating or poignant statement, she'd say, "Now that's the beautiful truth." I've expanded on that thought and taken her words a step further, recognizing that truth can also be brutal. I've now decided to speak and live out my Beautiful, Brutal Truth, whatever that looks like.

My prayer is that my story inspires you as you seek life in abundance. Begin dreaming again and start living your own Beautiful, Brutal Truth.

Ignite Action Steps

Here are a few things I'd love to see you do to make your own pathway clear:
1. Ask yourself hard questions about where you are in your life such as, "Am I less than fulfilled? Should I be doing more? Am I failing to live out my life's purpose? Will my gifts and talents die when I do?"

2. Accept the truth of the answers you get from yourself when you ask these probing questions. If the answers are "NO," great. You're already headed in the right direction.

3. If the answer to any of the questions is affirmative, ask yourself exactly what you should be doing, then take purposeful, prayerful, and intentional steps toward making the changes you need to in order, as my mentor says, "Live full and die empty!"

Jocelyn McClure — United States
Author, Inspirational Speaker
beautifulbrutaltruth.com
🅵 *jocelyn.mcclure*
🅾 *jocelyn.mcclure*

Dr. Raolee

"The disquietude of my mind calms as I inhale the
scent of courage and press on into victory."

My wish is that the narration of my journey will help someone dig deeper and get up each time they fall. Yes, life throws curveballs, and sometimes one may still be unbalanced when the next ball comes flying. Do not be held hostage by fear, be strong and courageous; find a reason and a purpose to rise, shine, and press into victory!

The Journey of a Sickle Cell Gladiator

If you looked through our windows, you would see a perfect family in a newly built 4,500-square-foot home with two BMWs™ in the three-car garage and contemporary furniture in the house like something in the magazines. Father and mother are in designer outfits, two beautiful daughters similarly clothed, and a cute white terrier puppy. Wow! Such a picture-perfect family. That is the image 'the mister' wanted to portray, and we all played our parts.

My face smiles, and I am bubbly on the outside, laughing, dancing, and cracking jokes, to make everyone around me comfortable. I put everyone's needs ahead of mine — doing everything that is expected of me. I am the mother, wife, friend, teacher, sister, confidant, etc. Zumba Mondays and Saturdays, MOPS (Mothers of PreSchoolers) every Wednesday morning, then midweek church service every Wednesday night. Ladies' Bible class Friday mornings and of course two Sunday church services every weekend, one to attend and the other to serve.

Once a month I unplugged with bunco, a women's game night in the neighborhood, held every last Thursday of the month at 6 PM. This was the time I truly felt free because it is not about the Lord, the husband, or the kids — it is just about fun with friends. I laugh out loud as I shake the dice and visualize my numbers. "Come to me, bunco," I whisper and smile, rolling the dice and yelling out "BUNCO!" Then I do my famous bunco dance, and everyone laughs because I always do that whether I win or lose.

One night was my night. I won the prize, Hallelujah! It was a victory and something shiny to momentarily dull my ache. What I won was not important. I could have won a pile of hay, and I would still have danced. That time I actually did win something decent: a nice table decor, though 'the mister' may not consider it posh enough for our luxurious home. I shrugged my shoulders and thought to myself, "I will regift it when the time comes; someone will have a birthday or a housewarming party. What does it matter? A win is a win."

I looked around, wishing I could toss back the wine like the other ladies who were laughing and speaking freely as the alcohol helped loosen their tongues. Different forms of small talk and overexaggerated laughter filled the room. I swirled my wine glass half-filled with cabernet, and I take a tiny sip, the one glass I would nurse for the whole night. How I would love to be on my second or third glass like the other ladies, but it would be reckless. I have sickle cell disease, and to help manage my condition, I have to take a plethora of medications. Drinking more than half a glass of wine would compromise me because of drug-alcohol interactions, which could perhaps send me to hospital.

With a smile on my face, I floated around the beautifully decorated home of our hostess, joining the side conversations going on. Every woman sure seemed to be having fun — our one Thursday a month, our girl's night out.

After the game was over, we picked at the different yummies that people brought. Although it was game night, it was also a potluck. But we only brought drinks, salad, and hors d'oeuvres because everyone was watching their figure.

"Hmm," I sighed. My heart quietly wept because it knows the truth — the truth of life at home; the one I constantly ignore and cover up with trivialities. "Hmmm." Again, I let out a long sigh because bunco was wrapping up and people were trickling out. I took another deep breath, inhaling very slowly then exhaling with another sigh. Finally, my friend Paula looked at me and asked if I was okay. With the smile I had perfected, I lied and said I was great. I picked up the beautiful wrought iron decor I had won and walked to the door, exchanging good night pleasantries with the ladies.

Heading for my slow walk back home, I declined all offers to give me a ride. It was a very cold night in Texas, but I walked slowly, lost in my thoughts, welcoming the chill. With fear in my heart I wondered, "How did I get here; in a marriage that is a dictatorship and not a partnership?"

Although I was surrounded by people for the most part, I felt alone in my world where the house was spotlessly clean and loud with silence. Everything in place, everyone in order, walking on the invisible eggshells and no longer recognizing ourselves in the mirror. What? Who said that? I think I may have, but I no longer knew the sound of my voice nor that of my kids.

My daughters were 6 and 10 years old and were afraid of their dad. Most times we talked in whispers so as not to upset him. Before I left for bunco, I had situated everyone, making sure the girls had their dinner and were showered before I headed out. The simpler I left things, the better; no complex 'honey-dos' (honey please do this...), 'the mister' hates honey-dos.

"Mummy, when will dad be going on his trip?" little Jade asked, whispering in my ears. "In two days," I whispered back. She happily went off to share the information with her sister, knowing that in two days they would be free to have their friends over for a long-awaited sleepover. It was never a good idea to have friends over when 'the mister' was around. It always ended up being an unpleasant experience for everyone, as his moods were unpredictable. Any noise or toy out of place always triggered a severe reaction, and I didn't want to traumatize my daughters' friends, so I let them know that they could only have their friends come over when dad was out of town. "Hmmm," I sighed again as I turned into my cul-de-sac. My heart started to race with fear, not looking forward to returning to my clinically clean 'home,' the model house where no one feels at home.

Life for the last five years of the marriage was especially difficult. 'The mister' and I had a fight at least once a week. He stopped traveling for work and having him under the same roof 24/7 was a nightmare I couldn't wake up from. The girls and I did our best to avoid him. My phone or computer was my best companion; I would play distracting video apps for hours to appear busy and avoid any dialogue. I had trouble sleeping, I was tired all the time, and I had lost interest in many things. I would go to work and be the best teacher I could for my students; helping my colleagues with their technological needs and trying to appear really happy.

In truth, my heart knew the truth. Life was mundane and meaningless. I went to see a 'shrink' and was diagnosed with depression. I spent a lot of my time hiding in my closet, writing poems, and listening to sad piano music. Although I was hungry to speak, I remained quiet to avoid a fight. Occasionally,

I would look at all my pain and sleep meds and contemplate taking them all, then heading to the pool in the backyard to complete my well-thought-out suicide plan. Drowning with an abdomen filled with narcotics would get the job done quickly. But I would think of my daughters and what a legacy of a mother's suicide would do to them. Then I would think of God's wrath and quickly discard the thought for another day.

I didn't think I could be happy again, but I just wanted to stop feeling miserable. I wondered what the future held, how long I had left in this life, this body, this hopeless marriage. When would the next pain hit? When would my misery cease and my smile stop ending with a sigh? I sometimes wondered how I could endure so much emotional pain. I often yearned for the other pain I know so well — the sickle cell pain that rips through me and causes me hospital admission. At least there is a drug for that; I'll get IV, oxygen, and maybe blood. The morphine, Demerol(™), or codeine (whatever the hospital chose that day) would put me in an abyss of nothingness.

I'm hungry to speak, but I bite my tongue. I am so tired, so tired all the time! Tired of the mental, physical, and emotional pain; the expectations of the cruel and aloof 'mister' that I always fall short of.

It would all come to a head through the stress of an 800-mile move. We had transferred to Atlanta from Houston six weeks prior, but I returned to sort out the rest of the things and get that pristine house that I disliked ready to sell or lease. It was past midnight and I had just arrived on the last flight. I walked into the garage and found a mountain before me; six huge trunk boxes were stacked on each other, almost touching the ceiling in the garage. OMG! I could not believe my eyes! I had asked 'the mister' to unstack the boxes so that I could sort out everything that needed packing or discarding. I was exhausted after a long day at work, facing the crazy Atlanta traffic, and heading to the airport having to practically run to catch my flight. The sickle cell pain was beginning to creep from my leg into my back and my right arm. I stared at the trunks in a trance, and I had my Ignite Moment knowing this was the last straw. I would not live whatever was left of my life the way I had lived the last 20 years, in a dictatorship of a marriage. 'The mister' knew my health condition, but again, he did not care.

I pulled out a ladder and climbed up to open the top trunk; I walked up and down the ladder to set things down, sometimes simply throwing them from the top. I did this for about two hours, dragging each trunk down when it became empty, but stopped as the excruciating pain became unbearable. I slowly walked back into the house and took some painkillers and laid my body down. The next day when I awoke, I knew with no shadow of a doubt that my marriage was over. I was afraid of my decision, wondering how I would survive when I was not financially independent. But the fear of the unknown could no longer hold me bound so I made my choice. I remembered hearing a talk by Les Brown where he said, "Too many of us are not living our dreams because we are living our fears."

I returned to Atlanta and began to 'plot my graph'— my escape plan and path to financial independence. The first step was freeing myself of the shackles of 'the mister.' While on a three-day field trip with my students, I sent him a text inviting him to be man enough to leave, as he had threatened so many times to do. By the time I came back, he was GONE, and I felt the mixture of relief, fear, and sadness overcome me all at once. But there was no time to dwell. I signed up for a Master's program in Instructional Technology and started to take my confident steps forward.

In conjunction with all the accomplishments I was pursuing, the miserable marriage and the separation stress took its toll. The move, compounded with settling into a new job at a new school in a new town, triggered painful sickle cell crises all the time. A few weeks later, Jade and I were heading home from school when she said, "Mummy, your eyes are yellow!" I looked in the mirror and I saw that the white of my eyes had turned yellow for the first time in my life. I tried not to panic and called my doctor, who told me I was jaundiced and had to go to the hospital. Sure enough, that trip to the ER resulted in me needing four days of admission to the hospital after an emergency surgery.

Since I had asked 'the mister' to leave, my daughters called to let him know I was in the hospital — bad call! Of course he came, but as soon as he was alone with me, he started his verbal abuse and aggression until a nurse had to ask him to leave. Alone again, my mind started to ponder on my journey with sickle cell and I quickly reached for a pen as the words for a poem came to me.

Sickle cell or sickle hell?
How can I turn my pain into gain and extend the infinite possibility of an
amazing life? How can I reverse my mutated genes and attract positivity...
The error of my red blood cells moves wearily through
my veins till they come to a screeching halt...
Out of nowhere or who knows where a paroxysm
of sickling zaps through my brain.
Then, sure enough, the roaring thunder takes its turn and chooses
a location in my skinny, fragile body, and it starts to pound.

Boom, boom, boom, constantly hammering...
The throbbing and the pounding go on and on...
Sickle cell, sickle hell?
Whatever way the coin is flipped, I have to fight the war in my body.
As a gladiator, a fighter! A sickle cell Warrior.

After I was discharged from that particular hospital stay, I returned every three months to have the same surgery for the next three years. During that time, I became separated from 'the mister' and I dedicated myself, come what may, to earning my Master's and Doctorate degrees. Sometimes I was in the hospital when I logged on to my laptop for my online class, often to the dismay of the nurses and doctors. Yes, I pressed on, I had a plan — **financial freedom!**

After my health appeared stable with no surgery for nine months, I took a job in Dubai to get as far away from 'the mister' as I could. Finally, in August of 2020, right in the middle of the COVID-19 pandemic, I received my official freedom from him in a Zoom™ officiated divorce court. As soon as the camera was off I gave the loudest guttural cry of relief and stepped into my victory.

I went skydiving in Dubai as an affirmation of my transformation. Life without 'the mister' was the best gift to myself. My body is healthy because my heart knows the truth. The disquietude of my mind has calmed as I inhale the scent of courage and press on into victory.

I moved back to Houston with my daughters who are now adults. Our home is small with a lot of mismatched furniture, but we are happy; TRULY happy because we are not defined by material wealth or things. It's funny that with less I actually feel more fulfilled and alive. I am now living my best life peacefully and full of freedom. I am not afraid anymore. Life is so different for me as I express myself through poetry, writing, and spending time with friends while being an advocate for others with sickle cell. I am living a life of purpose; I am not thinking of how to end my life but instead how to LIVE my life!

As you face the curveballs that life throws at you, know that you are powerful enough to catch each one, but others may roll off. Create your perfect home by filling it with life, love, and joyful activities. Let the person you walk beside be the one who would move mountains for you. Let your sighs only be those of happiness and always remember that people may not remember the words you speak but they won't forget how you make them feel, so be kind with your words. Inhale the scent of courage and press on to your personal victory.

New courage I find
My anxiety is calmed
In power I stand
I'm hungry to speak
With new boldness and belief
I rise and I shine

Ignite Action Steps

- When you need to make hard decisions, set emotions aside.
- A person's character is like smoke, and it cannot be concealed. Believe the way people show up in your life and never make excuses for them.
- Don't stay in a bad relationship to satisfy the status quo. You may think the stigma of divorce and a broken home will affect your children, but the opposite is true. Staying in an abusive relationship affects the psyche of them more.
- Improve yourself by learning and teaching yourself new things so that you can change your narrative — go back to school, take a course, or listen to motivational speakers like Les Brown or teachers like Oprah.
- Plot your graph so that you can change things, because if you don't make a plan to take charge of your life, then you give the power to another.

Dr. Raolee — United States
Author, Speaker, and Educator
in *www.linkedin.com/in/rao-olayeye-ed-d-65b84038*
f *rao.olayeye*
raolee.blogspot.com
⊙ *Raolee.write*

Atul Bhatara

*"Everyone wants to fulfill their truest
expression of themselves as a human being."*

**Life is a journey, and the first thing I want to share with you is that it's not
about where you begin but who you become. With support and self-belief
I had to overcome a lot to be who I am today. Don't restrict yourself by
letting your circumstances define you. Wherever you are in your life, this
is your beginning. Be kind and gentle with yourself. You have an inner
strength and when you speak up and use your voice for what's right, your
life can be filled with wonderful blessings and surprises.**

The Spark Within

My birth month was supposed to be April, but instead it was January. Yes, I
was a premature baby weighing less than three pounds, and the doctors didn't
know whether I would be able to talk, see, or walk. It took them 14 months to
diagnose me with cerebral palsy.

I was born in New York to first-time parents. My mother and father had
immigrated to America from India. Although my mom was a trained nurse and
my father a microbiologist, it was not easy for them to work in a foreign country
and raise a disabled child with health issues. But my parents loved me in spite
of all the challenges. They wanted me to have even more love, attention, and
family time so when I was 4 years old they took me to New Delhi to be with
my extended family. Even with the distance, they came back often to visit me.

Being surrounded by a joint extended family of aunts, uncles, cousins, and my grandmother in those early years in New Delhi was wonderful. We didn't have a lot of space or material comforts but there were a lot of people and I always felt loved. There were strict rules too because my grandmother ran a tight ship. I didn't go to school but she managed all the appointments for my physical therapy routine. She also taught me life principles like how to get up, how to dress, how to eat, and how to sit. She taught me that I could be and do whatever I wanted. I don't remember being exposed to anything negative or hurtful; it was a time full of positivity and cherishable moments.

The natural power of food was taught to me by my grandmother and aunt, although I didn't know it at the time. My grandmother always said, "You are what you eat." Many times my cousins or I would walk through the kitchen, absorbed in the rich, sweet cooking smells of aromatic herbs and spices. My grandmother or aunt would take a dollop of yogurt infused with cinnamon, turmeric, or saffron and swiftly smear it straight onto our little faces. We didn't know what ingredient it was and never questioned it, we just knew it was normal and good for our skin.

My uncles owned a wedding catering business in New Delhi, and I remember going to their storefront and watching them make sales and interact with customers, typically the bride and groom's parents. Sometimes I was even able to attend the weddings, which were not held in banquet halls but always under a tent that was put up in a park or on the street. The 'tent house' was a world of its own — intoxicating and intriguing, the table settings beautiful and the decorations spectacular. Often there was a swing on the stage for the bride and groom, and my cousins had to help me on and off, but it was always a great time and we each would happily take our turn. It was so much fun, like being in an amusement park. There was so much dancing to watch and everybody was happy.

Living in New Delhi enabled me to understand my culture and develop a relationship with my faith and religion. It wrapped me in a lot of unconditional love and I am eternally grateful to my parents for giving me this experience.

At the age of 7, I came back to New York, which was hard on me. I reappeared in my brother's life, and he had been an only child for many years so it wasn't an easy dynamic to deal with. I had forgotten how to speak English. I had to learn how to live in a completely different culture — the American way.

At school I was placed in 'special education' classes, and on one occasion when my teacher was trying to teach something, I started debating with her as though we were having a philosophical discussion. She said, "You shouldn't be in this class. It is too easy for you." There was no American Disabilities Act at that time (it wouldn't be introduced until 1990, three years later) but thankfully she believed in me and supported me because within two months I was placed into 'regular ed' and even skipped a grade. As a result of this unprecedented event a world of possibilities opened up for me, the magnitude of which I couldn't comprehend at the time.

I had challenges with writing because my fine motor skills were under-developed and it was hard for me to keep up. Spelling while writing was too difficult so I had to improvise. I got a typewriter, then one of the first Apple™ computers. When I was in sixth grade I was excited to get what would have been the first notebook computer. It had a black screen, blue font, and no lights. Using the computer gave me a way to study and write, but it also made me feel isolated from my friends. I understood very early the importance of socializing and I never wanted isolation to be an everyday occurrence.

The physical challenges I endured due to cerebral palsy were significant. At 9 I had my first of 14 operations and had to miss school because of all the hospital visits. I went through a lot of pain but it was a great experience in other ways. I enjoyed staying awake at night and talking to the nurses. It gave me a new appreciation for my mom, who was a nurse. She came to see me every day and then went to work at night in Mount Sinai Hospital in Manhattan. She retired after 30 years.

I looked for external validation from family, friends, and wherever else I could get it. People would only give it to me based on how they saw my phys-ical capabilities. They saw someone in a wheelchair who was dependent, and they looked at me as a person who couldn't do much without help. My asking for help was buried in guilt, shame, and victimhood. Being Hindu and Indian and having the principles of reincarnation and karma, everyone including me thought I'd done something wrong in a previous life and was being punished for a past bad deed.

I loved going to school. It was always an uplifting and beautiful experience for me. It gave me a chance to dream and visualize a future full of possibil-ities, and boy did I dream, dream, and dream some more. At age 14 I made the Arrasta honor roll in the eighth grade at Louis Armstrong Middle School in New York. It was a performing arts school that took in wheelchair students and was designated a 'Barrier Free' school.

I was looking forward to going up on stage and getting my honors pin for my mom and everybody to see. But, before the big day and to my surprise, I was told that they would come down and put the pin on me because it would take me too long to go up the stage stairs and I would hold up the line. This was not acceptable to me. I felt like I'd earned the recognition and deserved to be on stage. No one could take that away from me.

I mustered my strength and using both crutches and leg braces, I walked up on stage that day. It was one of my proudest education accomplishments and the effort of going to school in a wheelchair was worth it.

My parents were extremely proud of me. They always showed me love and support at home and at school and actively participated in my education. If any issues arose at school, my mom would come to the school to attend to whatever was needed.

My happiness from getting pinned lasted for many weeks and I was a hero among my friends, several of whom were wheelchair bound. This opened my eyes to the disparity between 'special' and 'regular' education. The special education system at the time paid no attention to a student's potential. Students with physical, mental, or behavioral limitations were grouped together without any aptitude testing, predetermining their capabilities in school and in life. I realized that the friends of mine who were in wheelchairs were never going to have the same moment of recognition because there was no access to the stage and nobody would recognize their potential.

At the next school assembly I brought this up with the principal, Dr Flowers, by saying, "I can use crutches but what about the kids who can't?" I was told the school's trepidation was due to not having the budget so I reminded them, "This is a performing arts school and all those children can't go on stage for awards, nor for any kind of performance or stage related activities, not even for graduation." They again reiterated that the budget wasn't available. I reminded them that under the 'Barrier Free' status, this was illegal. The status implied that ALL students had access to all educational or vital places. What was more vital than the auditorium stage in a performing arts school?

That was the first time I challenged any kind of authority for any reason and my first time fighting for something for others in a very public way. I chose to be a voice for the kids who would be graduating after me. The following year a lift was installed on the stage and every student in the class of '95 was able to experience their proud, ceremonial moment for everyone to witness.

As Les Brown says, "Habits are too light to be felt until they become too heavy to be broken." That experience taught me the value of speaking up and made me realize that I wanted to help others understand that just because it hasn't been done before you came along doesn't mean you can't be the person to do it. I want to teach people how to get in touch with their own inner voice and be able to stand up for themselves. To find that inner passion and strength. There were two things I learned: not to accept things as they are — just because it hasn't been done before doesn't mean it can't be done, and the importance of trying to be a voice for others and making an impact for years to come. When you have a proper cause aligned with the right vision at the right time in life, you can make history.

I have continued speaking up in my life when I didn't want to accept things as they were, such as taking the SAT (Scholastic Aptitude Test) at home because I was being homeschooled, and being allowed to have a person to write for me in college classes and exams. I still need help today for different things but I am no longer defined by it. Changing the way I think about 'help' has made me insightful and compassionate toward others and myself, and it has shaped my dreams. It has helped me know what's right and wrong, what's important and what's not.

I was 16 when my parents joined Amway™. They took me to one of the weekly meetings, and at the end the speaker asked what I later learned were the traditional closing questions. Who's new? What did you learn today? What do you believe is different about yourself? I was eager to speak and had a lot to say. Suddenly having all these people willing to listen to me was a brand new experience. I loved the company's positivity and its recognition system and learned more about business and life in four years at Amway than I did at business school. It was around the same time that the company started to expand in India. I learned many things and that helped form my foundational principles and fueled my love for business.

During my college years at St John's University in New York, I visited a restaurant near the city to have a drink with friends. I couldn't go to the restaurant upstairs because of my wheelchair and the inside seating area downstairs was a banquet hall, so a table was set up for me outside by the water. There was a magnificent view encompassing the marina on one side, the planes from La Guardia airport flying overhead, and the Grand Central Parkway — the essence of New York City.

Eighteen months later, I had graduated college and wanted to work on Wall Street but I couldn't deal with the schedule or the traveling so I decided to work for myself. The sights and sounds of the 'tent house' had left a lasting impact so I started evaluating similar businesses with my friend, Mandeep. We deeply analyzed 40 to 50 businesses but couldn't afford any of them because we didn't have the two to three times sales, as usually requested by the owners.

Driving along the Grand Central Parkway one day, returning from another unsuccessful evaluation, I felt dejected and frustrated. I was not a heavy drinker but when I saw the restaurant by the marina I said, "Let's go have a drink over there!" We drove in circles for 90 minutes trying to find an exit that would lead us to the restaurant. Finally, we found our way to the door but there were no signs of activity — it was completely shut down. Stuck to the door was a small piece of paper, "For Lease. City of New York" and another sign, "RFP." We didn't know what it meant, but immediately saw it as an opportunity. Cautiously optimistic we made inquiries the next day. RFP meant Request For Proposal so Mandeep and I got busy.

Six months later, on July 1, 2004, we opened World's Fair Marina Restaurant and Banquet Hall in that exact building.

We hold over 300 different kinds of weddings a year including week-long Indian weddings full of color, liquor, and dancing. I often say, "You haven't been to a fun wedding until you've been to an Indian wedding." Watching the couples come in and create the kind of wedding they want never gets old for me. Even though I don't know all the people at the wedding, by the end of it it feels like I do. The happiness I experience watching two sets of parents grateful that their children are going off on their journey is immense. I feel the excitement of the just-married couple, the bridal party, and the extended family and friends. No matter what kind of day I'm having or how my body aches, every time I enter the room, hear the music playing, and see all the little intimate moments that are created at the wedding, I am filled with joy.

With the family restaurant business closed due to the pandemic, I had more time on my hands. It was on one of those quiet days at home while sitting on the sofa that my cousin, Raj, who works for a financial institution, shared with me the contact information of his client's private label cosmetics laboratory. As soon as I heard such a possibility existed, memories of the textures and smells in my grandmother's kitchen resurfaced, and I knew what I wanted to do.

Inspired by Les Brown's words, "You can only have two things in life: reasons or results. Notice reasons don't count. Results matter." I developed my own skincare line called Atul Skincare™. My name Atul means 'unique' or 'incomparable' and these words form part of the product branding. The line is based on the principles of Ayurveda, which I learned from my grandmother and refined. I remember all the luscious and aromatic ingredients she put on our faces when we were kids and I use these in my skincare range. It was a brand new concept for the lab and after some persuading they agreed to give it a chance.

I am now devoted to being the founder of an 'inclusive' skincare brand. I want my brand to be a platform for individuals of all shapes, colors, sizes, and skin tones that unleashes their worthiness and magnifies their inner and outer beauty.

The journey of my childhood took me from New York to New Delhi and back. It consciously and practically shaped the outcomes of my life, the person that I've become, and the choices that I've made. Even though I've missed out on a few things in terms of experiences and timing of life events, I feel blessed for all my circumstances and the life that I have lived. I would not be sitting here today if others didn't cultivate the belief in me before I believed in myself. The foundational love and caring many people showered on me have been a vital part of who I have become. I learned at a young age: how you think about your abilities, your life, and yourself trumps everything else.

Throughout life we get signs of the direction to go in, and most of the time it's our mental clock that's adjusting to what's right in front of us. Even though I've faced challenges, my childhood has shaped me by giving me tangible signs of what I am doing today. Pay attention to the things that happened in your journey because they are always a reference point. There is always a way that the Universe ties it all together.

We all start out like a rough diamond, and as we go through life the spark within us ignites to reveal our brilliance. It's my hope and wish that the flawless diamond within you is revealed.

IGNITE ACTION STEPS

- To **conceive**, first **perceive, believe**, then **achieve**.
- Keep your mind's eye open: life usually has a way of working it out.
- A rising tide focuses on its strength. And the same is true for you.
- Don't sweat the small stuff. You will get through it as long as you don't make it bigger than it is or harbor resentment toward any situation or circumstances.
- Focus on strengthening what you have, not what's missing.

Atul Bhatara — United States
CEO and Founder of Atul Skin Care,
Entrepreneur, Motivational Speaker, Restaurateur
Atulbhatara.com
Atulskincare.com
🖪 *Atulskincare*
🖸 *Atulskincare*

SUSAN WELTON

"Sometimes we must encounter the darkness to become the light."

My hope is that my story will inspire people who have experienced trauma to embrace their healing journey. No matter how horrible your past suffering, there is hope. No matter how dark your world is, there is light; no matter how painful your life is, there is comfort. It's through embracing your healing journey that you transform yourself into your greatest potential. We all have the capacity to face our deepest fears and rise from them. Then, as a wounded healer, we can help others on their journey. Sometimes we must encounter the darkness to become the light.

LOVE SHOULDN'T HAVE TO HURT

Hope.

SLAM!!
The door crashed in my face again and I heard her scream my name. "Sung Eun, get out!" was still ringing in my ears. Alone in the dark, trembling and shaking with my heart racing, I faced the dirt road again. At least tonight it wasn't snowing. Was it true what my aunt told me, that nobody loves me? That nobody wants me?

As I clung to the coins in my hands I started to walk down that familiar dusty road in South Korea. The rocks cut into my bare feet. The pain of the beating from my aunt joined with the pain in my feet. It helped mask the pain

I felt from my uncle's abuse; abuse an innocent little 5-year-old girl couldn't begin to fully understand.

This walk started like the countless other times I'd been sent out to get supplies for the baby. I didn't know it at the time but this night was going to be different and would forever change the future trajectory of my life.

As I stumbled down the road, chaotic thoughts swirled through my mind: "What did I do wrong to be hated so much? Why was I such a bad person? Why did I have to suffer so much emotional, physical, and mental pain everyday?" It wasn't my fault my parents died when I was a baby or that I was sent to my aunt and uncle to be taken care of. But my hopeful, innocent heart didn't know any better than to keep trying to prove my worth and play my part.

I started to panic as I returned to the house with the supplies. Was I going to be met with more hate, rage, and abuse? Was I going to be safe and left alone, or was I going to get thrown out again? I never knew. Why was caring for me such a terrible obligation for my aunt and uncle? Why did they despise me so much? I was their slave and I resented that baby; their baby. The baby they treated like gold while they treated me like dirt. No child should have to go through this much abuse.

I was alone in the dark and in depths of despair and hopelessness. The pain from the physical and emotional abuse made me want to cry. Agony enveloped my entire being, choking tears from my eyes one cold drop at a time.

With nighttime encroaching and a lonely silence, I lingered to avoid returning home. That's when I felt this incredibly comforting bright Light surrounding me like a soft blanket. It hugged me and brought me out of the darkness. I wanted to stay with this nurturing Light forever. Suddenly, I felt it communicating with me, the message was, "Little One, you are going to be okay." I felt the Light and knew for a brief moment what love was — such comfort and peace in my heart. It didn't last as long as I would have liked, but it left me with hope for my future.

It was a defining moment in my early life that forever changed me.

Compassion.

I felt like throwing up I was so sick to my stomach. I unbuckled my seatbelt to slide from my seat to the floor and my whole 7-year-old little body shook from the roar of the engines of the airplane. I was so dizzy, disoriented, and dehydrated, but most of all I was scared to death because I didn't know where I was or where I was going. Fear took hold of me and all I could think about was my uncertain future.

The only thought racing through my mind was a memory of being told by my grandmother that I had a new family in America. She told me I was going to be adopted and was going to go away. I started bawling, asking her, "WHY?" How could she do that to me? What did I do that was so bad for them to send me away? I remember sobbing, dropping to my knees, and grabbing onto her skirt while wailing in disbelief. My whole world was crashing in around me and I no longer understood what was happening.

Who are these people; this new family in America? What's America? Why do they look different from me? What does family mean? What did they want with me?

My terrors and my fears were interrupted by a cacophony of screaming and crying babies, who, like me, were about to meet their new American families. As I looked around me, I was startled by how many there were on that flight. All I could think to do was to go to the babies and pick them up in an effort to try to comfort them. But there were so many. Their cries were overwhelming and only a few adults were present to care for them. I felt compelled to help so that they wouldn't cry. But I couldn't save them.

Still, my compassion urged me to help as many as I could. So, hour after hour, I went to pick up the little babies and tried to be their comforting light. After what felt like days of holding crying babies, I saw the bright light of day come shining through the windows of the airplane. It reminded me of the comforting Light on the dark dirt road a couple years before; the one that promised me hope for my future.

We landed in America, in Minneapolis to be exact, and I was met by my new 'family' — the Tuckers. They had smiles on their faces but I didn't know them. I couldn't speak their language and I didn't look like them. But I clung to the hope of what I felt intuitively — that perhaps a better life was in front of me. That was when I became Susan Tucker.

Empathy.

"Hey Chink!" "Slant eyes… What are you doing here?" "You don't look like us, where did you come from? From Ching Chong Ching?"

I was on the playground in elementary school and would often be the target of bullies. Beyond the ethnic jokes, I was also called, "Ugly." I couldn't under-stand why I was a target; why they were so viciously mean to me. I often waited until I was in my own bedroom and completely alone to let out my howling cries. Why was my life so unfair; so traumatic? Why did I have no one to trust?

I saw so many others who didn't seem to have my problems: getting picked on and emotionally abused. I built a protective shield to guard my heart from more pain — excruciating pain I'd felt for as long as I had existed. After all, who could possibly understand?

During these episodes of being taunted and tormented, I would always find empathy in my heart for other children who also were being bullied. I would find the same overweight girl hiding and crying underneath a slide, and I would attempt to soothe her, coaxing her to stop hiding from the other school kids. There were others, too — disabled kids and a boy with a limp who constantly received the brunt of the mistreatment on the playground. We all seemed to have an unwritten understanding, born from being the kids who were chosen to be bullied every recess.

I learned early on to expand my empathy beyond the bullies' targets. I realized that the bullies themselves probably had horrific lives and were tormented at home. I forgave them knowing that darkness consumed them and their only outlet was a little vulnerable person like me to beat on.

I had a vision during these early schoolyard torments. In the future, someday, I could see a reality where people would see my inner beauty, my inner light. It was the same Light I saw on the dirt road in South Korea, a comforting light of hope in the darkness.

Peace.

I'm laying in the sun and it is glittering through the trees. It's so peaceful that I can hear "Prairie Home Companion" on the radio in the distance. I'm watching a squirrel eat a nut in one of the trees nearby as my hammock gently sways in the breeze. I realize that life is good. There's no TV and no telephones for distraction so my thoughts can roam without interruption. I think about how lucky I was as an 11-year-old girl in America to be able to come to my family's wooded land to learn how to shoot a rifle. We left every weekend to get away from city life and into nature. It was shortly after learning to shoot that I also learned how to ride a motorcycle.

Being in a loving family with a mom, dad, and four older brothers was wonderful. My dad teaching me I could do anything a man could was one of the best lessons I took forward into my life. I had no idea the need to prove how tough I was as a girl was going to show up everywhere! I was a girl who continuously got beat up and got back up to go to the next round, like a female Rocky™. This peaceful family land is where I learned to become a co-creator through the use of my imagination and creativity. It was also on this family land, after being part of the Tucker family for a few years, that I learned I was 'safe.' The Tuckers were good people and I learned a lot from them. I wasn't driven by the need to be perfect when I was up at our land. This environment was an escape from the people pleasing and needing to be perfect. So often I feared if I was not perfect I would be sent back to hell. Looking back, the Tuckers never would've sent me back no matter how bad I was, but it was a fear that controlled me at that time. So, the need to be perfect was created out of survival in my childhood and has stuck ever since.

Perseverance and Resilience.

My heart was pounding as I fumbled for the keys in the dark to lock up the restaurant. I was panic-stricken and wondering to myself, "Why am I doing this?" It was 3 AM in the morning in downtown Minneapolis and I was trying to remember where I parked my car 14 hours earlier, running as fast as I could in my high heels to make it there safely. This was not an easy life. This was a challenge that hit me every day between the eyes, but it was up to me to rise to meet it.

My father's lessons would carry me through the professional challenges I faced in my 20s. I remembered what he told me when I was 12… "Susie, you will work twice as hard as any man will, because you live in 1. A man's world, and 2. In a white man's world." I grew up believing those words and therefore I proved that belief; it became my self-fulfilling prophecy.

The need to prove I'm just as tough as they are really sucked me in on this job. As the young, female assistant manager, working with two older male managers at a Japanese teppanyaki steakhouse, I was expected to do the grunt work. I couldn't show weakness and being a woman, I didn't feel worthy so I worked harder than my male counterparts. Often working over 80 hours a week. I worked long after everyone else left and closing the restaurant alone most nights left me in the chaos of fight-or-flight energy.

I knew this was not the career path for the rest of my life but it felt awesome to pay off my student loans in three and a half years. This brought me a sense of accomplishment. Over the next 20 years many educational experiences like that happened to me. Overcoming them and my past traumas prepared me to be ready for the Light of Hope to hit me again, just as I knew it would. That bright Light led me to joy and unconditional love for the first time. The bright and comforting Light I saw at age 5 was a message, "Little One, you are going

to be okay." God was preparing me throughout my life to meet my match…
my equally yoked match and bright light in my life.

Joy.

As I was escorted through the doors in the back of the church, "Here Comes
The Bride" was not playing. When I approached the front, I saw my hus-
band-to-be was crying. I'm sure they were tears of joy. Seeing this made me
emotional and I started to cry too. This journey of facing my biggest fears
brought me to the altar to marry my best friend on what was truly the best day
of my life. So much trauma and encounters with darkness happened throughout
my life to get me to this point.

Only God knows how much I love helping others so he put Kurt and I
together when we were the most damaged: two broken souls coming together
to do God's will and bring God's Light into a world of darkness. I have clung
to Hope and this comforting Light my entire life. I carried it all the way through
my existence and right when I almost gave up on humanity, at the end of the
tunnel I met my husband.

The journey of healing has helped me become Susan Welton. It feels right
to be in union with my biggest supporter and my biggest fan — my partner
for life. He is the only person who has loved me unconditionally from day one
and the only person I have ever let close to my heart. I trusted him from the
first conversation we had on the phone; six months after I turned 42. I have
felt his unconditional love for me every day since we first met and it's been a
whirlwind of a love story. Special in many ways because we both have a love
of life and desire to live it to the fullest as if every day is our last. The creative
energy we experience and the masterminding between us is out of this world!

Ha! That's what you get when two nerds fall in love.

Awakening.

The hope of my future is unlimited, overcoming so many fears from my past
and knowing my best friend, Light, and protector is by my side awakens more
in me. My jagged path to the joy and peace I have finally begun to discover
is a testament to the potential and hope in all of us. In truth, throughout each
difficult moment, I was so sure all I was feeling was fear. Yet, I now know that
underneath it all I had deep-seated and immensely strong courage and hope
that carried me through and allowed me to follow the comforting Light to my

destiny. If that courage and hope had not been within me all along, I could have never endured all I did.

For anyone who has experienced trauma, connect to the courage within you and embrace the Light that will lead you to the future you deserve. The best is yet to come! And always remember; no matter how horrible your past suffering, there is hope. No matter how dark your world is, there is light: no matter how painful your life is, there is comfort. It's through embracing your healing journey that you transform yourself into your greatest potential.

We all have the capacity to face our deepest fears and rise from them. Then, as a wounded healer, we can help others on their journey. Sometimes we must encounter the darkness to become the Light. You are that light!!!

IGNITE ACTION STEPS

1. Listen to the song "You Are Loved" by Stars Go Dim. Really listen to the message. It is both healing and poignant. Songs have the power to heal; find the song that touches your heart and fills you.
2. Don't play victim. Don't get stuck in your darkness. Embrace the light; we all have a light inside us. Set yourself free to be empowered and courageous.
3. Despite our childhood we are co-creators of our future reality. Your childhood does not define your future. Use prayers and meditation to know that all things are possible.
4. Find a mentor. We all need people to pull us to our greatness. JB Owen and Les Brown have done that for me.

Susan Welton — United States
Author, Speaker, Healer, Intuitive, Empath
www.warrioroflighthealing.com
Susan Welton (Madison WI)
Susan Welton
susan@susantucker.com

Jo Dee Baer

"Life is like a milkshake: Choose your ingredients wisely."

Health is not something you DO — it is who you ARE along life's journey. With every turn emerges the champion from within. Bring out YOUR champion in all six pillars of life: Spiritual, Physical, Mental, Emotional, Social, and Financial. Your health then becomes your wealth! My wish is for you to go DOWN within yourself, look UP to your true North, and reach OUT so you can truly empower yourself, your circle, and the world.

From Tummy Ache to Transcendent Health

My earliest childhood memory was my 3-year-old plaintive cry as I was awakened from a restive sleep: "Mommy, my tummy hurts. I can't go potty." My mother gave me a hug and a hot water bottle, and sent me back to bed with a loving promise that it would all get better. I believed her, even though we were both coping with incredible grief: the sudden passing of my father. For much of my childhood, I thought these pains were part of my M.O. (Operating Mode) but later in life I unleashed the link between the constipation of my emotions, (a pain in my gut), and my sub-optimal health conditions.

When I was still a toddler, I discovered that the pain in my tummy and my emotional pain was often expelled each time I sang soulfully. When I sang, my mother smiled, and I could see her sad tears transform to ones of happiness. My father bought our piano a year before his passing, when he prophesied: "This little sharpie will sing and play." My mother supported my talent with voice and piano lessons that she could barely afford by working two daily jobs and a third on Saturdays. She was overworked and grieving the loss of her husband, but her emotional and financial investment in me worked. That desire to keep my mother smiling eventually carried me professionally to the concert stages and opera houses of the world. I intuitively knew that my angelic soprano voice was the catalyst that helped my mother heal her depression from the loss of her soul mate.

Then at 24, my life truly turned into a tsunami. I was heading to a solo performance with the St. Paul Chamber Orchestra when a Lincoln Continental™ hit my Fiat Spitfire™ sports car broadside! I woke up the next day in the hospital, clamped in and facedown with screws in my skull connected to a surgical halo and the devastating prognosis of permanent paralysis. That is when my mother gave me a lifelong gift:

"Jo Dee, the doctors only know what they SEE, they don't know WHO YOU ARE!"

I felt her wipe away my tears, as she turned the pages of my Bible, never leaving my side, and poured in her love and belief into me. Six months later, I had fought my way back to standing, walking, running, and eventually two years later to athletic peak performance. A true miracle. On every step of my healing journey, I heard my mother's voice, which catapulted me to each new rung on my ladder of success.

My own journey to peak performance began with organized athletics — that included half and full marathons, and grueling triathlons — where I swam, ran, and cycled into a series of triumphs that have continued into senior adulthood: culminating in a 18th Age Group National Ranking in the Olympic distance triathlon event. I have SAVORED EVERY STEP along life's journey.

My mother's sage words: "Jo Dee, you KNOW who you are," became and have remained my life's mantra. They have inspired me to overcome my own emotional and physical demons along my life journey. My hunger to give back was ignited from this experience and has grown my life's mission — I *know* I was destined to do this. As Les Brown says: "Accept responsibility for your life. *Know* it is you who will get you where you want to go. No one else."

I was filled with gratitude for the love my mother poured into me at so many moments of need. Then, the moment came when it was my turn to pour the same love back to her. I was a wife and young mother of two in diapers when my mother was diagnosed with Stage IV pancreatic cancer. I was in the bathroom grabbing a hand towel when she called to deliver the news. My world stood still. My heart was pounding as I slumped to my knees, and all I could do was sob as I grabbed toilet paper from the roll until the roll ran out. Despite her tragic news, I refused to stay still for long. I became relentless in finding SOMETHING, ANYTHING that would elongate her 'six weeks to live' diagnosis, so I decided to fly back from Atlanta to my childhood home. While I was there, I visited my local library of little Laurel, Montana, and found a book full of Edgar Casey's 100-year-old natural protocols that dated back to the 1800s. I felt exhilarated as I dusted the book off and ran through the library to the checkout desk, determined to use what I had found and help my mother beat the odds. Knowing this was a protocol for the liver, my mother and I got a gut-wrenching laugh about the role reversal that occurred as she had once changed my diapers and now, I was helping her with similar parts of her anatomy!

Six weeks passed, and triumph was ours to celebrate. Even as terminally sick as my mother was, I witnessed alternative healing and the 'magic' that this practicum had for true healing and transformation. Her hair returned, her skin renewed, and her eyes were restored with a healthy gleam. Casey's natural healing remedies gave my mother nearly *three years* of quality life.

This love and life that allowed me the chance to help cure my mother was the igniting of my life's purpose; something I would be pushed to explore in an unexpected way. After 11 years of marriage, my life's 'milkshake' suddenly included single motherhood and working two jobs to support my two young sons, Carl and Evan. I picked up the pieces and worked with a prominent direct sales company, consulting in natural health and beauty during the day. In the evenings I capitalized on my classical singing talent. Because of my quest for healing and hope for others, I found a 'life ingredient' in a larger audience as an expert in health and wellness.

What I learned from my mother's legacy was transferred to my sons as I supported their swimming gift in elite competition. I was compelled to give them a 'two parent' lifestyle so I poured myself into their 5 AM and afternoon swim practices, their hours of study, and my work. It was not uncommon for me to be seen sleeping between swim meet sessions, on the bleachers, using a swim bag for a pillow! I grew through the grind with my daily ritualistic mantra: Wake Up, Be Amazing, Rinse, and Repeat!

One morning, after only two hours of sleep, I crawled out of bed in my pajamas to take my sons to 5 AM practice. After dropping them off, all I could think about was getting home to that coveted two extra hours of sleep. Providence saw it differently! Suddenly in a highly trafficked intersection… POP! I had a blown rear tire. With the adrenaline flowing, I popped the trunk of my pink Cadillac™ and saw a full arsenal of cosmetics as a barrier to entry to my spare tire. I had not unpacked my car from my business trip the night before! As I neared the end of the unpacking process, a police officer came to my rescue. Grateful, I asked how he knew I was there. "Ma'am," he replied, "you were just on the early AM radio and TV." He told me that the famous DJ, Moby in the Morning, had proclaimed, "YEE DOGGIES!! There is a lady in a pink Cadillac and pink pajamas changing a flat tire on Spaghetti Junction!" Only then, did I realize that I was still in my pajamas! Turns out life's milkshake includes choosing your clothing wisely and keeping your sense of humor!

It was all worth it, though. My relentless passion, love, and knowledge as a holistic nutritionist gave Carl and Evan their own 'six pillar' edge in their athletic journeys — Collegiate All American, world-record-setting Olympic swimmers: Carl from Georgia Tech and Evan from the University of Tennessee. They are now both successful corporate vice presidents in their respective companies.

I had successfully boosted the well-being of my sons. True wellness for ME, however, came later. I was one of those women who put the oxygen mask on everyone else before putting it on myself. The trauma I felt in my body from my father's sudden death, that 'tummy ache,' created a physical chronic condition that carried into adulthood. I was part of the original class of Title IX: "Equality in Women's Sports," yet I did not fully embrace wellness until the 1990s when two 'situations' with melanoma, and two more near-death auto accidents gave me the wake-up call I needed to practice what I had promoted to my family and hundreds of thousands of others.

I had to re-engage my mantra: "Jo Dee, you know who you are." This finally became my life's crystal clear 'hungry' credo: "Health isn't something you DO, it's who you ARE along life's journey."

Our bodies give us warning signs: a tap on the shoulder, then a two-by-four, and ultimately a Mack Truck™. You cannot exercise your way out of a bad diet, and you cannot exercise your way to health. My situation with melanoma occurred because I had become ridiculously active and created an 'overachieving' goal of competing in a marathon a month: training 60-80 miles a week. This regime compromised my liver and toxified my body. I stared down the barrel of baldness and considered wearing the orange wig that had been part of my 'fan' costume as a University of Tennessee ardent swim mom. When I told my son that I was going 'away' to heal, he lovingly said the natural way was better — much better than that WIG! I went into a vigilant protocol, integrating what I had discovered for my mother in the Laurel Library decades earlier. My health BECAME me.

For the past two decades, I have rejuvenated and renewed myself from these setbacks, and have become relentless as a 'peak performer' in athletics. Every day, I do some sort of aerobic exercise — running, swimming, cycling — plus Ashtanga yoga that complements my outdoor exercise and diet. If I am on the 'road,' I use the gym, swimming pool, and, if need be, a hotel stairwell turned Stairmaster™.

Eating right has become a passion for me. A Green Miracle Drink (a mixture of raw fruits, herbs,and vegetables), gluten-free grains, complex carbohydrates, and no sugar, are the essentials of my diet. I often eat out and there is literally no restaurant where I can't find something healthy and fun! I augment my diet with daily vitamins. Just like supplemental accident insurance, vitamins are supplemental insurance for you and your health: Uno Cuerpo — Una Vida, meaning One body — One life!

I believe that there are two levels of 'wellness' followed by a more pervasive unhealthy lifestyle, where poor nutrition and overeating lead to obesity and unhappiness. We 'sabotage ourselves' because we run from the emotional hunger that lies within each of us. We make poor choices in food and exercise, and we convince ourselves that we can't reverse the changes that this lifestyle makes to our body. If we live this way, the 'Mack Truck' destiny is inevitable.

My hunger for giving back to others truly has become my life's mission. My wellness walk BECAME who I am, and I continue to spread the message to the world, empowering people to find optimal health. Energy creates vitality, which transcends to longevity. I believe that my family, my strong work ethic in the mental and emotional pillars, my personal physical pillar mantra: "No food tastes as good as health feels," and my spiritual pillar of faith in *Yahuah* (Hebrew for 'God'), have made all the difference in my life, and put me on own personal road to optimal wellness. The 'magic' and hunger for holistic health continue to emanate from my mother's wisdom to this day!

I often smile when I cook vegetarian delights from the cookbook entitled, *Laurel's Kitchen.* My mother gave me a legacy — vision and hope — and her words ignited a passion in me for healing which has now been over four decades. I developed a basic model of eating for wellness: three levels for three stages of life. *Level Three* is basic existence: we are running on the need to just subsist and survive, get through stress, and make it to the end of the day so we can collapse in bed with a beer before we have to do it again. We are running to get a bite, ordering fast food, or opening a couple cans and boiling up some pasta because that is all we think we can handle doing. This is the fast track to morbid obesity and premature death, but there is hope, I promise. *Level Two*, I believe, is attainable for everyone. We can seek out garden fresh organic vegetables, enjoy smaller portions, and choose natural whole food found in nature.

Of course, it took something bigger than myself to take me from being at Level Three to what I call the Jo Dee Way: *Level One*. When I knew there was a life inside of me and knew I was responsible for the health of my unborn baby, I transformed. It wasn't instant by any means. At first, I pushed myself to embrace a Level Two lifestyle, and remained there for several years. Then my near Mack Truck experience finally pushed me to the brink. It was then I chose to develop my own protocol that has helped to transform massive lifestyle changes in millions of people.

Now I am the fastest cart in the grocery store — and still get a little thrill at checkout when the cashier says, "This is the healthiest cart I've seen so far today." I follow a 'hungry for health' simple rule: I shop around the periphery of the supermarket, staying away from the canned and processed foods in the middle aisles. I scan and read the last ingredient on the label and then decide if it is for me. And I almost always AVOID the middle aisles, though I still go there for mops, detergents, and paper towels.

Prioritizing your health becomes a daily decision, and once committed, can be successfully navigated around any occasion and relationship: NOT the food. Health becomes H.O.P.E. and who you ARE along life's journey. I have had the honor of assisting my weight management clients in collectively losing close to a million pounds, replacing the emotional pain that has been left in the middle aisles of the grocery store with a hunger to give H.O.P.E. to others. Many sweet milkshakes of transformed lives! For, "No food tastes as good as health feels."

Despite the moments where I could have been taken out of the game, the hunger inside of me ignited my ability to triumph. I went from being permanently paralyzed, disease-stricken, and constipated with grief to living my life's purpose. I am a 67-year-old Certified Health Coach and Holistic Nutritionist of 40 plus years; one who people say looks 20 plus years younger. These compliments support my contention that anyone with the will and perseverance can overcome any adversity.

I got here because I listened to my mommy who energetically soothed my tummy at age 3, made my life's milkshake 'all better,' and gave me H.O.P.E. She taught me that you must choose your ingredients wisely. You must always share your voice with the world. You do not have to be a classically trained musician like myself to make your voice heard, just realize your unique gifts and use your voice to express it. Les Brown says: "Do what is hard, and your life will become easy. Do what is easy, and your life will become hard." Be relentless in your pursuit of health, happiness, and wholeness. Have a HUNGER to Ignite all six pillars in your life: Spiritual, Physical, Mental, Emotional, Social, and Financial. When you commit to you, you have found your true North in life.

Remember what my mother said, "They only know what they SEE, — they don't know WHO YOU ARE!"

Ignite Action Steps

Go DOWN; look UP; go IN; and reach OUT.

1. Go DOWN to Heal: Your mind, body, and spirit.
2. Look UP toward Opportunity: look for those doors marked 'PUSH.'
3. Go IN with Positivity: It is not what happens to you, but how you respond that will continue your successful life implementing the Law of Attraction.
4. Reach OUT for Empowerment: Go outside yourself to be an influencer, impact your circle, and change the world.

Jo Dee Baer — United States
Certified Health Coach Jo Dee; Holistic Nutritionist A.B.D.
www.healthcoachjodee.com
healthcoachjodee
healthcoachjodee
coachjodee

Ermos Erotocritou

Ermos Erotocritou

*"Once we identify the restraints that hold us back,
we can smash them, unleashing limitless potential."*

People are often restrained in many areas of their life. They remain in toxic relationships, trudge to jobs they are not passionate about, and feel trapped in bodies they are ashamed of. Many are held back by negative mindsets. Their lives are on autopilot with no clear trajectory, and they are simply going through the motions. I want you to believe that you can overcome any challenge, heal, and UNLEASH the power you never knew you had. It is your duty and obligation to share this unlimited potential with the world. By reading my story, my wish for you is that I inspire you to do this for yourself: become *Unleashed*.

Unleashing My True Potential

On the surface, it looked like I had it all figured out. Married with two wonderful daughters I adored dearly, a career I absolutely loved, traveling around the world, the nice house, nice car, and a generous bounty of friends. What more could anyone ask for? Everything around me suggested I should be happy, so I fooled myself into believing I was.

In the year I was turning 50, it all began to unravel. I started to realize that my perception of freedom was nothing more than restraints that were holding me back from being happy; true happiness, not the pretend kind that people post with forced smiles in a fake, made for social media moment. Just because I couldn't see the bars didn't mean I wasn't caged.

Two years prior, new leadership at the company I worked for began to deteriorate the culture that attracted me and kept me there for 20 years. Massive terminations, centralized controls, and in some cases a complete 180-degree reversal on the company's values sent shockwaves through the entire organization. What was once heralded as a family atmosphere where people truly enjoyed congregating had become what I fled from 20 years prior — a cold, heartless corporation that people joined only to earn a paycheck. What was once a passion, and something I woke up early for feeling inspired by mentoring, coaching, and building relationships, devolved into a "job" full of endless meetings and corporate messaging. All the creativity and freedom was sucked out of my career. I was no longer happy.

When the time came to part ways, the same man that hired me 20 years prior was there to send me on my way. We were in different roles now but he was still my boss, even though I always considered him a friend. It was a terrifying moment full of emotion and uncertainty. Although it felt like a stinging blow, there was a part of me that felt free. One of the restraints had just been smashed.

I saw my success in the amount of service I provided others. I prided myself in always being accessible. Once I was liberated from a job in which colleagues, clients, and bosses had access to me 24/7, I cleared my mind of the clutter and began to see opportunities that were in my blindspot previously. I started to notice other areas of my life where I was restrained. My perception of happiness was merely a facade of complacency and comfort. I would tell my colleagues that comfort is the enemy of progress. Yet there I was, being a hypocrite in my own life.

The next major change would be the hardest of them all. The rising conflict and uncertainty in my marriage had reached a tipping point. The previous gut punch felt like an amateur boxer had taken a half-hearted swing. But the moment I realized that my marriage needed to end felt like a blow from Mike Tyson in his prime. Iron Mike clenching his fist, veins popping from his freakishly oversized arms, sized me up and thrust his entire body weight behind an explosive blow. That gut punch knocked me out cold. Even though there was little communication, no affection, and we grew apart over the years, it was still a dark, petrifying moment. I went through despair, denial, shock, and constant numbness. I would lie awake, sometimes for days, staring at the ceiling, my mind and heart racing, out of control with no relief in sight.

As an only child growing up, I was constantly seeking friendships. Rainy days were the worst days as it meant I would be alone that day. My solace would come in the way of television and imaginary hockey games played out with hockey cards and a marble. Yet at the end of my marriage, I was more alone than at any time in my life. It seemed impossible to cope with my feelings and the fear of a life alone. "I'm turning 50 in a few months," I thought to myself, "Who wants to date a 50 year old?" played ominously in the back of my mind.

Everything culminated into two dark weeks of despair and I would cry at the drop of a hat. Losing a job after 20 years. The realization that my marriage was over. COVID-19 lockdown constraining me in the same house as my ex-spouse with both her parents. Stepping on the scale and realizing I was more than 30 pounds overweight. Fighting two legal battles simultaneously. Hitting the half century mark. As if that wasn't enough, I discovered I was adopted in a very unexpected way; yet another shock to my system. My drama was so blockbuster that Oscar-winning actor Leonardo DiCaprio could play me in my biopic. I had no clear path to a future career and no prospects for a new relationship. I worried about how my daughters would handle the marital breakdown. I had hit rock bottom. I was alone with my thoughts; horrible, uncomfortable thoughts. Clinical depression had set in.

I spent time imagining the worst case scenarios that could unfold for me. I focused on divorce statistics and thought about what it would mean to be single again. Being an only child taught me independence and how to live alone without feeling lonely so I tried hard to remind myself of this experience. Finally, after weeks of helplessness, being lost, and feeling like a zombie, my years of positive mindset conditioning slowly began to creep back in. I would break down what happened in order to understand my pain and make it go away. After accepting the obvious, that my marriage was over, I began to feel a sense of liberation and hope for the future. Another restraint had just been smashed.

I can still remember my moment of revelation as vividly as anything I had ever experienced before. The house was deathly silent as everyone was still asleep. I was lying on my couch all alone; the same gray couch that acted as my bed for the past six years. It was 5 AM, the time I normally awoke to get my day started. My stomach was grumbling as I hadn't eaten in two days. It's impossible to eat when your life is in complete free fall. The 5 AM Club™ strategy, which helped me jump-start my busy days, was working against me now. Instead of being productive, it gave me more time to wallow in my fear and self-doubt. The COVID-19 lockdown exacerbated my situation. I was isolated from the world. I had yet to tell anyone about my pending divorce because I was still in shock, had the fear of judgment, and wondered if it was really a conversation I could have over the phone.

Questions of doubt, self-pity, and remorse consumed me 24 hours a day: "How did I fall so far, so fast? Was this it for me? Was my life over as I knew it?" I couldn't shake the feeling of anxiety. I was physically exhausted from weeks of sleep deprivation and mentally exhausted from the unrelenting stress of the unknown. It felt like someone was constantly sitting on my chest: it was hard to breathe and impossible to concentrate. On the verge of tears, feeling vulnerable, raw, and alone, I laid there and began to listen to my inner thoughts of hope. Facing one challenge after the other, I started to contemplate that all of this could be a test to make me stronger, better, happier, and more resilient. I suddenly realized that everything I once cherished as my bedrock of freedom was actually a set of invisible chains holding me back.

Could it be that my perception of freedom was actually a cage cloaked in comfort? A 20-year career that I loved with a passion had morphed into a suffocating corporate job. Losing my job wasn't a setback, it was a setup for my comeback. All the ideas about starting my own business were now on the table. The possibilities were infinite as I began to dream of unleashing my limitless potential. Why was I depressed over the breakdown of my marriage? There was no love there. No affection. No future. Many dread turning 50 because it's a sign of getting older, but I decided that I could control what 50 would look like for me. Finding out I was adopted wasn't a negative. I loved my parents that raised me because they truly are my parents. Finding out I have half siblings is a blessing. I have an extended family that I look forward to meeting and loving. I wasn't losing anything, I was gaining everything. Many people fall in love after age 50 and have never been happier. This was an opportunity to find my perfect partner. She doesn't need to be perfect, but will be perfect for me. I knew I had the wisdom to create exactly what I want and don't want in a relationship. I realized that my legal battles are temporary and once over, I would be free. Truly free. Free from any and all restraints that were for so long invisible to my eye and mind.

Embracing my positive mentality helped me. I was transformed in what felt like an instant. I realized that things weren't happening *TO* me, but happening *FOR* me. Like a phoenix rising from the ashes, I felt liberated. My heart was pumping harder and happier than ever before. My body felt lighter as the suffocating weight on my chest lifted and breath filled my lungs for what felt like the first time in forever. I had a renewed hunger for life. The whole world opened up and I was euphoric. I felt Unleashed!

Although active for most of my life, I was certainly not in good shape. I was ashamed every time I looked in the mirror. I was disappointed in my lack of discipline and self-control. I was overweight and had a bad relationship with food. I exercised but not consistently enough to see results, and if the results *were* there, the layer of extra pounds did a good job of hiding it. I decided to be in the best shape of my life by my 50th birthday. Another restraint, the restraint of getting older was shattered into a million pieces. I began intermittent fasting, eating healthier, and working out every single day. Undeterred by gym lock-downs, I bought the missing pieces I needed to work out from home. The money I'm saving from my gym membership will pay for all my equipment within a year. I used to believe that home workouts could never replace the gym. I was dead wrong. My workouts are better than ever — without membership fees, the commute, or waiting for gym equipment. I only need a set of dumbbells, a pull-up bar, and a bench.

I watch Caroline Girvan on Youtube™ and it's free. She taught me that you don't need heavy weights and machines to get amazing results. She looked innocent and sweet but turned out to be tough as nails. She's the best thing that ever happened to me on the road to getting fit. I lost 32 pounds by my 50th birthday and achieved my goal of being in the best shape of my life. I looked younger and felt like I was in my 20s again. It was absolutely exhilarating. The feeling of trying on new clothes and not having to hide excess body fat made me giddy with excitement. I picked up golf and walked the 18 holes effortlessly. Where there is a will, there is a way. I wasn't going to let anything or anyone stop me from reaching my fitness goals.

I filled my days watching motivational videos and reading self-help books. I took long walks to clear my mind. Walks began as a form of exercise but by adding motivational content, they became therapeutic. I marinated on business ideas to get my mind working in a positive manner while simultaneously blocking out the whirlwind happening in my life. Your mind cannot hold a negative and positive thought at the same time. When discussing a negative topic, I will now preface it with, "I will discuss this for 15 minutes and then we'll talk about something else immediately after." This allows me to vent without getting bogged down for too long. By making conscious choices like this each day, I keep finding new paths to greater potential. I joined and 'binge-listened' to the Clubhouse social app where I met wonderful individuals who helped me transform my life. Connecting with inspirational people now gives me more to aspire to.

A blessing of going through this ordeal is the benefit of discovering who your true friends are and who were just coming along for the ride. My cousin, who I had only seen periodically because 'I was too busy,' reached out and insisted that I stay with him and his family on the weeks I was obligated to be out of the house. I was not deserving of this much love and support from a man that reached out to me so often and who I turned down almost as often. But there he was, accepting me with open arms, providing unconditional love and understanding. At first, it was a convenient place to lay my head at night, tired of the cold and lonely hotel rooms that I was used to staying in. This was an injection of love that my very soul was desperately aching for at the time. There are no words to express my gratitude. I'm truly thankful and blessed to be part of his cherished family. Being able to express my feelings was monumental to my healing process. My one regret is that I didn't reach out for help sooner.

All the love my cousin and his family gave has inspired me to give this gift of love in return. I want to take what I have gone through and all I have learned and use it to serve others. I want to leave a legacy and simultaneously help those that are struggling with their own challenges, to cope, overcome, and unleash their best Self. My lesson learned is my ability to accept my failures and keep moving forward. Les Brown says, "You don't get in life what you want; you get in life what you are."

I now understand when they say, "Strong trees need strong roots." If water is easy to find, the roots will not grow deep, and the tree will fall over easily. If a tree digs deep to find nourishment, that tree can withstand any storm. Challenges make you resilient. What unwittingly constrained me had suddenly sculpted me into a better, more confident person. I wear my scars like a badge of honor. They are trophies that make me stronger, make me better, make me complete.

Confronting and then breaking the restraints in your life is never a clean process, but once you embrace the pain with the promise of something greater, you will discover your true potential waiting to be unleashed. Your future is in your hands, and you have the power to be the director and star of your own blockbuster movie. When you Ignite your true Self and unleash that unwavering desire for life, you attain your ultimate potential.

Ignite Action Steps

- Wake up and read one chapter of a book. You can read two books per month by doing this.
- Exercise daily. Exercise releases endorphins, makes you feel better, and as your body transforms into a leaner and fitter version, your confidence

will soar. If you can't work out, then go for a walk. Consider walking the golf course. Park further away from the door. Take the stairs instead of the elevator.

- Try intermittent fasting. The benefits include weight loss, stabilized blood sugar levels, resistance to stress, suppression of inflammation, decreases in blood pressure and cholesterol levels, improvement in resting heart rate, and most importantly, improvement of brain health and memory.

- Positive mentality: As soon as you catch yourself thinking negative thoughts, consciously think of something positive. Eventually having a positive mindset becomes an automated process that happens subconsciously.

- Explore career opportunities that make you feel alive and give you purpose. Discover your hierarchy of values. Once you discover your values, everything in your life becomes more clear.

- Share your feelings. As men it's normal to keep our feelings bottled up inside. The weeks of hell I experienced were partly self-inflicted. After reaching out to my close friends and talking about my many challenges, I was able to heal. My advice is reach out, call that person, connect, and find those people who support and care for you. It will make a difference and change your life.

Ermos Erotocritou — Canada
Serial Entrepreneur, Business and Performance Coach
www.yourunleashedpotential.com
📘 *www.facebook.com/profile.php?id=845235432*
in *ermoserotocritou*
📷 *ermoserotocritou*

ASHLEY PATTERSON

"Prayer changes everything when you have the heart of a child."

I wish I could tell you how to connect to the Higher Source, but that would not be fair. I can give suggestions and I am happy to tell you about my journey. My hope is that you seek Him, Source, or Spirit in your own way and at your own pace. No one can force the connection, and no one can tell you what is right for you. The answer is inside of you. As I seek enlightenment and practice positivity in each action that I take, I pray that you seek the things that fill you with love, joy, enlightenment, and positive well-being in the most peaceful and gratifying way.

THE POWER OF PRAYER

I never thought much about prayers growing up. Some of them were funny, some were boring, some were confusing. Either way, I did not truly understand the purpose of prayer. I grew up thinking that you have to pray when you go to religious events, before Thanksgiving dinner, or when things got bad, and you needed some help. Prayer often felt like an uncomfortable obligation when someone asked you to do it on the spot. After all, no one gives you time to prepare or a cheat sheet. For the longest time, that was my unspoken belief about prayer. No matter the circumstance, prayer did not resonate with me. I did not really see the point.

As I grew into adulthood, I began to question prayer and its function in a cynical way. I would hear things like, "You have to say this or that, or God will not hear your prayer." I often wondered why some people would pray for the same things over and over and over, and then complain that they did not get an answer. Why don't they stop praying if there is no answer? It was so confusing to me to see their dedication for something that they complained was not producing any results.

When I looked up different definitions of prayer, I found that prayer could be seen as a request for help, or an expression of thanks addressed to God or an object of worship. I also found that prayer was a part of the structure of a religious service, or an earnest hope or wish. Though these definitions are not necessarily wrong, they only further fueled my cynicism of the act. In search of the truth, I began to seek answers through scripture. Similar to prayer, people would tell me to start reading from different places within the Bible. Someone told me to start with the books of John and Acts. Someone else told me to start with Proverbs. There is a reason why the Bible is assembled the way it is. I chose to start on page one.

My first thought was, "Lord, help me."

Unintentionally, I developed a routine of writing in my journal at night, then reading first thing in the morning. I split my journal in half, labeling the first half 'Past' and the second half 'Future.' In the Past section, I wrote about whatever happened that day, or what I thought about. In the Future section, I listed my goals and dreams.

Every morning, I would wake up, wash my face, brush my teeth, then climb back in bed and sit up against my headboard relying on my book light until the sun rose to read at least five chapters a day. I was asking for help, but I did not truly understand what I was asking help *for*. As an example, I could not ask, "help me build a house," or, "help me get this job." All I could ask for was help. I did not know at the time that prayers are understood even when we can't find the words to articulate them.

As I read page for page, things in my life began to change without my awareness. I was going through the growing pains of releasing my old self and allowing my new wings to spread out for the first time. I used to think that when the old me would shed, I would be happy, but it was quite the contrary. I would wake up overwhelmed, unsure why I randomly felt sad and confused; especially since I knew that I was blessed. Yet each day, I would open my Bible and read word for word and begin questioning things. I would wonder, "What does this mean? Why is this story in the Bible? Do other people see what I see, and wonder what I wonder?"

What I did not realize is that simply speaking to God, informally, was okay.

I did not have formal prayer training, or scriptures memorized, so instead I spoke from the heart, and I asked like a curious child. I would ask the questions like a bread crumb to the prize. "What does this mean? What does that mean? Where are we going? Can I have a sign or a snack?" Just like children do asking random, rapid questions.

The adult in me felt like my life was disconnected in so many ways, and my prayers took the form of half-hearted wishes. One morning I woke up feeling defeated from mental fog. As tears rolled off the side of my face onto my pillow, I said weakly, "Help me. Please help me understand!" I was tired of being tired and feeling unclear as I tried to decipher the Bible for application. After I ran out of tears, I turned over and went into a deep sleep. When I woke up, I turned again and took a deep breath — my first breath of hope. I felt better. I got up, made the bed, and carried on with my day, unaware of what was coming in the near future.

Soon enough, after a networking event I received a phone call. "Hey Ashley, how would you like to be trained by Les Brown?"

"Ummmm… okay?" I said with hesitation.

Prior to being asked, I had only vaguely heard of Les Brown. I had no idea of the following he had and the many lives he touched through his motivational speaking. About a month later I was sitting in a virtual class with about 15 other people as Les Brown interacted with us and critiqued our speeches.

"I'm not sure if I belong, but I'll stick it out. It's only a couple months and the people seem really nice. Maybe someone can help me practice," I thought.

I went into the Zoom™ chat box and found another participant who seemed comfortable and seasoned. I thought she might help me.

"Do you want to be my accountability partner?" *Please say yes, please say yes…*

"Me?" she responded.

"Yes," I replied, hopeful.

"Sure," she seemed surprised that I would ask her, and it ignited a new friendship.

Weeks went by and my partner and I continued to push each other to become better speakers. But I was still weary of the process. *Is this what help was?* I was almost ready to let this gift go in spite of my prayer. The day I decided it would be my last class, I reluctantly logged in, hoping it would go by fast and I'd only have to be half engaged. I cannot remember all that was discussed. I sat there semi listening, checked out and tired from a long day. As I watched the sun go down from my office window, all I wanted to do was take a shower and climb into bed. Yet at the end of that call, something new happened. Les Brown said, "Let's pray." In shock, I bowed my head.

Snippets of his deep reflection sang to my soul. "Father, we thank you…" "I know this is what I am supposed to be doing because when I do this the pain goes away…"

In that moment I could feel my eyes begin to water as my tear ducts filled up. It was like Les and I were in a room together with no one else around. I began to daydream as I sat in the office with my eyes closed listening to his prayer. It felt like Les was my long-lost grandfather and I was a kid comforted with the warm sun and his company. It was as if we were sitting on a porch side by side, dangling our feet as he put his arm around my shoulder and brought me comfort and peace. As long as my eyes remained closed, the dream remained vivid. With his voice in the background, I felt safe. I knew this is what I was supposed to be doing because when I heard his prayer the confusion went away.

As I opened my eyes, the tears finally fell as I saw him crying. I'll never know if he had the same thoughts I did, but one thing is for sure, our tears were the same.

Weeks went by and more people began to populate the Zoom call. What went from about 15 people turned to 30, 45, 70, and so on. It got to the point where I wasn't sure if I wanted to stay in this course because of how large it had grown. Something was missing.

I'm sure the friends I had made could pick up on my energy because it was JB who called me and asked, "How are you feeling about the class?" I responded, "I am not sure." I was learning so much, yet it wasn't what I expected. I really missed our small group and the interaction of a smaller crowd. Plus, I couldn't understand why Les had stopped praying. Didn't he know that was my favorite part of class; that his prayer brought me comfort and peace?

"Why don't my own prayers bring me comfort and peace?"

About a week later, I sat in my office looking at the picture of the tree of life on my wall and rehearsing what I would say in my interview with the great Les Brown. "Hi, my name is Ashley Patterson, founder of Elite Acuity…" I kept repeating it as if I would forget my own name and company title.

I received a text from his son asking if I was ready for our interview. I texted back yes, but I wasn't. I quickly opened my laptop, clicked on the link, and found myself in front of Les Brown. To my surprise, he was talking on the phone with his body turned so I could only see the right side of him. At first, I thought to myself, "Am I early? Was he not expecting me?" until I heard the conversation.

"Yes, I'm getting ready to start an interview. Yes, get me some almond milk.

Yes, two gallons. No, one gallon. Yes, two one gallons. And bring me some of those Atkins™ snacks too. Yes, I still have time to hide them."

Immediately I burst into laughter. I picked up the Atkins carton off my desk and quietly waved the bottle in front of the screen for him to see. "You too, huh?" he said with the biggest smile.

I immediately relaxed, as worry was replaced by excitement. I couldn't stop smiling and giggling inside like a tickled adolescent because I was on camera with a legend... who was placing his grocery list. He was human, just like my imaginary grandfather.

We introduced ourselves and spoke about my endeavors with Elite Acuity. He asked me many questions and gave me an impressed look like, "You go girl!" He then asked me, "Are you a speaker?" I shook my head no. He looked puzzled, "I don't know why not." I didn't know if I was qualified to call myself a speaker. Before I knew it, Les eagerly said, "Let's get started," and within 10 seconds I was in front of the Facebook™ world speaking with Les Brown. My nerves came rushing back. "What am I doing?" I asked myself.

The 15-minute interview felt like 60 seconds. He ended with the question, "Did they call you Smiley growing up?"

I responded, "No, they called me Ms. University."

Once the cameras were turned off, he asked, "Were you nervous?"

I responded with a deep sigh, "YES!"

He smiled and said, "I couldn't tell. I can't wait to interview you again after your book comes out." With that we said our goodbyes and I promised that I would see him the next night at class.

I spoke with my accountability partner about everything that happened with Les Brown. I told her about how I'd said I was not a speaker. When she heard that, she became FURIOUS. I could feel her hands reach through the phone and grab me by the collar.

"DON'T YOU EVER SAY YOU'RE NOT A SPEAKER! YOU'RE DYNAMIC. DON'T YOU EVER SAY NO AGAIN!"

My eyes widened, "Okay okay, I won't."

That night I lay in bed tossing and turning, wondering why I said no. I'd spoken before, but did that qualify me as a speaker? When I woke up the next morning, I still felt uneasy. I went through my morning routine to get my day started. For inspiration to clear the drowsiness, I began to play some music. My grandma's favorite song came on and I began to sing in the bathroom as I put on my makeup and styled my hair:

The lyrics of the songs rang out, "Yes, he knows my name. And oh, how he walks with me. Yes oh, how he talks with me. And oh how he tells me that I am his own."

As I was looking in the mirror singing those lyrics, I broke rhythm and declared, "You ARE a speaker!" Was God using Les Brown to wake me up?

Later on that day I had a candid conversation with a friend about manifesting the future. At first, I denied the power of manifestation, and thereby denied the power of prayer, until he made me take into account all that had happened within a 12 to 14-month period. He said, "Just think about it. What have you accomplished in a year?" I got up and grabbed my journal and turned to the Future portion. Page one, nothing accomplished. Page two, nothing accomplished. Page three, my mouth dropped, I did that. Page four, oh my goodness I did almost all of those things. Page five, my mouth dropped further to the floor, I am a speaker, and I did get trained from the best. *He was helping me.* Within a little over a year, I accomplished over 15 things in my Future section, including being mentored by a legend.

I realized then; *God knows my name.*

I have heard the phrase, "The Lord works in mysterious ways," and to me, that means that whatever is happening in your life does not make sense now, but it will. It took the pressure of putting my vision out into the world and embracing the reality of my talents for me to realize the powerful truth: I had been praying all along. Each time I had a conversation with God, each time I simply asked a question, each time I chose to reflect, I was harnessing the power of prayer and walking toward my purpose. Today, although my understanding of prayer has changed, my vision has not. I have made a promise to practice every day in reminding myself of the power of prayer. I am enough. After all, I am Ms. University. ;-)

A friend once told me that, "God will meet you at your level of effort." I have come to define prayer as spiritual communication between God and myself. It's a two-way relationship in which I speak and then I listen. When I began to take pride in *my* prayer and put effort into seeking Him, there He was, waiting for me with open arms, ready to provide the peace and comfort as we sit together, walk together, talk together, and create together. I'm excited to give gratitude and tell God about all the things that I have learned: a child's conversation with her grandfather. The reality is, prayer does not require a structure, proposition, or title. We are only required to pray from the heart and listen with eagerness. Then, in His mysterious ways, always in due time, God will answer our prayers.

I share my story so that you can understand what can happen, unconsciously and sometimes under pressure. I allowed my old habit of denying my talents to shine and come out through answering a question. There are some of you out there that deny yourself of greatness because you feel that you don't measure up. Success is not what you have accomplished compared to the people around you, or those that you admire. Success is the reflection that you project when you have persistently reached to fulfill the vision that God has placed on your heart. Prayer will help you get there.

Ignite Action Steps

- Take some time and space to identify what prayer means to you. Define the relationship that you choose to have with the Higher Source.
- If you don't have a journal, start one. As you reflect, also take some time to dream. Write out your goals and let your past greet your future before you let it go. It's only polite.
- Sometimes, we need someone to remind us of who we are and the gifts that we possess. Get an accountability partner that is ready and willing to remind you to operate in your gifts.
- At times, the thing that we are getting ready to walk away from is the very thing that is the answer to our prayers. Keep your mind and heart open to the possibilities that are rooted from your prayers.
- Acknowledge what you are willing to let go in spite of your prayers; this will help you make the right choices for yourself.

Ashley Patterson — United States
Founder and CEO of Elite Acuity, LLC
www.eliteacuity.com
AshleyPattersonElite
asheliteacuity/
asheliteacuity

Dr. Yasmine Saad

Dr. Yasmine Saad

"Give great voice to who you are IN LIGHT and not in spite of those around you."

My wish is for you to transform the muddy waters of your life and blossom into the beautiful human being that you are, giving life to all the potential within you, in light and not in spite of those around you. Most people have a message for you but may say it in a way that is hard to hear. The urge to build yourself against these messages may exist, but through embracing them, you may discover greatness within you. Love is hidden behind everything that happens to you, and when you connect to that love, your potential will unfurl like petals opening to the sun. Life is a blessing and filled with gifts designed to propel you into your future with strength.

Giving YOU Your Greatest Voice

Have you ever sat next to someone you love and felt all their pain and frustration? No words spoken: the feeling is there, you know the pain, the sadness, the frustration. I grew up feeling other people's pain. I was particularly attuned to my mother's. The first five years of my life I watched as she negotiated the fear of living during the Lebanese civil war, surrounded by falling bombs. We moved back and forth between Lebanon, Athens, and Aman, yet everywhere we went, the threat to our life and the fear that came with it was there.

In Lebanon, there were the bombs. In Athens, the earthquakes. In Aman, our hotel was taken hostage by terrorists, and we were stuck fighting for our lives as they burned down the hotel we were in. I was too young during the hostage crisis to remember, but I can only imagine what it must have been like for my mother to protect the life of her infant baby while the flames were burning.

In Athens, I remember hiding under the living room coffee table when the earth shook; trying to figure out where to go next to protect myself. One day, when the earthquakes were stronger than usual, we had to leave the city with our neighbors in their tiny car, as it was too dangerous to stay close to our building. We went to a deserted field and waited… and waited. It felt to me like the end of the world. There were no buildings in sight and the atmosphere in the car was grim. I felt everyone's fear as well as my own.

Needless to say, by the time I was 5, fear and angst had become familiar emotions. So was boredom. My mother liked the house to be quiet and didn't want me to watch TV, so she pretended that the TV was broken. She would spend a lot of time reading. My dad was traveling for work most of the time and we were far from other family members. As an only child, I was all by myself; bored and lonely.

I delved into a deep and rich internal life. I colored and played, pretending that I had a friend or my cousin playing with me. I would take turns being Yasmine, then the other person. I did my best to entertain myself, but my life was filled with the contrast of boredom alternating with periods of angst and fear. Although, I did feel my mother and father's love deeply. I treasured being together as a family — that was my fun. My mom says that I was 'happy-go-lucky,' and as long as I was with my parents, I was happy.

Riding the waves of happiness, dullness, and fear while observing my mother and her reactions, I became a witness to how emotions get built, transmitted, and stuck within us. Little did I know that those emotions were stuck in me also.

Growing up, I remember looking out the window seeing life passing by as children were playing, wishing that I had a group of friends to have fun with. I was not adventurous and didn't feel like I belonged, growing up in different countries. We settled in France when I was 5, but I was so different from the French children. My culture, values, relationship with my parents, and way of speaking were alien to them, and I was constantly being reminded of my differences. Children laughed at my unique use of the French language. I was also teased for how close I was with my mother, but that didn't matter. I loved being with my mom. Yet, she had to adjust to so many changes in her life and was carrying so many deep-felt emotions. Often, I felt 'blah' not knowing why. Looking back, it is obvious that in those moments I was feeling her sadness and sense of loss in the atmosphere we shared.

There was so much pain in my family although everyone appeared happy. They laughed outwardly, but when I was alone with them, I also felt their grief. I remember feeling my mother's angst while also feeling her strength. It was hard to understand as she *seemed* happy, and I felt loved by both my parents. But something was muted in our existence at the time. Looking back, I think a lot of emotions were pushed down, both happiness and dullness sharing the same space. I somehow tuned in to the 'blah' of life — the lack of life — as if we were going through the motions of life rather than actually living it.

I didn't want to bother my mother, as she already had too much on her plate. I became shy and introverted, not wanting to inconvenience others. I had become accustomed to delving into a creative world to escape the boredom or negative emotions around me. I also became an observer of my mother and very early on started helping her feel better, longing for happiness, joy, and life in the house. When she was stressed, I would tell her to sit down, and I played a recording of the Boléro de Ravel to help her de-stress. She was so appreciative of my efforts and was so loving. "Ma chérie, ta présence est tellement apaisante," she would say. "My darling, your presence is so peaceful."

My knack for calming others carried over to school, as classmates came to me for soothing and commented on my melodious calm tone of voice. Some, however, made fun of it. But I didn't receive it as aggression. I was somehow observing it all and understanding, very early on, people's psychology and their pain.

My other strengths, however, were of greater focus in high school. I was obedient and good in math and was put in a mathematical section in a private school so I could excel. At 16, sitting in a math exam, imagining what my life would be like, I realized that I would be miserable going to business school and managing people's money. I hated the prospect of the stressful business school curriculum in Paris, the place we had settled after all the stressful events of my early life. Having sat and simmered in this pain since I was child, I knew that I wanted to create a life for myself filled with joy.

I thought and asked myself, "What do I like?" The answer: "I like helping my friends." It was set: I was going to become a psychologist. I was so excited about having found my calling. I no longer had to worry about my math performance and the stressful days ahead in business school. I felt like I belonged in the field of psychology. My life had already been my training ground and understanding others came easy to me. I felt like I had wings!

Proud of having found my vocation, I came home and told my mom. She replied, "It is made for you!" It felt great to be seen and validated in my choice.

I then told my dad and he thought that I had turned mad. Giving up the prosperous life that business school could help me achieve and instead attending a mainstream university to help people with psychological problems made no sense to him. He was worried for both my sanity (hearing others' problems all day long), and my financial safety, and asked me "How are you going to support yourself emotionally and financially?"

Determined to do what I wanted, I 'gave great voice' to one of his main principles: be the best in what you do. I went on telling him that I would be the best at it, without knowing what it really meant. At the time, I just thought: "Everything is possible, therefore I will figure it out." Based on my mother's encouragement that doing what you love is most important, I believed that if I followed my passion, I would succeed.

Life fulfilled my intention. I became a psychologist in Paris, cum laude, at 23 years old. I loved the field of psychology and my profession. However, I wondered who would go see a 23-year-old for advice. I thought that I needed many more years of experience in order to be taken seriously. Many of my cousins went to the United States to study and I dreamed of a campus life like theirs. I learned that a PhD in Clinical Psychology from anywhere in the U.S. would entail five years of clinical experience, which was not the case in Paris. I set forth to New York and embarked on a new journey.

By myself, without the words of people around me, I discovered who I was: I was brave, courageous, loved people, and had an ease to understanding psychology. I *felt* people and was able to translate those feelings into words. I was intuitive and discovered what life was like for the first time. I was no longer an observer; I was a participant in my own life.

I also loved the multicultural aspect of New York City, as I could integrate all my cultural background and work in many languages. I felt at home. Everyone was like me from a different cultural background. Having a feeling of belonging, I blossomed like a flower. Giving great voice to what my heart desired opened all the doors for me, especially the doors to myself and my potential.

Without realizing it, I also 'gave great voice' to my father's main principle: be the best. Upon graduation, the chair of my dissertation gave me the most glowing recommendation, listing me among the top one percent of all students he had taught in his 30-year career. I choked up and was in awe when I read the letter as I had no clue about my value. Psychology came easily to me so I thought my way of operating and supporting others was the norm.

When the 9/11 tragedy happened in New York City, I quickly understood that my childhood experiences of angst and dread were my training ground.

Having lived through these fears as a child, I could, as an adult, help others deal with the trauma of the terrorist attack with much ease. I came to understand that everything that I experienced in my life was a preparation for the future: from my father's teachings of excellence and my mother's teaching of following your heart, to my observing and experiencing the intricacies of emotions and how they are trapped within us. I was in awe of my life journey from a bored, 'blah' child, who lived through terror and angst, to a blossoming psychologist who had been given all the ingredients to innately help others.

As I became aware of the purpose and meaning that experiencing the terror of war brought me, I embraced and had so much love for the 'blah' child in me. I came to understand how that was all necessary. I am very grateful for those experiences, as I can now help others move from any bored, sad, traumatized emotional state to the light. I am proof; a product of the transformation.

I now realize that everything has a purpose and can help you transform the muddy waters in your life into beautiful lotus flowers. When supporting others, I often help them see the messages behind their family's words. If I look at my story, listening to my dad was not a matter of choosing not to pursue psychology or follow my heart. It was about seeing his love and taking into account his warnings: listening to others' problems can affect you negatively, and providing financial security for yourself is important. His words of concern were his way of caring.

I developed a way of listening to others that led me to understand the message behind the pain and not be affected by the pain. I also embarked on building a group practice and became one of the top three rated psychologists in New York City, which provided safety for me. In addition, the path through the acculturation process to finding one's own place in society and cultural identity was the best training to give me the tools to help my patients with their feelings of worry and not belonging.

Looking at my life, I still cannot believe how all the pieces of the puzzle came together and are still coming together. I am particularly in awe of how my mother's pain set forth my purpose. If it wasn't for her and our close bond, I would not be on a mission to help others transform their pain. I know what it is like, I have felt it, transformed it, and do not want anyone to live in it, although I understand its function. I now have a respect for the purpose of emotions and a respect for people's journey.

I believe in 'giving great voice' to who you are in light of the messages given to you. Do not take these messages as a negative. Rather, look at what they are there to teach you. I could have totally gotten upset with my father, blaming him for not understanding me. Instead, listening to his concerns and keeping them in mind as obstacles to overcome on the path I had chosen, was the best guide.

My life has been such a journey of transformation. Everything that I experienced, my childhood's angst and terror, feelings of not belonging, my mother's pain, my father's push for excellence and strict attitude, were all gestures of love coming my way preparing me for my future. I have come to see that love is hidden behind everything that happens to you. I invite you to look at your life that way and see what you discover.

We are shaped by the feelings within us and by the feelings that surround us. The words of others, the emotions they emanate, the lessons they teach, all are gifts. Les Brown said in one of his quotes, "Don't let the negativity given to you by the world disempower you." I would like to expand it and say, "Give great voice to who you are IN LIGHT and not *in spite* of those around you." You are not fighting against them to achieve your purpose. You are bridging their concerns with your desires to live a protected, prosperous life.

Life is filled with messages, with love in our hearts, we can hear them in a way that lets us bloom. Listen for love, empower yourself, and unleash your potential!

Ignite Action Steps

Here are three questions to ask yourself to transform your muddy waters into a blossoming flower:

1. What do I love?

Love does not have one strict definition. But what and who we love says so much about ourselves and our purpose. What we love is what we need for our path. Tune in to what you love in everything that you do. Look at the foods you are craving for example. They are meant to give your body what it is missing to be supported. Asking yourself, "What do I love?" opens the doors to you and your life.

2. What is blocking the way to doing what I love?

We often have fears and lots of 'shoulds' that block us from believing that following what you love is the path to take. Identify the emotions and thoughts that block your way and look at them from a different perspective. What if they were showing you something for you to overcome to achieve more strength, happiness, and safety in the world?

3. What is it here to teach me?

What if your friend's hurtful comment was bringing light to your shaky self-esteem? What if you went on a journey of building a solid self-esteem and became thankful to your friend for that hurtful comment, as without it, you would not have realized what your next step is to be strengthened on your path? I encourage you to approach everything that happens to you as an attempt to prepare you for your future and to deepen your connection to your path.

Wishing you a wonderful journey! If you need any support, I invite you to reach out.

Dr. Yasmine Saad — United States
International Best-Selling Author, Top 3 Licensed Clinical Psychologist in
NYC, Founder and CEO of Madison Park Psychological Services
madisonparkpsych.com
f *yasmine.saad.397*
📷 *dr.yasminesaad*

Suzanne A. Nakano

"A genuinely radiant life cannot be bought. It must be cultivated."

You may be pursuing a path that is not in your best interest and not realize it because it's disguised as a pursuit that people might believe is worthy. Through "Living Life in Radiant Bloom," I hope you will align your life with what truly invigorates you and leave behind what hinders you from the greatest good. As you do these things in increasing measure, you will realize your fullest potential.

Living Life in Radiant Bloom

I do not hear Him audibly, but I feel Him move in my soul.

One such moment happened when I invited my friend, Noriko, and her mother, Michiko, to dinner at my Tokyo apartment. Michiko, a spry 60-year-old with a take-charge personality, raised champion orchids and traveled the world to study them.

After dinner, I asked the flower expert, "Do you know what's wrong with my cosmos plants?" The leaves had shed, and the remaining stems were black and dry. I was ready to toss them out.

"Bring me a rubbish bag," she ordered, while studying the branches. Then, with the twist of her wrists, she began to snap away most of them and threw them into the bag.

"Mom!" Noriko gasped, "Aren't you stripping away too much?"

"You have to remove what is dead to stimulate growth." She turned to me. "Keep watering the plants, and they'll bloom nicely."

"That's interesting," I thought. "Pruning is also a spiritual discipline."

Then I felt a stirring in my soul. "Ask her how much she prunes," God said to me.

So, I asked.

Without pausing to think, she replied, "Eighty to ninety percent."

"Eighty to ninety percent?! God, is this how much you must remove from me to stimulate growth?" At that moment, I realized my Divine Gardener had recently done such extensive pruning in my life. He showed me that my career had to be cut.

It was a job at an international conglomerate that I had worked hard to get. I knew people in the financial industry who would have given their eye teeth to have my career. They had also pursued my position, which they considered worthy, but they weren't hired. The company had rigorous employee screening and background checks, and they sifted the industry's top talents to assemble the best teams. The silver lining was that the people and projects were creative, pioneering, and of the highest caliber; and we were treated to the first class of everything.

I had thought I could be a faith-filled example to my colleagues. But the workload overtook all else. Sometimes I got home at sunrise to jump in the shower and return to the office for a 7 AM presentation, only to remain in the office to make the next project's deadlines. I was excited about being a part of a team that would explore various real estate-related investments in China and fixated on that part of the job. Pioneering investments in China was the carrot on a stick that kept me plowing through.

The Asia Pacific financial division, headquartered in Tokyo, was the conglomerate's main revenue driver, and our team produced phenomenal growth. But success had come at a high cost to all of us. Ignoring doctors' advice to get some rest, our director, Steve, spent a month in the hospital but continued to work from his bed. Another concerning incident occurred during one of our daily meetings when a younger coworker collapsed on the wood floor. She quickly got up, apologized, and went back to work. The intensity of our work environment impacted everyone's health. I wondered how much longer I could hold out.

Then I got my answer. While working late one night in my apartment, my heart suddenly started pounding and reverberating like a timpani. I pressed both hands to my chest, trying to will it to stop. But my heart continued its erratic thumping. "I'm going to die!" I thought. I grabbed my phone and called the front desk clerk, who called for an ambulance. As terrified as I was, the embarrassment and worry over inconveniencing others weighed heavier.

My building's staff and the emergency medics were in my apartment within minutes. The medics strapped me to a gurney and wheeled me out through the corridors. I was mortified to be bound into a ride I didn't want.

Lying motionless on the hospital bed in complete exhaustion, I could hear and see the ER doctor, but I couldn't answer him.

While losing the battle of my desire to respectfully answer the doctor to my lack of energy to move my mouth, I raised a white flag, "I give up." My self-talk continued, "Snap out of it! What are you doing living this insane life? No one cares if you die. Your life is meaningless." At that moment, I resigned myself to the fact I would have to leave my job or die an early death.

Then, I felt a stirring in my spirit. The hairs on my arms stood up. God spoke, "The only worthy aspiration is getting closer to Me, not getting closer to what the world might consider 'achievement.'" I felt lovingly embraced rather than reproved. Flat on my back with my focus locked on God, my soul relented into His arms.

"Okay, You got me. What do You want me to do?"

The answer came. "For starters, go and encourage people in China."

For years, I had dreamed of going to China to encourage the believers there. I had read and heard about their persecution and their fervent love for Christ through it all. The thought of supporting these Christians pierced my heart.

The fear from my uncontrolled heart-pounding gave way to a deep-seated commitment to use my every breath to love others the best way I could. This health scare ignited a hunger in me to leave the corporate mindset and give my all to serving others.

It took a month to settle my office affairs. On my last day of work, I was sitting at my desk, which faced away from the grand foyer with its 30-foot high ceiling and 2,000-square-foot wood floor, when I heard the loud thud of something heavy hitting the floor. The sound echoed throughout the expansive office. My 50-year-old coworker, Takino-san, who had no known health issues, had collapsed as he walked across the foyer.

As Steve rushed to Takino-san's side, he motioned for those of us at our desks to stay put. He called an ambulance and, with the help of the front desk workers, carried Takino-san to the employee rest area. One of my coworkers told me that Steve had attempted CPR on Takino-san, but to no avail. Takino-san died from a massive heart attack.

His death filled me with sadness. I remembered how his eyes lit up whenever he told me about his Hawaii travel adventures. Since he knew that I was from Hawaii, he would make graceful hula hand motions at me as he passed my glass-walled office.

A few hours after the ambulance came for Takino-san, I went to the employee rest area. His necktie and polished shoes were neatly placed alongside the wall. This sight hit me like a splash of ice water on my face. Those shoes along the wall could have been mine.

The sound of Takino-san's body hitting the floor would both haunt me and serve as an unforgettable reminder: my demanding work had distracted me from my greatest good and best path. I had made the right decision to leave, letting go of what had been disguised as a worthy pursuit.

God pruned the branches of my life that weren't bearing fruit for Him, like the process in the following scripture:

> I am the true vine, and my Father is the gardener. He cuts off every branch in me that bears no fruit, while every branch that does bear fruit he prunes so that it will be even more fruitful. — John 15:1-2 (NIV)

Michiko's instruction that day in my apartment had given me hope: "Keep watering the plants, and they'll bloom nicely." This was true of my cosmos plants and of the radiantly blooming life that I longed for. God responded to my desire: "Keep doing good, and you'll bloom nicely into your designed brilliance."

After having my Ignite Moment, I dove into my passion — investing love in others. As friends gathered at my apartment for my new weekly hula dancing lessons, the white, pink, magenta, and purple flowers were so dazzling that my friends marveled, saying they had never seen such strong, lush cosmos plants. As the women entered my apartment each week, they would head straight to the gorgeous flowers and "ooh" and "aah" at them.

Through Michiko's skilled hands, the struggling plants gained new life to bloom magnificently. Similarly, through the masterful work of my Divine Gardener, I was set free to experience a fresh vibrancy.

A genuinely radiant life cannot be bought. It must be cultivated.

After leaving the company, I booked a five-city China tour. A month before my departure, I emailed my itinerary to a Hawaiian friend with Christian contacts in China. She replied, "I will confirm your meetings and get back to you." I packed whatever I could find to encourage those I would meet. Then

I waited. And waited. And waited. But there was no response. A week before my departure, I emailed my friend again. But no answer came.

On the day of my departure for my first 'underground Christian' adventure, I stared at my email hoping for confirmation. Her response finally arrived the moment I had to leave for the airport: "They will call you at your hotel. Don't say Christian words on the phone because the government might be monitoring their calls." The government monitored some publicly open churches, but the believers I would meet with gathered in private, without the government's knowledge.

English-speaking Chinese Christians called me at each hotel. After one such contact, a tall, attractive woman in her 30s tapped softly at my Beijing hotel room door. She used the name Grace. She had traveled for hours to meet me. We talked at length about our backgrounds, and I learned that many of the Chinese Christians were highly educated teachers like Grace. Even though we had just met, our hearts immediately bonded as we shared the same concerns and desires. When I asked how I could pray for her, she said, "Please pray for my family and church, and their future." We prayed for those things together and agreed to continue to pray for each other. We embraced, then Grace left the same way she entered, quietly with an abiding love about her.

One of the Bibles that I had given to Grace had been a gift to me with my name engraved on it. I am looking forward to the day I learn how that Bible produced spiritual blooms in someone else's life. Perhaps a bouquet or field of blooming lives.

When I consider how much has flowered in me since Michiko's pruning and watering lesson, I feel like my lush cosmos plants. One of my blossoming areas is leading a women's group, The Aloha Angels. We visit those who need encouragement.

When one of our group members, Carol, suffered a heart attack, the Angels gathered in her hospital room. She was asleep, and her husband was at her bedside. We prayed and then sang our usual medley of songs. God filled the room with peace. While we were singing, a nurse came in, checked Carol's heartbeat, and announced, "She's gone." Carol had unfurled into endless radiance as we sang.

Carol's husband profusely thanked us, saying, "I'm so grateful that she was sung into Heaven." A week later, I received a card from him: "To the Angels, Thank you for singing Carol into Heaven. I can't think of a better way for her to have met Jesus. Don't stop doing what you do. Aloha, Harold."

My flowering joy has grown to encompass donating appreciated equities to various causes through a fund I established. This fund was designed to encourage greater and wiser giving.

God's pruning and watering in my life have produced other blooms as well. I enjoy providing annual financial awards and materials to public school students, housing and welfare assistance for those in need, and community safety support.

God has even brought the physical bloom full circle since I left the conglomerate. I am surrounded by the beauty, wonder, and fragrance of nature when I teach *ikebana* (the art of Japanese flower arranging) — one method of which is to incorporate the natural growth of plants from bud to bloom in the arrangement. This art form is a valuable reminder that God's cultivation produces radiant blossoms.

Just as suddenly as God had pruned a career from me, He also unexpectedly provided me with the opportunity to participate in this book as a miraculous bloom. I would never have imagined, in all the cosmos, that my story would be published to encourage others.

Another recent and unforeseen blessing was God planting songs in my heart. They bloomed out of nowhere! Songwriting has long been buried at the bottom of my desires because I do not know the mechanics of writing a song, which is why I am certain this miraculous flourishing was from God. I presented one of the songs I had sung into my iPhone™ to a music producer who created background music for it. I was in heaven at the recording studio! I was living one of my dreams: to share peace and joy through music. The producer explained how the song could be improved. My next step is to gain a greater understanding of music creation and revise my song. God gave me this peace-releasing bud to nurture.

God's pruning stimulated my growth in areas of true and greatest value — investing love in others. He took me from nearly dead, like the black cosmos branches, to a blooming season beyond my imagination.

To live a truly beautiful, abundant life, don't despise or reject the Divine Gardener's pruning process. Let Him work *in* you and *through* you to produce a life in radiant bloom.

Are you hungry for change? Then let the pruning begin!

Ignite Action Steps

- What areas of your life do you sense a need for 80-90 percent pruning to stimulate your growth? You may ask family, friends, or mentors to help you identify areas (e.g. environments, habits, and unhealthy relationships).

- List any obstacles that may be causing you to resist the pruning needed to generate positive changes. Ask yourself: "What must I do to break free from them? How can I overcome them? What is preventing me from acknowledging the hindrances and removing them so I can blossom into a radiant life instead of remaining in a withering one?"
- Living life in radiant bloom means accepting God's pruning and watering for your optimal growth and health, as well as encouraging others to bloom. What are your God-given gifts and talents — abilities you naturally do easily and enthusiastically do, and that people have complimented you on? Your talents can also be identified by asking yourself: "If I did not need money, what would I do?"
- How can you cultivate your talents to produce beauty in the lives of others?
- Communing with God can produce a radiance that sets you apart from others without spending money. If you wish to possess this radiance, then extricate yourself from environments and situations hindering your growth and embrace the habit of daily nurturing through scripture meditation.

Suzanne A. Nakano — United States
Encourager, Prayer Warrior, Investor, Realtor, Certified Commercial
Investment Member (CCIM), MBA, Japanese Flower Arranging Instructor,
and the woman from Hawai'i with a passion to release others'
"aloha" (love, joy, peace) blooms.
www.suzannenakano.com
🔹 *SuzanneNakano*

Stacie Shifflett

STACIE SHIFFLETT

"Sometimes the right thing to do is the hardest."

When faced with a crisis, we often lose sight of the wisdom of Hope. We hide her behind our fear, our anger, our grief, but she is there nonetheless, patiently waiting for us to remember her presence. My intention for you, dear reader, is to never lose sight of Hope in the face of a challenge. She is a fine traveling companion as we traverse the winding road to recover ourselves. I invite you to pick her up from the rubble that may be your life and gently place her back into your heart to Ignite the healing within. Listen to her gentle voice as she asks you to count your blessings and reminds you to gaze forward to the promise of a brighter future. Hope. She truly does spring eternal.

THE END OF ME

Anger. We've all experienced it in its varying forms and intensities. Sometimes it is a mild irritation that quickly fades without consequence. Sometimes it's an explosive force that shatters its vessel, splintering and propelling parts in many directions. This is where my story begins, when the implosion of my 28-year marriage fully ignited my rage.

In the beginning, I found some comfort in the proverb, "Hell hath no fury like a woman scorned." Oddly, it validated my emotions. It resonated with me. But I soon realized that I needed to choose a different guiding phrase to carry me through the coming months. Rage was not going to be productive, something I concluded quite quickly one evening after kicking in my kitchen cabinets during a complete meltdown. Unbridled rage, it seems, can be a destructive force.

That wasn't the first time I had experienced a pain so deep and sorrowful that I wondered if I would ever recover. Twenty-two years earlier, my first son died as an infant. I truly believe there is no pain greater than that of losing a child. It is the ultimate tragedy. So, when my decision to divorce clearly became the right (although most difficult) choice for me, I told myself that if I could survive the death of my first child, I could endure this. But how? I felt like Humpty-Dumpty, shattered with all of my little broken pieces strewn about. How would I ever collect them all and reassemble them back into a happy, fulfilled human?

I needed the opposite of destruction: creation. In the few months that followed, I redirected much of my anger into building a new foundation to regain some stability in my life. A home of my own, that's what I needed. That endeavor gave me a much-needed purpose and consumed my attention in a productive way. A home in town. Check. High speed internet. Check. A king-size bed. Check. A television in the bedroom. Check. No antique furniture! Check. The list went on.

However, don't think for a minute that my anger was only directed in a positive way. Oh no. Quite the contrary. Some fully bore the brunt of my rage. At times, yelling quite profanely was about all I could do. I wouldn't say it was misdirected or unwarranted per se, but it certainly wasn't healthy for anyone — including me.

Seven months after moving into a lovely neighborhood and leaving behind the farm that had been my home for two decades, the gears of change were again in motion. I moved my parents from out of state into a home around the corner due to my dad's declining health. Shortly after that, my son, who lived with me, departed for an out-of-state college leaving me cursing empty-nest syndrome for its poor timing. Then my father died. I lost my mother as I knew her when my dad died, as she never recovered from his death.

Of course, the stressors and heartache associated with divorce underscored all of these radical lifestyle changes. I knew my ex had a new family but the announcement of his plans to wed was devastating. I remember the day I received this news. It was Thanksgiving Day, the day I was released from the hospital for a serious infection from which I was still recovering. As I read the letter, which must have been sent while I was in the hospital, I literally collapsed to the floor, unable to bear the weight of that news, sobbing uncontrollably for what seemed like an eternity. I felt ripped apart, alone, abandoned, betrayed, unlovable, unappreciated, and discarded. I felt I had been gutted like some wild animal and left there to die without mercy. It was not a 'good' day for me.

To outsiders, I appeared to be doing well. Friends knew I was facing challenges and most admired me for my grit and perseverance as I weathered these trials that arrived one after another like angry waves hitting the shoreline in a storm. They saw me as strong, but I felt that every time I regained my balance, I was knocked down again by the uncertainties of life.

Through all of this, I created a network of friends and an active social life. Fun distractions became my forte and provided welcomed relief from my situation. Being busy allowed me to ignore, for a while anyway, the fact I was continuing to fall apart piece by piece on the inside. Alcohol was always on the guest list throughout my adventures. I often joked that I had worked hard to build up my tolerance to liquor and I certainly wasn't going to put all that effort to waste by slowing down! I embraced and enjoyed some really memorable experiences during this time filled with deep belly laughs and lots of love. I needed some happy. I cherish these experiences to this day, and they are deposited forever into my 'positive memory bank.'

Life proceeded that way for a couple of years. I was operating under the theory that the anger would eventually weaken, and the hurt would simply fade away naturally with the passage of time. Not so much. We cannot escape painful emotions festering on the inside without taking new deliberate actions. When left untended, like weeds, they eventually take over shrouding any beauty trying to peek out through the chaos.

Many nights I staggered into bed, curled into a fetal position, and released all of my agony into my pillow. I cried and screamed, hoping the neighbors wouldn't hear, clutching my belly from the pain in the pit of my stomach brought about by such deep turmoil. I would eventually drift off to sleep, finding my sweet escape alone in the safety and comfort of my dark room. Day would come and I would awaken, opening one eye to greet the sunlight — my head throbbing: my mouth dry. "What was that *smell*? Oh, great. I must've vomited during the night. There's a wine stain on the carpet from the glass I now see laying on the floor next to the bed. Guess I better get up, clean myself up, clean all of *that* up, and rally for a new day. Again. Nothing a bottle of water and two Tylenol™ won't fix."

I thought about suicide at times. I didn't really want to die; I just wanted the pain to stop. I tried to imagine a future without that pain, but I couldn't. How could I find the closure I sought when I knew in my heart that there was no closure that would comfort me? The word 'hopeless' came to mind often. But then Hope, that little voice in my head, would remind me that I wanted to be there for my family and that I would, indeed, find joy again. She breathed an internal knowing into my heart that there was a brighter future ahead of me. She reminded me that I had survived grief before and that I could do it again.

Part of me realized that I had to stop this cycle. The anguish that echoed in the emptiness within me was exhausting. The message that something had to change became louder and clearer as the days and months wore on until one day, I breathed out the words, "I am so done with this." I knew that I had to do something differently or this would be the end of me. I was not willing to be 'ended,' so I scheduled an appointment with a woman in town who had been recommended as she blended traditional coaching with energetic healing techniques. I'm a big believer in alternative approaches as they have worked for me in the past for maladies that traditional doctors or therapists were unable to cure with conventional methods.

The first time I met her she asked me, "What brings you here?"

"I'm tired of being angry," I said. "This anger has to go."

It was a lovely session, and when I say lovely, I mean that I could literally feel her love for me — a complete stranger. No judgment. Only heartfelt compassion that was palpable. I booked a series of sessions with her which helped immensely over the coming weeks. I marveled at her ability to 'see' me. I implemented energetic techniques and read books she suggested, and it helped. These sessions ignited my desire to fully reengage in personal development work, which I had done years earlier but discontinued while focused on my marriage, building a prosperous career, raising my family, tending to my beautiful show llamas, and all manner of the busyness we call life.

I began to read voraciously and watch documentaries, intentionally exposing myself to topics such as spirituality, neuroscience, quantum physics, and energetic healing modalities. I began to slowly narrow my social circle choosing instead to shelter alone in the safety of my home. I spent a year meditating daily, sometimes for hours at a time, seeking answers and connection in the quiet. I was in awe when I began to feel the energy moving through my body as I meditated — how information was provided to me clearly and concisely; how that information would lead me to the next step in my healing process if I simply listened and heeded the guidance. I didn't know where this journey would take me, but each time I listened to my intuition and took action, the next step magically appeared on the winding path guiding me toward some unknown outcome.

One evening, I watched the documentary, *I Am Not Your Guru,* with Tony Robbins and sat in amazement witnessing him guide people in crisis through transformation. I popped online and saw that another of his events, Unleash the Power Within, was scheduled for the following month in Florida, only a short flight away. Without hesitation, I registered and made my travel plans knowing that I would become a 'Platinum Partner' (whatever that was) when I arrived. As predicted, I signed up for the program and through that partnership spent two years traveling the world with Tony and other 'Plats.' That experience opened an entirely new world and depth of information to me and offered a community of people with similar mindsets. It provided a new way of thinking, a new way of doing deep personal work with the goal of understanding my emotions, my actions, human needs, human psychology, and so on. To this day, I call Tony my 'gateway drug' as those events set aflame my passion to learn all I could about the human condition.

I then heard the teaching of Les Brown. He shared such great messages that echoed the philosophies and ideas of many of the great thinkers past and present. Les says, "Dealing with life means taking advantage of each new challenge as an opportunity to learn and accomplish something new," and that's exactly what I did well beyond my time spent with Tony. I nurtured new friendships and created opportunities to work with amazing teachers, coaches, energetic healers, meditation masters, gifted mystics, sages, and scientists of all kinds. In the process of learning about myself, I obtained multiple certifications in coaching, Theta healing, neuro-linguistic programming, and other topics and modalities without knowing how I might put these new skills to use beyond my personal healing. I achieved some of my biggest breakthroughs during my Theta Healing™ classes under the guidance of my very gifted teacher. All this accumulation of knowledge and understanding of the human condition, my path to profound healing, was reshaping itself into a mission that started calling me, and I heeded the call in spite of not knowing how it would manifest or what contribution I could possibly make. What I *did* know was that it is possible to leverage crises as a catalyst for change. I had lived it and witnessed my struggles Ignite my soul toward deeper learning and understanding. Through the lens of Hope, we can see the gifts crises offer us and actually come to appreciate those struggles for the lessons therein and the virtues obtained through these experiences. They bring wisdom and amazing possibilities into our lives.

It takes courage to do 'the work,' but Hope is there to help us as we sort through the old pieces of us: toss those that no longer serve us away without regret or guilt (key point here), polish the ones that do serve us, grab new shinier ones aligned with our new selves, and assemble them into a whole joyful being living a purpose driven life. It seems unlikely during our gloomiest days that we can create something even better than before, but I can tell you that my life has been enriched and expanded in ways I never thought possible through this process.

My journey to get to this point has taken years, much like the Chinese bamboo tree Les speaks of in one of his motivational speeches. You see, when you plant a Chinese bamboo tree seed, it requires water, fertilizer, and faith daily to yield the desired outcome, which cannot be seen until *five years later* when the seedling finally breaks through the dirt. Then it grows at an astonishing rate! Why does it take so long to sprout? The outer shell of the seed is so hard that it is difficult to germinate. Progress takes time. Perhaps another lesson we can learn from this is to soften the hardness of our heart to facilitate our personal growth.

Now, I realize that my life is mine to enjoy. I see the world in a new way, an awakened way, and I feel called to help teach people that reaction is NOT action; instead, focus on regaining balance and peace of heart. My biggest lessons have been to apply contextual thinking versus reactive thinking and to raise awareness to view things more objectively. his has allowed me to, in turn, help others on multiple levels in their lives to find peace and harmony and to elevate their level of consciousness. I know supporting others this way will make a difference for as many people on the planet as possible, to think clearly for themselves and live a joyful and fulfilled life.

My message to you is simply don't stop; don't give up Hope. The way forward is to tend to your own fertile ground on the inside. Keep watering your dreams. Fertilize them by expanding your knowledge. Remain rooted in faith. Embrace the promise of Hope during the darker days to allow your possibilities to grow. Let the beauty of each moment shine brightly in the sun.

Postscript: It is also worth sharing with you how I came to be involved in this book. I was meditating with the intention of determining the next best step for me to move forward. I was offered one word, 'Write.' Not the first time I had been prompted to write, but it was the first time that I surrendered to it and acknowledged to the Universe that I would without question. Within a few short hours, I received a message from a dear friend letting me know that her friend, JB Owen, had a few openings left in this collaborative work. Needless to say, I stopped and took notice with wonder and amazement. An email introduction was made, and within 48 hours I was welcomed into the community of this project. To echo, the journey isn't a straight line, and you may not see results as quickly as you would like, but don't stop. There is no 'quick fix.' Do the work and grow tall like the bamboo tree as eventually it does all begin to fall into place like magic.

IGNITE ACTION STEPS

- Cry. Dance. Sing. Meditate. Pray. Laugh. Rest. A lot! Move the emotions through and out of your body so they don't become trapped within creating depression, anxiety, feelings of separation, and even disease. And release your worries in those moments to fully enjoy the present.
- Read. Listen to audiobooks. Enroll in a class, seminar, or workshop. Hire a coach. You have the power to change your beliefs, the way you think, and the trajectory of your life. As Les says, "If you don't program yourself, life will program you." So, take charge of your programming!
- Forgive yourself. Love yourself. Be patient *with* and kind *to* yourself. This is a journey of discovery. Celebrate your wins and epiphanies and give yourself the gifts of forgiveness, acceptance, and appreciation instead of guilt, criticism, and self-loathing.
- Adopt a meaningful mantra; a statement of guidance to keep you focused and reinforce your personal goals by incorporating them into your daily practice. One of my favorites is "The Four Agreements," from a book by Don Miguel Ruiz. Two of these, *not taking anything personally* and *not making assumptions*, were absolute game changers for me.
- Learn to pause. When confronted with an emotional trigger, take a moment to connect to your heart and react consciously with well-intentioned purpose rather than from a place of raw, unbridled emotion.
- Start a gratitude practice. Take time each day to express gratitude for your blessings. Don't feel blessed? Think again. Be grateful you have two legs to carry you as some do not. Be grateful you can pick up a book and read the words on its pages. Be grateful you have food to fill your belly and clean water to drink. Become consciously aware of the *good* things in your life and focus on those. As you begin to focus on the good things, you begin to see and experience more and more of them.

Stacie Shifflett — United States
Certified Thetahealer®
Master Practitioner of Neuro-Linguistic Programming
Professional Neuro-Shine Technology Coach™
Certified High-Performance Coach™
www.ModernConsciousness.com
Modern-Consciousness-101509125567383
moderncosciousness

JACKI SEMERAU TAIT

*"Circumstances that seem disastrous are often the very
thing needed to bring us to our higher purpose."*

There are going to be things that happen in your world that feel insurmountable. You may be at the end of your rope and have nowhere to go. But it is my hope you will see that those moments are your chance to get out of your own way. Stay in that moment, look up and see where the opportunities lie, using all the gifts and talents that God has put inside of you.

THE FOUR DOLLAR STORY

I was sitting at my desk in my home office and could feel the pit churning in my stomach. My third client that day had called to cancel their real estate search. Two of the transactions I had in process were canceling. The stock market had just plummeted less than a week earlier, and the fallout was now hitting my business. Staring at the screen on my laptop, hopelessness was starting to creep in.

The writing was on the wall. In a recession that was initiated by the real estate industry, it's natural that those making a living in real estate were hit first and hit the hardest. That was me. Things were shifting and I needed to adjust.

I was no stranger to my world shifting. When my marriage began to fall apart years earlier, I felt the ground falling out from under me. Looking at my daughters, ages 2 and 4, I knew that I had to reach deep down inside of myself and go to work. If 100 percent of my effort wasn't going to be enough to save the marriage, I needed to spend that energy on making sure my girls grew up healthy and whole instead.

To do that, I had to make myself whole first: something my daughter made clear without even realizing it. The girls were playing together while I was lying on the dining room floor just across the hall. I had eyes on them to make sure they were safe, but that was all I could muster. My depression was so deep I couldn't engage with them; their little world unfolding in front of me while I simply looked on. My intuitive oldest daughter could tell that Mommy wasn't alright and came over to console me with a cup of imaginary tea. She asked me if I was okay. I just laid there, not even able to answer her.

Tears began to fall sideways down my cheek. In my mind's eye, I can still see her looking at me with a desire to 'fix it' — which only broke my heart even more. After a moment she left me there and went back to playing with her sister. I wanted to join them, but the weight of my depression made standing feel impossible as tears kept spilling out. I was helpless in that moment. It was then I realized my depression was completely owning me.

Seeing the disappointment in my daughter's eyes gave me the strength to rise up to a sitting position. I saw how my absence was letting her down; how my inability to function was leaving her and her sister with only the shell of a mother. It was that moment when I knew I needed to make a change. To find help. To take control. A spark of determination happened deep down inside of me. I decided to pick myself up.

That's when my powerful journey into self-development began as I went to work on changing myself into the best person I could be.

Shy of my 30th birthday, I officially became a single mom. I knew that I didn't want to repeat the preexisting patterns that led me into a deep depression, failed marriage, and victim mentality. It took years of treatment, therapy, faith in God, and an amazing counselor to help me learn how to elevate my life experience. I stepped away from the victim mentality that had plagued me since I was a teenager. I saw that the things in my past that had held me down were actually blessings that created me into the woman I had become.

For four years, I labored on a journey that led me away from depression and into empowerment as I rode a wave of financial success. Then, right as I was finally feeling emotionally strong, my secure financial base was about to get wiped out from the recession.

I started looking for resources to help me get through the upcoming hard times. What I found was a shock to me: hundreds of websites targeting single moms, promising resources or grant money access — all SCAMS. It infuriated me to see other people manipulating single moms for their personal information and out of their hard-earned dollars.

I was angry! I was feeling so frustrated from searching that I had to walk away from my computer thinking someone needed to *do* something about it! Someone needed to create a website with trustworthy information for single moms that would *help* them! Someone needed to create a community where single moms could network and *share* resource recommendations that would give them the tools they needed!

As I stepped past the mirror, I caught the reflection of myself and that 'someone should' thinking forced me to stop and really look at myself. I realized at that moment that I *was* that 'someone.' A tingling rippled through my veins as a feeling of peace and purpose washed over me. I had no idea what it would look like or how I would make it happen, but an idea had been planted and I just knew I had to act on it. It was time to take all the things I had learned in my journey of self-development and begin to share them with others.

In addition to helping single moms connect with one another and find trusted resources, I wanted to help show them that they can rise above their circumstances. They can move out of life patterns that aren't serving them and into the greatness that God created within.

I knew it was possible. It was possible to be an overcomer, to step into the greatness that God had created in me, and to live a higher purpose in this one life I was granted. And if I could do this, I knew that EVERYONE had the ability to tap into that greatness and elevate their life experience. But empowering others meant stepping up and stepping out of my comfort zone.

That is how the idea for the *Strong Single Mom Network* was born.

Unfortunately, at the time, it remained just that; an idea. The very thin thread that was holding my financial world together broke in June 2008, and I was floundering. By September, I was facing the hardest financial choices I've ever made: pay my mortgage or put food on the table for my girls.

I did my best to keep up with whatever bills I could. I made a game of the fact that I was the 'coolest mom' because I was feeding us macaroni and cheese for dinner every night. I can still remember the feeling I had going to the grocery store and picking up a bulk package of macaroni and cheese, milk, and butter in order to provide our meals for the week. I remember standing at the checkout, swiping my debit card, praying I had enough to cover the grand total of less than 10 dollars. And I remember the embarrassment and sense of failure whenever the payment didn't go through.

I did all this while still showing up professionally as if all was in order, masking my stitched together clothes and worn-down shoes with a bubbly, energetic smile that hid my reality.

Foreclosure notices started to appear in my mailbox. There was no way around it, I was losing my house. I decided to short-sell the home rather than let the bank foreclose. I packed up my things, my kids, and my pride, and moved back in with my parents — not easy for a self-sufficient woman who had enjoyed a successful run in her career. I truly thought it would only be a few months while I got back up on my feet, but a few months turned into two and a half years.

Thankfully, amazing things happened during this time. Because I had temporary relief from a mortgage and all the other responsibilities of homeownership, there was space to reinvent myself professionally. I branched out and shopped my marketing and advertising skills to small businesses in different industries.

My amazing parents allowed me the space to hide myself in my room and begin building an online home-based business. They weren't entrepreneurs, nor did I come from a family of generational wealth. For my parents to allow us to come into their home and let me take a brief breather from contributing financially to the household was a blessing far above and beyond anything I could have expected.

From the corner of my bedroom, I went to work creating the Strong Single Mom Network.

It was *a lot* of work. There were no pre-made, all-in-one software solutions to create a website with a membership portal, a CRM, and robust features, such as housing videos and other media. In the past, all my marketing experience was in strategy, not necessarily implementation. It was an overwhelming task, but I met it with determination.

Every day I would go to work learning about what was possible. Then I would take that knowledge and research what was available. Each morning I would get the kids off to school. Then I'd come back to that room in my parents' house, sit at the small corner desk, open my laptop, and work on creating. In time, through much trial and error, I was able to piece together enough software to make my vision become a reality.

On Mother's Day 2009, a year after 'looking in the mirror,' the official Strong Single Mom Network membership website was launched.

The connections that the network created were above my wildest imagination. But in the meantime, I couldn't quite figure out how to monetize the business. Membership was free, as I was unsure how to put together a paid membership. I did have Supportive Business Partners: a level of sponsorship businesses could purchase in exchange for a marketing presence on the website.

Still, it remained a passion project at the time, as I was focused on regaining my finances and moving out of my parents' house. I continued to work with marketing clients and was wrapped up in trying to increase my income while hoping and praying all my hard work would pay off. And so it went for the next year; the push and pull of running a membership site that I loved while trying to make a living for my family. I was drowning in the instability of it all.

I woke up with a knot in my stomach one day a little over a year after launching. I'd been logging onto my bank accounts daily, only to see the balance dwindle. On that particular day, I learned I was overdrawn on one account; the other had a flat zero balance. Sitting on my bed, still in my pajamas, I opened my wallet and found four single dollar bills. I was scared.

As I flipped through those last four dollar bills, I realized that they represented the entirety of my net worth. I started thinking about my daughters who were to start attending a new school in just one week's time. Their previous school required uniforms. But this new school was one where they could wear their own clothes.

How was I going to afford to buy school clothes for my children?

My parents had already chipped in and bought the girls backpacks as well as all the items on their school's supply list. But I would need to figure out how to get the girls proper school clothes, or else send them off to a new school in their worn-out play clothes.

I allowed myself to have a proper breakdown. I had learned that in order to stay strong, sometimes I needed to give into the need to lose it all. I gave myself an ugly crying, yelling, snot-running '30-minute breakdown.' Then I got up and pulled myself together. On that day, I needed to be presentable in time to go to a business coffee meeting. I was meeting with a member of a networking group to which I belonged. He had a potential referral for me, and I was in need of clients. Showing up at the coffee shop, I went to the counter and ordered a cup of water. There was no way I was spending my last precious four dollars on an expensive cup of coffee.

During the course of the meeting, my friend could tell that I wasn't my usual happy, energetic, glass-half-full self. He asked me what was wrong, and I found myself unable to put on a happy face to lie and say, "Nothing."

Out spilled a short version of my story. I told him about the slow payments from some of my clients. I shared about my last four dollars. But I didn't share my stress about the lack of funds to buy the girls' school clothes; that felt too humiliating to admit.

It was then that my friend offered me a lifeline. He had just come from the bank and happened to have a large amount of cash on him. He reached into his wallet and handed me 300 dollars. I couldn't help but to tear up out of relief and gratitude. His generosity meant the world to me and that my kids would get school clothes after all.

Over the next year, I was able to connect with a couple of amazing opportunities, one of which was with a tech start-up. My income increased to the point that I was finally able to move out of my parents' house and into an apartment. That little apartment felt like a castle to me because I was back up on my feet. I was able to provide for my children again.

Over time, many things changed. Once again, I became a full-time real estate agent. I married a wonderful man. We moved to a new town with the girls and started all over. And I have been able to rise to the top of my industry in real estate, as well as create and lead a coaching program to help real estate agents succeed through the power of relationships, building a referral-based business they can rely on.

During all of that, the Strong Single Mom Network continued to grow until we had 10,000 members. It was running itself. That's one of the great things about an online business. Once the systems are established, it doesn't take much to maintain it. Until something goes wrong. And boy did it go wrong! Six years after launching, the hosting company that housed my membership site went out of business. There was no warning. Everything I had worked so diligently on was gone.

For years, I let it be. We still had our presence on Facebook™, which I half-heartedly maintained. I felt defeated. But everything inside of me couldn't let the Strong Single Mom Network go completely.

As I end this chapter, I'm excited to tell you about a whole new chapter for the Strong Single Mom Network. We have relaunched a whole new site, complete with a premium Empowerment Membership. Finally, my vision of helping single moms around the globe find ways to connect with the greatness God has created within has come to fruition!

I understand now why it took so many years. You see, when I first launched the network, I was still in the middle of my mess. I was trying to lead from a place that wasn't fully developed. God had work He still needed to do in my life to bring me to a place where I was finally ready, willing, and able to own the greatness within.

Now that I'm here, I can truly reach in to help others.

God didn't create us to be powerless observers of the things that were happening to us. He created us to be powerful overcomers: to learn to be better, to rise above, and serve with all the greatness and gifts He has blessed each individual with.

When you experience this reality, your life will forever change. You will have the ability to overcome your hardest realities and turn them into your biggest victories. And once you do, don't be surprised to find yourself in a position where the 'someone should' mindset comes to you.

When that happens, it's time to take a long, hard look at yourself. Chances are, you ARE that someone. It is possible that YOU are the one being called. This could be your opportunity to step into a higher purpose.

IGNITE ACTION STEPS

Look for the helpers. You aren't meant to go on your journey alone. Don't be afraid to accept help from others, and don't be timid about offering help when you find yourself in a place to do so. In the times of adversity, look up and remember that life will often conspire to get you out of your own way. As one path is shutting down, look for the one that is opening up. It may not be easy to step into a new path, but it will be worth it. Sometimes that shift will happen rapidly. Sometimes it will lead you on a journey that will last a lifetime.

Jacki Semerau Tait — United States
Founder, Strong Single Mom Network, Lead Real Estate Agent, Team Three
23, Realty ONE Group Mountain Desert, Success Coach, and Founder of
Real Estate by Relationship coaching program
www.StrongSingleMoms.com
www.StepsToStrength.com
StepsToStrength
jacki.semerau.tait

JAMEELA ALLEN

"By persevering through dark days and illusions of your weakness, you will achieve your dreams."

I am sharing my story so that you have an example of what life could be like if you just push through your fears and obstacles. I want to inspire anyone who has felt defeated while trying to accomplish their hopes, dreams, and goals. In order to achieve big goals, you need to persevere and persist. Anything worth having is going to take a lot of effort. Believe in yourself, and never give up no matter how hard it may seem. With a goal, hard work, and consistency, you can accomplish anything you dream of.

PERSEVERING TO MY OWN CADENCE

"Daddy, take me to the barber, please!" I begged in tears one snowy winter evening. At just 5 years old I had an ability to make decisions that most children wouldn't have the luxury to. I wanted my dad to take me to his barber to cut off all of my hair, because unlike my two sisters, I didn't like getting my long, thick hair pressed by my mom every week. The hot comb against my tender scalp left me jumping out of my seat every time she fired up the stove and got the comb ready. She stood over me and every few minutes she shouted, "Hold your damn ear down, Jameela, before you get burnt!"

On my first day back to school after I got my hair chopped, I entered the classroom with my new 'hairdo.' My teacher kneeled down to me at eye level and smiled. I heard a little preschooler say, "I like your hair, Jameela," as I took my seat on the circle time rug. I thought the same thing as I touched my ears to make sure I had on my earrings and girly bracelet that my mom gave me for my birthday. I felt liberated with my hair so short. I loved my new look, but most importantly, I loved that my dad allowed me to make choices as a preschooler.

I was allowed to drop out of pre-K because I no longer wanted to go to school. My parents allowed me to stay home while they dropped my other three siblings off to school. This was the beginning of me marching to my own cadence.

I eventually came to love going to school, receiving perfect attendance and citizenship awards. I was always involved in school extracurricular activities because my parents couldn't afford to pay for four children to attend ballet classes or swim lessons. As the leader of the safety patrols in the fourth grade, I was the person who was assigned to make sure everyone was on their duty post in the AM and PM. My whistle hung permanently around my neck because it was my job to call the cadence when practicing formation and marching in the annual safety patrol parades. I loved having a sense of responsibility and enjoyed having a position of leadership. My friends looked up to me; just like they do today as a business owner and coach.

During the mid '80s, the Washington, D.C. streets where my school was located was infested with prostitutes, drug dealers, and addicts on every other corner. Junior high school was a place of protection and security and it created structure for me as a teenager. At Shaw Junior High School, I joined the marching band, choir, and the drama team. For safety reasons, we were not allowed to go outside except for band practice. We marched up and down the streets four times a day, Monday through Friday before school, during our scheduled band class, recess times, and after school. We were protected by our leaders, our principal, and fellow band students. Our protectors would strategically surround the perimeter of our lineup to defend us from random gun violence and the distractions of the street hustlers that were posted on every corner.

We were invited to travel as guests to several different states to participate in huge parades because of our reputation as the best sounding band in D.C. I loved the structure and routine and I only wanted to be associated with the BEST. Hearing all of the spectators on the sideline scream and root for us made me feel proud, excited, and honored. It was a relief that people knew that our hard work paid off as we continued winning awards and getting invitations to show off our sound and straight lines. We strutted down the long streets blowing into our instruments for the world to see, knowing that our family and friends were watching us on their televisions screaming our names. We worked hard, we showed up, we corrected our mistakes, and we had a vision to WIN. I learned firsthand the power of discipline and consistency which made us damn near perfect because we showed up every day to fine-tune our performance.

At 14, I got my first job working at McDonald's™. The expectation was that I contribute to the household bills, so I chose to pay my mom 200 dollars a month toward rent and be responsible for my own phone bill. My mom's expectations of me were to be independent and financially responsible. That small gesture of me helping out afforded me many opportunities because now as an adult, I am a responsible steward over my businesses; something I credit to my mom.

In addition to McDonald's, I worked for NASA part-time in 12th grade. I was making $3.25 per hour and suddenly realized the power of money. I was amazed to see my bank account jump from $50 to $500 because of my work ethic as a teenager. I would write out goals for my money as I deposited my paychecks. I remember the first item I chose to buy was a fax machine. I can't remember why, but I did it and I was proud!

After working in an office setting at NASA, I knew I wanted a job that would allow me to be free and move around in the workplace, so waiting tables was what I gravitated to. My first interview at Houston's™ restaurant, I was told "No," because I had no table waiting experience. I chose not to accept that, got extra training and practice in waiting tables, and eventually got that job. It taught me a lot about providing service to the customer. I learned quickly that the better the service the higher the tips, as I saw my tips jump from the basic 15 percent gratuity to 30 percent from some of my returning customers who would wait well over one hour to sit in my section. Waiting tables is how I purchased my first home at the age of 26. I saw the power of taking care of people — it's reciprocity at its fullest.

I learned a few things about business while working at Houston's. They vetted their new team members: only hiring experienced, friendly, competent people with bubbly personalities who would literally work as a team from day one. At Houston's we worked so much as a team that frequently customers would jokingly ask who the server was because we all helped out at each other's tables as if they were our own. Most nights I was selected to be the person who checked out the servers before they left to go home, the 'Sheriff' they called me, just like little Jameela who captained the safety patrols.

As good as I was at my job in the restaurant business, it wasn't where my passions truly laid. My mother would often say, "You didn't go to college to wait tables!" Even if I was making good money, I knew she was right. I went to college at West Virginia State University (WVSU) to pursue teaching, knowing since I was 17 that I wanted to own my own childcare center. My freshman year of college, I was working in the campus Child Development Center and saw how my director operated her center. I was extremely impressed with how clean and structured the center was. The entire experience for families and young children was exceptional from the time they walked through the front door. This was totally different from the small unkempt Child Development Center in my neighborhood that I was used to. I remember how important I felt when the President of the university picked up his child from my class. He would tell me how much his daughter liked me and how she would pray for me during her bedtime prayers. That was the beginning of my journey of falling in love with working with children. I enjoyed it when I walked into the classroom and the children ran up to me and grabbed my legs; I loved reading to the children as they snuggled on their cots during nap time. I appreciated listening to the parents rave about how happy their children were in my care. I learned firsthand how to provide value to parents as I highlighted their child's day just by having a quick chat during pickup. I never imagined the experience I gained from working at that center would stick with me some 18 years later as I opened my own business. Today at my childcare center I implement some of the very same policies and procedures that my director, Mrs. Davis, enforced at WVSU.

In my senior year in college, I received a letter from the education department outlining what I needed to do to prepare for student teaching. I was approaching my last semester and I was extremely excited to be graduating. The letter stated that to graduate I had to pass the *Praxis 1* test that consisted of reading, writing, and math. I took the test without preparing because I felt confident I would get the results I needed. As I set out my schedule to prepare for student teaching, all I could do is visualize what my life would be like after graduation as I transitioned into becoming a schoolteacher. I wanted to buy a new car because I was tired of driving the '85 Chevy Cavalier™ that got me back and forth to school from D.C. for five years. I was ready for a more modern car that I thought would match my new teaching salary.

Then my test results came, and my heart dropped. I was 20 points away from passing the math test. The next time I took the test, I was seven points away from passing, the third time, 10 points away. I started to get frustrated because the reality of me not passing the test in a timely manner to receive my student teaching assignment was making me anxious. Before I knew it, my time at WVSU was up. I was humiliated because I had to return to D.C. without a student teaching assignment or graduating.

Once I arrived home, I decided to get serious. I ordered study guide materials,

I contacted my high school math teacher to tutor me, and I never stopped retesting, even though it cost over $100 each time. I remember meeting my math teacher during his lunch break and after school for tutoring. I would stand at the chalkboard day after day practicing geometry, statistics, and probability problems. I was determined to pass that test. No one told me to keep at it. I was hungry to get my degree and start my career, so I just wouldn't stop; especially because I was so close to passing. My perseverance was relentless, and I took the test over 17 times before the magic happened.

My life changed at last one fall evening. I decided to go back outside to check the mailbox after I had already settled in from my job of waiting tables. Something told me, "Go check the mailbox, Jameela." I put on my jacket and shoes and headed to the entrance of my complex where the mailboxes are lined up. As I peeked in the small box, I saw the ETS (Educational Testing Service) envelope once again, buried under my monthly bills and junk mail. I decided not to wait until I got back to my house, opening the envelope while standing at the mailbox. I felt the brisk fall air hit my fingers which caused me to shake a little while I ripped open the letter. My heart was beating fast as usual — I had done this over a dozen and a half times before and still my heart always skipped a beat. Except, this time it was different. This time I would walk away with lessons learned. This time, I would have tears of joy versus tears of sorrow or defeat. I saw something at the top of the formal letter that I had only hoped for time after time, retake after retake: a red stamp across the top of the page with six large letters that said "PASSED!"

I never knew the meaning of perseverance and the doors that it would open up for me until I saw those letters. Nor did I know what that experience of never giving up would prepare me for when I decided to quit my good government job to start my own childcare business.

The next big obstacle I had to overcome blindsided me just months after I had signed a 15-year lease to operate my childcare center to service over 130 families. I was devastated when I received the phone call from an employee that a sheriff had posted an eviction sticker from the courts to vacate the premises. I took five deep breaths because I felt my chest tighten up as I listened attentively to what my employee was saying to me while I was out shopping for my childcare business. The building was in foreclosure because of overdue mortgage payments and a lien was put on the property. The landlord owed a million dollars in taxes. I was heartbroken, already overwhelmed with being a new business owner, feeling attacked, and now taken advantage of.

The thought of vacating the premises wasn't an option in my mind. I knew I had to prepare to fight and persevere once again. I had faith as small as a mustard seed and I continued to breathe through the moments that felt uncomfortable. I got laser-focused on my ultimate goal of owning the building; trying not to look in the rearview mirror. I went to work! I had to kick down doors when bank after bank denied me a mortgage loan to purchase the property. Each letter I received said the same thing: I had been denied because I didn't have enough business credit and operational experience. This was the year of the housing crisis and banks were not giving out loans even to business owners who had been at it for years. Yet, because of my persistence and determination, my excellent credit history, and the fact I was the current tenant of the property, I ultimately found myself at the settlement table with my attorney, signing my name to become the OWNER of that same commercial property with the eviction sticker that was once on the door. It all happened because I was determined to fight for my destiny!

I continued to persevere when COVID-19 hit and I had to close my business for several months not knowing if I would ever be able to get back to pre-COVID-19 enrollment and staffing. I could have closed my doors just like thousands of other small businesses. I knew in my heart that I needed to keep at it regardless of the circumstances, regardless of the lack of income, regardless of the smaller classroom sizes that were mandated by the governor. I continued to ignore the *illusions* of permanent failure and got better and wiser as a business owner.

Over the last 15 years of writing my own paycheck, I could have given up so many times because I kept getting knocked down in the ring: stumbling blocks in my business, a failed marriage to the man of my dreams, and my daddy being diagnosed with bladder cancer. Each time I had to get back up despite the bumps and bruises. I heard in my mind, my mentor Les Brown say, "When you think you are down for the count, Jameela, try to land on your back, because if you can look up, then you can get up."

I was determined to stick to my vision and goals during those dark days. I have learned that perseverance is an essential quality for success in life. There will be a lot of discomfort, but we have to push through when confronted with complications. I am a successful childcare business owner today because I decided to not let the illusions of failure hinder me. I turned my dream into a seven-figure, award winning childcare empire. I am extremely honored to be able to provide employment for my team, who allow me to work on my business verses in my business; a business that received the Prince George's Chamber of Commerce: Small Business of the Year Award because of our outstanding contributions to the community.

There were many times I felt defeated and at my wit's end. I always went back to my belief that perseverance creates magic. I pushed through many obstacles to achieve my success. I took notice and modeled what I experienced during my earlier years: from safety patrols to marching band, from Houston's to that Praxis exam. I utilize those lessons learned through my journey to help others persevere through dark days that are only illusions of weakness. Keep at it, keep trying, no matter how many times you have to fail or no matter what fears try to paralyze you. Never stop; never give up on your goals and passions; you will make what appears impossible... possible. *By persevering through dark days and illusions of your weakness, you will achieve your dreams.*

Ignite Action Steps

Have the mindset that you can accomplish whatever you want, regardless of the obstacles you have gone through. Here are eight ways you can accomplish your goals:

1. Never give up on your goals; when you feel defeated, ask for help.
2. Let past successes give you hope when confronted with obstacles.
3. Always be a good steward over your finances because you never know when your credit score could be the deciding factor for something big. Credit is POWER — it's a snapshot of how responsible you are.
4. Know that if someone else is doing what you are dreaming of, you can do it too.
5. Never ever allow 'No' to stop you. You must get many 'Noes' before you get a 'Yes.'
6. When life knocks you down and you feel defeated, ignore the negative voices in your head that will tell you that your goals and dreams are impossible. Perseverance, hard work, and consistency will always trump those illusions.
7. Understand that the choices you make will shape what type of lifestyle you have.
8. When obstacles blindside you, take five deep breaths to process what is happening.

Jameela Allen — United States
Speaker, Author, Childcare Business Coach,
CEO Themba Creative Learning Center LLC
www.jameelaallen.com
Jameela Allen   Jameela_Allen

DR. TYRA GOOD

*"Connect to your #GOODWithin and allow your
glow to light someone else's journey."*

**I hope this story allows you to see the #GOODWithin yourself and others as
we all strive to thrive. I wrote it to help shift our perspectives from seeing
people as who we assume they are, to seeing them for who they really are.
I want to reignite the human gaze to the possibilities and power that are
birthed from a nurturing environment that is rooted in strength, resilience,
and joy. I want to instill a hunger within you to cultivate a life filled with
your own God-given #GOODWithin.**

To the youth: **You are strong and powerful, and greatness is within you.**

To the adults: **You are portals of hope and paths to possibilities for this
generation.**

I AM THAT #GOOD

Sounds of joy, cheers, and applause filled the air as a sea of blue caps and
gowns could be seen reflected across the Mecca Yard. It was graduation day at
Howard University. This renowned institution of higher learning in Washington,
D.C. is considered the Mecca of Historically Black Colleges and Universities
(HBCUs) for its prominence and its proven history of cultivating the genius-
ness of great Black minds. The parallels to whom some consider the holiest

city honors the sacredness of this belief. It is a place of unity that centers on oneness, identity, and self-discovery rooted in Black culture throughout the African diaspora.

On that hot spring day, my fellow classmates and I channelled the artist formerly known as Prince and partied like it was 1999. In the midst of the celebration, a water fountain of tears began to stream down my face. They started out as a trickle of rain sprinkles before quickly progressing to an uncontrollable downpour that was enough to fill the three rivers that beautifully confluence in the 'Steel City' of Pittsburgh, Pennsylvania.

Four years earlier, (I still remember it vividly), "Tyra, the mail is here!" my mom yelled from the other room as I sat at the kitchen table completing my homework assignments. My hands instantly became sweaty as my body temperature rose and my mind filled with racing thoughts of what-ifs. Tap, tap, tap, tap. My fingers pulsated on the kitchen table as I nervously agonized over tearing the perforated edges off the envelope to reveal the contents inside. The future was in my hands, literally in the envelope that I was holding. You see, I have always been a diligent student, immersed in my schooling, not initially because I loved it, but because I was always told it was a meal ticket to success. To freedom. To happiness. To peace. To riches. To the #GOODLife. That envelope was tied to having all those things.

The promise of a quality education is sold as a 'golden ticket' opportunity to a better life, especially to youth like me growing up in communities plagued with violence, broken school systems, and lack of access to high-paying jobs. Being raised in that environment had its challenges. In fact, not all, but many of the schoolteachers didn't believe that students from my community could be successful. Constant messages from general society conveyed most people didn't have high hopes for those born into these situations. I was determined to not let that be me, so I became obsessed with academics and learning new things. I participated in extracurricular school activities, joined several school clubs to develop my leadership skills, and did community service work. I was determined to create an impressive package for my college applications.

"Well, are you going to open the letter, Tyra?" exclaimed my mom. I can still recall the zipping noise as I ripped the perforated edges with my heart beating rapidly. My mother looked on as I read the results from my Scholastic Aptitude Test. My head slumped and my shoulders tensed as I let out a big sigh. My mom could tell by my posture and the look in my eyes that the results were not good. She quickly went into comforting mom mode, consoling and reassuring me that everything was going to be alright. Thoughts of inadequacy and 'you're not good enough' trampled through my head. This was the third time that I took the test in an attempt to get a higher score so I could receive scholarships for colleges. I felt discouraged and defeated.

During my schooling experience, I often felt disconnected from the curriculum materials and struggled to find myself within the stories of heroism from cultures that did not resemble my own. In fact, the word on the street was that 'No good things come out of this high school.' You would either end up across the street in the cemetery at a young age or down the street in the penitentiary.

My well-rounded academic record had me accepted into most of the schools that I applied for, including Howard University. To secure my attendance, I had to attend a three-week summer enrichment program and take a remedial reading and writing course my first semester. I was dedicated to my dream of attending an HBCU institution, and knowing I would have a support network close by, Howard University became the perfect choice.

My first day at Howard, U-Hauls™ and caravans filled the streets and loading docks as parents gave their children goodbyes, hugs, prayers, and well wishes then released them further into adulthood. Moving in that day felt both scary and liberating. It was the beginning of my journey in discovering the #GOODLife.

"Ready or not, here I come, you can't hide… Lest I must confess, my destiny's manifest." Lauryn Hill's voice rang loud from the dorm room windows, while the sounds of the rap group Luniz, "I Got 5 On It" permeated from another window. I was struck and smiling as I realized no one was criticizing the music, telling us to turn it off, or questioning the not-so-perfect English in the lyrics. It felt like a place meant for people like me; the place for us all to shine. The excitement and energy were high as hundreds of nervous and curious freshmen embarked on a new journey of educational freedom and self-liberation together.

My freshman dorm, Bethune Hall, was named after the great educational pioneer, Mary McLeod Bethune. She devoted her life to ensure the right to education and freedom from discrimination for African Americans and opened one of the first schools for African American girls. Laughter, joy, and smiles encompassed the student lounge room as awkward introductions were made while we united and shared stories of our families, high school experiences, and repping what city or state we were from.

In the midst of the soulful conversations, the voices began to fade into a faint whisper and my gaze became fixated on this huge mural drawn on the wall. It was a photo of an African American woman, a line dividing the two halves of her brain. From one side billowed images of money, the scales of justice, and other career-centered ideas. From the other side floated images of a mother holding her child in a loving embrace. This woman was contemplating whether to pursue her career goals to climb the ladder of success or to have a family, raise her children, and be a homemaker.

The picture intrigued me because of the dueling decision that women so often seem divided between. I wondered what I would do if I had to choose between those two contrasting roles, and I decided at that moment that I *wanted* and *would* have both: a prominent career and a loving family combined. Living in a dorm named after a trailblazing woman who was a wife, mother, entrepreneur, humanitarian, and a civil rights activist ignited a hunger in me.

From the moment I stepped foot on Howard University's campus, I was embraced with love, empowered, and wrapped in peace. The culturally affirming sounds — from the music to the marching bands, movements from the campus block parties to the university dance team, and images from the murals to the prominent statue monuments — cultivated a sense of true belonging before a textbook was even opened. A connection to my true generational roots was being rebirthed as I discovered my identity in the legacy of my great Black ancestors. An identity rooted in strength, power, and overcoming harsh life struggles.

At Howard I was groomed for greatness within a community tied to a legacy of resilience and fortitude. We were immersed in the teachings and readings of W.E.B. Du Bois, Carter G. Woodson, Thurgood Marshall, Sonia Sanchez, Toni Morrison, Bell Hooks, and Ella Baker, just to name a few. We participated in the Million Man March and other social justice causes that spoke to the power and strength of Black people. We sat at the feet of and engaged in critical conversations with authors, poets, activists, entertainers, industry-specific professionals, and business owners across all sectors. Not to mention the infamous Howard University homecomings that were headlined with the hottest music artists, culturally affirming events, and graced by a legendary lineup of Who's Who in the political and social arenas. Thousands of people planned their October getaways to commence in Washington, D.C. to join in on our 'Coachella-like' experience at the Mecca. Tunes of jazz, hip-hop, R&B, and reggae vibrated through our souls.

The transformative experience proved to be a cognitive reframing and reclaiming of who I was. I connected to the affirming cultural narratives and discovered my #GOODWithin. I was being cultivated in this journey of discovery and validation. The weight of my past doubts about my abilities were melting away like chocolate in a fondue pot while ironically unpacking the meaning behind Washington, D.C. being known as the 'Chocolate City.'

I imagined that I felt as the prodigal son must have felt in the Bible when he was welcomed back home by his father waiting for him with open arms. There was no more straying away from the mirror of imperfections and inadequacies told to me by society, images, or books. I felt I could see and embrace all of myself, feeling more beautiful than ever before in a sea of people who are as beautiful in the same way. If I was hiding in high school, desperate to keep the truth of my academic doubts from ever seeing light, Howard was where I shone the brightest light upon myself, every aspect of my being. My mind, my motivation, my melanated skin.

I felt seen, valued, loved, and validated in my own skin. Lifelong friend-ships were planted that have blossomed into cherished family memories. Those experiences ignited in me a deep hunger to thrive, and to make the same kind of success possible for others.

My experience at Howard University broke off the shackles that I didn't even know were there. It freed me from the poison of seeds planted by low expectations from society and the school system; seeds nourished by my low self-esteem and internalization of negative beliefs. My HBCU experience uprooted the weeds, cut away the thorns, and watered a new beginning that quenched my thirst for pursuing my purpose.

As I stood to receive my undergraduate degree with magna cum laude honors, my mind traveled back to the last four years of overcoming doubt, fear, challenges, and the loss of my father; times when I thought reaching this accolade was all but a dream deferred. At that moment, I screamed, "Momma, I made it!" as my voice joined in celebration with my friends' shouts of joy. I was sure they were reflecting on their own perseverance, pulling from their #GOODWithin. It was precious confirmation that I had stepped into the true understanding of me, and I was unapologetically proud of everything about me.

Abolitionist and political activist, Harriet Tubman, forged new paths to freedom for herself and others. I too, have a drive to allow others to liberate themselves from negative stereotypes and limiting opinions about who can be successful, especially the views of youth from marginalized communities like mine. As an educational revolutionist, I create radical spaces of hopefulness that center on culturally affirming life experiences and academics that foster true self-actualization. I want others to experience the validation and freedom that comes from discovering their 'self' within liberating learning environments.

Les Brown says, "Wanting something is not enough. You must HUNGER for it. Your motivation must be absolutely compelling in order to overcome the obstacles that will invariably come your way."

As I have blossomed into my own revolutionary activism through teaching at the collegiate level and bridging the gap between my community and academic career, I now mentor youth and other adults to help them see their opportunities for reclaiming how they will be defined. In doing so, I have reclaimed the definition of 'hood,' which is a slang term for the word neighborhood that is often referenced in a negative cogitation to describe the ills of the inner city. My definition of H.O.O.D. is **H**ealing **O**ur **O**ffspring **D**aily. I believe that we have all had life experiences that have caused us to pull from our #GOODWithin so we rise above and grow through our adversities. This takes an intentional focus and a collective village of supporters to help us heal along our journey, as we seek to impact generations. As a transformative educator, I cultivate these healing learning environments.

Teaching is my form of activism. I teach through a social justice lens that addresses issues of educational inequalities to help current and aspiring educators unpack their stereotypes and biases and the racialized history of the opportunity gap that is often experienced by students from historically marginalized communities. Through my work as a practitioner-scholar, I introduce ways to learn about people impacted by poverty and race so creative solutions can be implemented to eradicate these inequities. My students explore the concept of equity as an approach to redesign teacher preparation so they can be transformative leaders in schools and communities around the world. Reimagining and redesigning educational spaces rooted in love allows me to genuinely work every day within my passion and fully connect my deep commitment in educating culturally and linguistically diverse students and their families. This has all become *my* #GOODWithin.

Famed African American poet and social activist, Langston Hughes, who is a graduate of the HBCU Lincoln University, wrote the acclaimed poem, "Harlem." The poem metaphorically questions the impact of societal pressures and oppression and what can happen when someone's dream is deferred. My experiences at Howard University ignited the possibilities for me to become an educational pioneer, just like Mary McLeod Bethune. I invite you to also positively impact someone else's journey by igniting the #GOODWithin them through the work that you do so they will not have to experience a dream deferred. The reality is, no matter who you are, when you choose to be that #GOOD, you are destined to be undeniable. And, as Les Brown says, "Be so good at you, you can not be ignored."

IGNITE ACTION STEPS

As you embrace your #GOODWithin to Ignite your transformation in cultivating liberatory and radical spaces of healing and hopefulness, I provide a few action steps so we can do H.O.O.D. work together within our spheres of influence to impact generations to live their #GOODLife.

1. **Healing:** Alignment of our mind, soul, and body creates energy that fuels and ignites us toward our greatest possibilities. By allowing ourselves to connect to the #GOODWithin, we provide space for inner and outer healing. Allow this power to strengthen us, so we give to others from our overflow.

2. **Our:** Ubuntu is an African word that means 'humanity to others' and serves to remind us that, 'I am what I am because of who we all are.' We can practice 'being self through others' by making sure our interactions with ourselves and others are uplifting, validating, and affirming to our cultural and communal roots.

3. **Offspring:** As we are all stewards of this earth, it is our collective responsibility to nurture and embrace one another, especially our future generations. We can engage with others through group or peer mentoring about a specific topic to ensure we are sharing our life's journey and lessons learned.

4. **Daily:** Life throws challenges at us every day, so we must be beacons of light to ourselves daily to stay encouraged and uplifted as we seek to inspire and Ignite the hunger in others. We can do this by greeting and smiling at someone through our daily interactions, by calling or texting someone on the phone that you have not talked to in a while, or by praying for them.

Dr. Tyra Good — United States
Speaker, Author, Education Consultant, CEO of GOOD Knowledge
Connections, Associate Professor of Education, Executive Director
of the Center for Equity in Urban Education at Elms College
www.drtyragood.com
🅕 *drtyragood*
🅞 🅧 ✍ *tyrathegooddr*

Nik Reyno

"Don't let your limiting beliefs keep you from being an answered prayer!"

My wish for you is to see possibility, hope, and beauty even in what seems to be the darkest and most painful of places. Reflect and recognize that in and after sickness comes awareness, appreciation, and intentionality. After loss comes gratitude, perspective, and the drive to do something meaningful. From disappointment comes reflection, inspiration, and openness to the unfamiliar. My prayer is that you find peace in knowing when this broken world does what it does, God has already done his part in equipping you to be victorious against all odds, to inspire others in such times.

Before I Knew It

"Don't shop at Walmart, come shop from my Papa!"

I was a joyful marketer from the time I was a little girl, excitedly running through homes my grandpa was showing to potential buyers and enthusiastically helping him sell toilet paper from our garage for his home-based business. I was raised by go-getters, compassionate servant-leaders, and resilient entrepreneurs. My family made sales and service a part of life to cultivate genuine relationships, making it fun to dream big, set goals, and game plan to achieve them. I grew up listening to motivational radio stations and educational TV shows which turned into CDs, videos, and audiobooks. Les Brown, Zig Ziglar, and Jim Rohn were familiar voices early on. When my siblings and I caused trouble, we were disciplined by having to read pages in a dictionary. We were enrolled in martial arts to further drill in that high caliber of discipline, respect, and excellence among a variety of extracurriculars. We also enjoyed spontaneous family trips, thinking that was the norm.

It wasn't until I got older that I recognized the work it took to enable our family's abundant lifestyle and flexibility. As Les Brown would say, "Do what is easy and your life will be hard. Do what is hard and your life will become easy." Though we often went on vacations, it was evident how hard my family was working to make that all happen. I was a preteen when my mom taught me to help do the books for our family businesses. By then, my siblings and I weren't just playing in our parents' warehouses anymore, we were helping out; and, boy, was there a ton of work to go around.

Along with the skills my parents encouraged, I had a childhood obsession with drawing and writing that I carried into middle school. I was ecstatic when my parents supported it, enrolling me in classes to further develop my talent. I looked forward to those heart-to-heart conversations with my dad about my growing passions. He was excited to hear that on top of becoming a pediatrician, I wanted to be an artist and author before I turned 30. During the long drives home from high school, my dad asked me and my brother to think about where we wanted to see ourselves in five years. I remember him sitting us down in his office, encouraging us to type out our goals to achieve our five-year plans. I struggled a bit trying to figure out what I *really* wanted to do, worrying about making my parents proud, because it was in high school that I established a deep love for empowerment, leadership, and public speaking also.

I went into college defaulting to the medical route since pediatrics was my spoken goal since I was a kid. It seemed the 'easier option' versus navigating all my other passions and interests. Yet, I felt frustratingly indecisive as college life opened my eyes to endless possibilities and homelife was starting to do the same. While home between classes, I was invited to sit in on a meeting my parents had organized with their business colleagues. Before I knew it, my parents were signing me up for my first official network marketing business. This was the first of many where I was encouraged to connect with professionals, learn from speakers, and gather the business tools of direct sales that I could apply to our private family businesses.

I dove headfirst into public speaking, inviting peers and mentors to empty classrooms to hear me share all the things I had learned. I loved being able to see people's faces and physical reactions to the information I eagerly doled out. Being acknowledged for my ability to speak and explain things clearly had me feeling euphoric, and for the first time, I was seeing tangible possibilities and envisioning a whole different future for myself. I really didn't know what to do for sure, but I wanted the freedom to figure it out.

It took a while for me to find myself after I moved away from home. It felt weird to be completely free to do whatever I wanted to do. First, I chose to study art, and goodness, did that create tension! Then, feeling guilty for wasting my parents' efforts and support, I considered pursuing a career in physical therapy to stay within the medical field. That would have been great, had I not struggled so extensively with all the advanced science and math classes. Law? Nope. Confrontation and legal jargon are just not my cup of tea. Trying to appease my family's stress over my lack of direction, I made my way back to working in the family businesses.

In my third year of college, while I was home visiting one weekend, a salesman showed up. My mom encouraged me to sit down to listen to what the man came to offer. In a nice, tan, professional looking suit, he pulled several brochures from his briefcase: life insurance, investment options, and retirement solutions. I felt very sophisticated being able to follow along, so at home and inspired. Before I knew it, I was enrolling into my second independent business.

For several reasons, that run didn't last long, but soon, I was enrolled into another, then another, and another. I got in touch with all the things I did, and didn't, want to align with as I reflected on all the lessons and tools I gained from each opportunity. I disliked seeing profits prioritized over people; I loved the flexibility of being able to work from anywhere. I wholeheartedly support helping people surpass their goals by genuinely sharing great products and services backed by a trustworthy compensation plan. Grateful for the life I had been privileged to live, through my parents' hard work and dedication to their businesse, I pursued my passions excitedly, running my own race.

Before my senior year in college, my finish line shifted when I became a mom. Captivated by my tiny human's face and brilliance, I knew I had to figure out a way to give him the world. As I sought extra income, my brother tried to recruit me into another direct selling company, but I refused to see, try, nor consider anything for months because I didn't trust his judgment. Yet, nine months later as I was struggling with my postpartum body, everyone in the family kept insisting I see my brother's product presentation on health and wellness supplements. My ego and protective instincts kicked in. I sat in on the presentation with the intention of finding all that was 'wrong' in the products and company to convince my family to stop and let me be.

In that presentation, I was shown a discovery channel documentary and the heart and vision of the company owner. The information blew me away! Before I knew it, my husband was eagerly signing us up to get involved in the business. I panicked, considering all I've come to know about direct sales and this being my husband's first experience. I wanted to make sure it'd be a positive one. It only took a few short weeks before I had my own incredible product testimonies of an insane increase in breastmilk supply and rapid weight loss. So, I quickly built our customer base, rose ranks in the company, and felt like I had found a long-term vehicle to build for life.

For the last eight years, that company was a big part of my and my family's life. We traveled thousands of miles, attended countless events, and connected with incredible people. Four months into that business, I had earned tickets to fly out to a leadership training in Texas. A man on stage, Mr. Kevin Mullens, spoke of a 'relationship with God,' that drew us in. He was teaching people how to apply kingdom principles in the marketplace. He poured into me and my husband as we bought several copies of his book, *More Than Enough,* to share with our friends back home. We noticed many of the top earners in the room were Christian. It was because of Mr. Kevin's heartfelt support that we grew curious. We called on a friend who invited us to her nondenominational Christian church where we gave our lives to Jesus and got saved. We were baptized, born again, and married that following year. We served missions with an incredible supernatural ministry school after that. It was also that year when I got to personally connect with the one and only Mr. Les Brown.

Les and his children came to Los Angeles, California for an event. As soon as I heard his laugh... game over! I was on a mission to talk to him so I could properly invest in training with him. Les lovingly directed me to his son, Mr. John Leslie, who listened to my passionate story about growing up listening to his father's teachings. John Leslie immediately shared that if I could get myself to Florida that coming weekend, I would be his special guest in their exclusive training for high-level published authors and established speakers.

With my husband holding down the fort, I flew out to Florida and was greeted by John Leslie at the event doors. It was incredible to get so much personal training in such a small, intimate group. I earned my "Speaker-in-Training" certificate and got invited to attend a follow-up event where I met and learned from Les' daughter, the amazing Ms. Ona Brown. She called me out as the youngest in the room, at 26, and it sunk in how blessed I was to practice and work with people of such high caliber. The Brown family honored my childhood goal, challenging me to write my first book.

While I was inspired and excited, I also was battling personal loss. My husband and I were open to more kids, but I suffered two miscarriages, which had me feeling ashamed, afraid I was to blame, and unsure of how I'd be judged.

I resolved to focus on the positive, grateful for my husband's unconditional love and support, as I kept myself healthy so that if it was meant to be, I'd be ready. Our prayers were answered with the healthy pregnancy of our second son, but the internal battles had already taken such a huge toll, and a frivolous lawsuit tangled me into more grief. I stressed myself out not eating, sleeping, or showering; constantly worried about what it all meant for me and my family. I couldn't stop crying and kept feeling like my childhood asthma was coming back, which I later learned were panic and anxiety attacks. After a trip to the Emergency Room, I opted for therapy for the first time and developed a new-found respect for those who've experienced postpartum difficulties and anxiety.

The year 2020 did quite a number on my family, like everyone else. We lost loved ones, said unexpected goodbyes to friends, and made life shifts we never saw coming. I quickly fell into a deep depression as the direct selling company I loved was bought out and I couldn't align myself with the changes. I felt defeated as longtime customers called asking if I had extra products to pass along; in need of them but unable to afford a monthly supply. I was crushed realizing I failed to teach people how to properly work the business to earn the income needed. I had allowed my limiting beliefs to keep me from stepping into leadership to help people create true leverage by capitalizing on genuine connections, simply sharing what they evidently loved.

The hits kept coming. When I was let go from my jobs due to COVID-19 losses, I was determined to stay hopeful in at least finding part-time work to support my business goals. People loved my resume and interviews but had no funding to hire me. I filed for unemployment and discovered someone tried to fraudulently use my social security number in their unemployment claims. I was told the fraud investigation could take six to eight weeks or six to eight months. Then I encountered another delay when the report was improperly filed — three months wasted with no recourse nor exception! I lost it. I don't even remember what happened the following days. I apparently blanked out, going through the motions for my kids as I spiraled even further than before.

My therapist recommended I see my physician to be evaluated for anti-de-pression and anti-anxiety medication. That was really hard to hear and accept. I was disappointed in myself, but I knew I had to be open to doing something different to get different results. So, I reached out to friends and mentors from church. Hearing their personal experiences, struggling with similar issues, I felt encouraged to at least hear what my doctor was suggesting. He said I checked all the boxes and that he felt comfortable starting me on the lowest dose to see if I could wean myself off as soon as possible.

A month into taking those meds, I broke down one day and fell to my knees, crying out saying, "Father God, none of this looks like you. You're a God of abundance and joy. There's none of that here. Everything I've done has gotten me to this point. I don't like any of it. I'm done doing this my way. I surrender my ego, my selfishness, trying to be perfect in being everything for everyone. I want what you want for me, Papa!" I was tired both emotionally and physically and finally felt ready to be still, to listen. I knew that His plans for my life would come into fruition and, if I didn't get in His way, I would triumph.

I woke up with a renewed feeling of connecting with others and turned to social media to 'catch myself up.' I came across a post from a mentor, whom I've had on my vision board for seven years. She shared a meditation app that had helped her get more restful sleep, so I tried it. I got such great REM sleep that I woke up to a drool-covered pillow. I went back to social media to thank her, but instead came across a song by Dan and Shay called "Glad You Exist," and I teared up, danced with my kids, and laughed for the first time in what felt like a really long time.

I cried writing my mentor a thank-you message and was beyond grateful when she responded with such delight and intentional encouragement and support. Before I knew it, we were making plans to start a Bible study to connect regularly. My heart was bursting, and I was jumping up and down when my husband came home from work, eager to tell him who I was connecting with.

For two weeks, my mentor and I were regularly Facetiming™, Zooming™, and praying for God to lead our days. Then, despite being anxious, I boldly told her, "I pray that God leads us to a business or a way to get paid to pray for people, uplift people's stories, and tangibly contribute to people's life goals." She looked so stunned. I thought I had offended her and apologized in a panic. But she shook her head laughing, saying, "I can't believe you just said that because God's been telling me to tell you what I've been a part of, but I was afraid to trigger you and jeopardize our new friendship."

I stopped her and said, "If you have a business, take my credit card, sign me up! Whatever you're doing, I want to be a part of it."

Then, she name-dropped and said, "Do you remember Kevin Mullens? He went into co-ownership with a new company." I basically tossed my phone in disbelief that the person who literally changed the trajectory of my life was my dream mentor and new best friend's business partner, in a NEW company?!

Suffice it to say, I came in like a wrecking ball, revived in every possible way, surprised with how quickly things moved along. I was determined not to study everything to avoid analysis paralysis. I genuinely invited people to just see the information to see what spoke to them without worrying about 'supporting me.' Before I knew it, I had not only multiplied my investment several times over, but those I invited were inviting others and many of them were making comma-filled paychecks in a way they had never done before.

I was so fired up, I started opening up to strangers on social media; Clubhouse is the app I opened up in, to be specific. As an audio-based platform, I got to have incredible conversations with people all around the world. As divine timing would have it, God brought me full circle connecting me to an encouraging woman named Ms. Katherine Vrastak. She reached out to me saying she was working with Les Brown's publishing company and asked if I wanted to be a part of Les' next book. I immediately felt like God had answered yet another prayer, confirming my lifelong dream to work with Les Brown, write a book, and fulfill the goal-oriented work ethic my parents had instilled in me. I set up an appointment and met with the renowned Ms. JB Owen. The rest is history in the making.

Life has definitely become exciting and there are so many new opportunities unfolding right before me. My newest business is now the business of me! I am devoted to the life God has in store for me and I am thrilled to see what's next.

As Les shares, "Life has no limitations except the ones *you* make." So, get out of your own way and be *your* answered prayer. You were created and equipped to bless people in ways that only you can! Be still and reflect on the things you've loved in life. Recognize your gifts and share your heart unapologetically. Be bold, selfless, and motivating; and, before you know it, your story will inspire someone else's miracle!

IGNITE ACTION STEPS

1. Surround yourself with a healthy, genuine community that will lovingly support and hold you accountable. Accept help!
2. Give yourself and others grace.
3. Be vulnerable and willing to lay things down to be open to receive.
4. Be still enough to listen.
5. Once you have the clarity to move forward, do what Papa Les says, "Shoot for the moon. If you miss, you'll still land among the stars."

Nik Reyno — United States
Artist, Speaker, Author, and Interpersonal Intelligence Coach
linktr.ee/nikslettering   anrlifestyle.navanglobal.com
 reynonik *nikslettering*

Holly H. Kalua

Holly H. Kalua, RN

"TODAY is TOMORROW's successful YESTERDAY."

Today's decisive actions create a future legacy that you are retrospectively pleased with. So, what will you do with your TODAY? I want you to be empowered: boldly pursue your purposeful life through intentional actions where you joyfully experience your heart's desire coming to fruition. Whether it's navigating your career path, enhancing your relationships, or like me, on a fertility journey to build your family, you have the self-determination and resilience to confidently achieve your dreams.

The Pink Carnation

"Congratulations!"

I was gently handing off another beautiful baby, to another exhausted, glowing mother, smiling at her joy while concealing my pain. Ahhh, this is the life in a paradoxical predicament of working as a 'baby nurse,' while struggling with personal infertility.

As the oldest of five children, I wanted a break from raising kids; so, when I got married at the fertile age of 19, I immediately got on birth control — not realizing its untoward effects. A few years later, when I decided to start having children, I found out it wasn't as easy as flipping the fertility factory's switch on. I checked my temperature daily, diligently charting all my physical baby-making details, but to no avail; I was still in a gestation-free zone. Because my body 'attacked' the sperm on their first lap around 'my pool,' we had to try IUI, Intrauterine Insemination, to bypass my unwelcoming chamber. As I stood hopeful staring at the pregnancy test in my hand once again, I was met with the same disheartening minus sign.

In contrast to my personal anguish, professionally I was on the rise. I finally landed my dream job I had hoped for since becoming a nursing school student: getting a full-time position as a maternity nurse! I had the privilege of coaching parents through their labor and delivery experience and ultimately teaching them how to care for their baby. While I knew I had found my calling, the pangs of the past decade of infertility struggles would well up inside when I'd catch the couple's eyes locking on each other as they shared tears of joy for their long-awaited precious baby.

I believed my glorious day could be just around the corner — I'll continue to be patient. Oh, it was going to be perfect! I would learn all the tips of how to enjoy my future pregnancy and was fairly confident that I could care for my own newborn. After all, I had provided compassionate and customized care to each of the various 'models' of babies that popped out over the years.

Dreaming of the glorious possibilities was all well and good, but I realized that my best laid plans were just evaporating into the morning mist as I headed home to an empty 'nest' after another busy night of 'stork deliveries.'

I had experienced the loss of several early pregnancy miscarriages, which were very difficult, but the most gut-wrenching one was the day they put me in a maternity patient gown to complete the pre-op prep for Dilation and Curettage known as a D&C. I was in the maternity ward waiting room, in the same hallway as the laboring women and the crying newborns! Lying on the gurney, soon to be hauled off for my D&C, I silently cried out, "God! Why is this happening?! You have the power to protect the life within me! I am trying to 'be fruitful and multiply,' but instead, I am waiting to go to the operating room to have my incomplete miscarriage erased from existence."

The top of my medical chart looked like there was a cryptic code posted front and center, 'G5 P0,' to protect the innocent, but in reality, it was more like a billboard declaration: I had repeatedly failed to birth a baby, and frankly, I was pretty old to even be trying. As if having the 'G5 P0' meaning Gravida (pregnancy) for the 5th time, Para (live birth) zero – (still not a mom) label wasn't enough, you couldn't miss the dreaded *red-letter stam*p 'AMA' (Advanced Maternal Age)! It's how they routinely labeled all the over-35-year-old maternity patients, those deemed obstetrically obsolete and high-risk for pregnancy.

"I am not AMA!" I told myself, "I still have a chance to be relabeled as 'Mom,'" half-heartedly believing my own declaration as I was now over 40 years old. Trying to conjure up hope, I recalled barren 'AMA' women in the Bible, Elizabeth, Rachel, and Rebekah, who woefully thought their opportunity to bear children had passed, only for God to then bless their wombs and allow them to have their miracle babies. I thought maybe that would be my story.

It is not uncommon for women who are struggling with infertility and loss to avoid situations that increase their emotional pain — such as attending baby showers, shopping with pregnant friends who want to look at all things baby and bump, and driving out of the way to avoid family planning centers. Since I was essentially in a 'pregnancy immersion program,' talking about labor, deliveries, babies, and breastfeeding for 12 hours straight at work, I was able to walk by pregnant women on the sidewalk downtown and not feel too anxious about the encounter.

However, attending church was a whole other matter! It's not that being childless was unacceptable or even a question of not being blessed by God, but it was the annual church celebration of mothers that would bring me to my knees in tears — and prayer.

Every year, the Saturday before Mother's Day, they would call the children up front to each pick up a few pink carnations to give out. They'd ask for all the mothers to stand and wait for the children to bring them a carnation, honoring them for Mother's Day. With big smiles, the children would first run over to their mothers, hug and kiss them, hand them a carnation, and then head off to find their aunt, grandmother, or family friend. I contemplated skipping that one day to avoid the pain, but somehow, I was compelled to be there — I longed to be included in that special celebration of motherhood.

I'd take a deep, sad breath in and slowly release a despondent sigh, feeling my face start to droop, and the tears well up; trying not to audibly sob or bring too much attention to myself. I stayed hunched over, looking down — for fear that one of the children would come over and ask if I was a mommy; that I would have to answer honestly and say "No" and see them skip off to give someone else a pink carnation.

Those misty-eyed days were temporary, but the fateful day that was about to unfold would permanently change my life. I was working my typical night shift when I tried to move a new mom from the gurney to her bed after her Cesarean section surgery: 1-2-3! Ouuuuch! I felt a painful pop in my left shoulder and within 72 hours, I could not lift my left arm without excruciating pain.

After going through physical therapy, shoulder treatments, and two surgeries, I was still not restored to take care of patients again. As a nurse if you can't lift or move patients, then you can kiss your 'patient care' career goodbye!

No! Is my nursing career over? According to the Human Resources (HR) person on the other end of the phone, it essentially was! "Holly, go look at the hospital job board to find a new position that you're eligible for as you are being relieved of your current role. You have two weeks to secure the new one; otherwise, you have to go home on disability."

I refuted the new label that HR was handing me — 'disabled.' I had more to give and many more patients to care for! I chose resilience. Leaping into action, as the 14-day clock was ticking away, I was embarking on a new career path. I reached out to hospital directors, marketing myself in hopes of finding a nursing role that didn't require lifting patients. Thankfully, I found the Case Management (CM) department that invited me to apply for a position they were just about to post. I was offered the job even with no experience! Wow! I was praising God for providing the necessary insight and this amazing blessing! I realized that I no longer had to passively accept what life dished out.

That pivot into CM was the catalyst that took me on my journey of leadership and entrepreneurship where I was able to care, inspire, encourage, and support more people than I ever could have, continuing to solely work as a bedside nurse.

In my new day-shift role, I was in a better place to focus on my reproductive health challenges. After years of surviving profuse menstrual cycles due to the complications of fibroids, I sought help from my OB-GYN doctor. She stated the treatment for my uterine fibroids is to cut them out of my uterus via abdominal surgery. With angst, I asked if that surgery would preclude me from using my uterus to get pregnant and carry a baby. Her response, "Of course, but as a single woman at your age, you're not going to be using your uterus to have a baby anyway, right?"

Wait!!! Whaaaaatttt?!?!

Ugh! That bright red 'AMA' stamp on my chart was haunting me again! I knew I was more than what the clinical community was labeling me to be. I couldn't believe my ears; horrified when I realized how potentially close I was to either saving or losing my ability to have a baby!

Once I gathered my thoughts, I then asked her if there were other alternative treatment choices and she coolly answered, "No, none that I am aware of; I am a surgeon, I do surgery." I sadly left her office not knowing what to do. Should I continue, in the hopes of having a baby, living my life practically glued to a bathroom each month as my fibroids made my period so heavy, I couldn't leave the house? Would doing so change anything; alter the odds that I would be a childless woman? Or, should I just surrender my uterus over to the surgeon and give up on my life's dream of finally being a mom?

My very next cycle answered that question when I ended up in the emergency room with heavy bleeding. My OB-GYN was on vacation, and I received emergency care from another OB-GYN physician. During my follow-up examination, he took a peek and exclaimed, "You won't need open incision abdominal surgery! I can easily remove this feisty fibroid with a same-day laparoscopic surgery, and you'll be left with only a few tiny bandages on your abdomen."

The outpatient surgery was scheduled soon afterward and before I knew it, I was rolling down the hall on a gurney off to get my physical life back. When I woke up in recovery to see my physician's face smiling, I couldn't imagine what was going on. I felt my abdomen — no holes or stitches. Did he *not* do the surgery? He shared the great news, that he was able to remove the fibroid intravaginally and did not have to poke holes in my abdomen or cut into my uterus! Praise the Lord!

Okay, that does it! As a nurse, I was a great patient advocate but had almost failed at protecting myself. Patient empowerment is a right and a responsibility of *mine* — not a privilege to earn. Although I had been resilient and intentional in my career, I was merely a submissive supporter of my personal health. The idea of empowerment doesn't just apply to our careers; it carries into every facet of our lives. This medical triumph of mine proved it.

I have refused to be limited by the labels I was given. I rejected the stamp of 'disabled' to bravely take on a new career path and empower myself to ultimately become a supportive leader. I questioned the validity of the stamp 'AMA' and found a solution that didn't cost me my chances of motherhood. Had I not first grappled with my own limitations, I may never have been pushed toward shedding them and becoming something greater.

Yesterday is proof that *Tomorrow's* success depends on what we do with *Today*. Knowing this, I integrate the lessons of both my personal and professional emancipation into the way I serve others. As a Registered Nurse and Certified Human Behavior Consultant, it was a natural transition for me to become a Fertility Coach. I now advocate, "You are people *first*, and patients *second*." I use this model to effectively guide couples on their family-building journey. I also teach them how to compassionately communicate with each other by gaining new understanding of each other's personal needs.

This serves as a platform of strength and wisdom for the couple to transform into one empowered unit confidently facing life's challenges with endurance. With decreased stress and an enhanced awareness, they are able to integrate a true sense of liberation into their lives. Their perspective to navigate their fertility journey is no longer based on a victim mentality, feeling out of control of their bodies' reproductive capacity. Instead, they gain insight into what and how they can positively impact their goal.

The most empowering thing of all is that I now choose my own labels, including the one of my deepest desires: Mom. Here I was, back in the same church's annual Mother's Day service with carnations being handed out. Again, I was in tears, but this time, it was because I held one in my hand. I don't know if I have ever seen a flower more beautiful.

Now I sit here writing this, pen in hand, with misty eyes, as my precious baby girl has just turned 12 years old — a budding little lady who calls me 'Mom.' What will her own journey be like? I pray that she will be blessed with a sweet and loving daughter like she has been to me. As this chapter of my life continues, with such abundant joy in my heart, I set my pen down and breathe in a peaceful sigh and the sweet fragrance of my beautiful pink carnation.

Whether it's your personal or career path, you are not on a passive tour; indecision *is making a choice* for inaction. The realization that you do not have to remain a victim of your circumstances liberates you to see that where you are presently is simply the stepping-stones of choices and reactions that you have made in the past but can now conceive of, proactively designing the blueprint of your future with passion and purpose.

With this understanding that you are in charge of *your* life's path and free to reject labels that others place upon you, you will unlock your inner power, strength, and courage to boldly navigate forward with intentionality — acting on your own authority, governing your decisions and actions to create your personally fulfilling journey.

As you reveal the new empowered and amazing you, with only inspiring and positive labels of *your* choosing, imagine how you will flourish living an exceptional future of life's journey! As both Les Brown and JB Owen have shown me, unlock your potential and Ignite your soul for life's infinite possibilities.

Ignite Action Steps

Stamp it Out — It's Not True! Today's circumstance may not have changed from Yesterday's, but Tomorrow's can when you realize how empowered you are to create your future path. What is one self-limiting belief that you can rewrite with an alternative statement that stamps over that negative one? Great! You have just discovered the truth! Say it out loud like you are running for President ;-)

Map it Out — A Plan for You. Create a road map with potential key decision-making points you'll need to make along this journey. For a fertility journey, consider how much time you can afford to try natural family-building approaches before contemplating assisted reproductive techniques. My clients fill out the M.A.P.P.I.N.G. road map independently — each freely rendering personal unencumbered thoughts. They then discuss their decisions as a couple, respectfully reviewing the 'whys' behind incongruencies in their choices, agreeably seeking a common approach going forward. A new customized map with these aligned concepts is not only getting the couple on the same page, but also it's especially helpful when communicating the fertility plan with providers.

Figure It Out — A 360-degree Review. Optimizing fertility starts with identifying key components and circumstances that, if improved, would enhance preconception health. Changes in household and external environmental exposures, nutrition, and lifestyle factors and managing psychological stress will not only be crucial for boosting your fertility, but it will also significantly contribute to having a healthy pregnancy, postpartum period, and a healthy baby. This holistic fertility approach may also take social and spiritual needs and desires into consideration.

Reach Out — Secure Your Crew. Know someone who's not within an arm's length of your uterus — who could be a neutral advocate for you two? You need a safe zone to be able to transparently share your perception of the challenges and opportunities of your fertility journey without judgment. A confidant(e) who can validate your concerns, provide encouragement, and be your advocate — yet willing to broach the tough topics and questions. A friend, a Fertility Coach, or anyone you choose to have by your side for as long as it serves you. I've enjoyed guiding and supporting couples from preconception through pregnancy and the delivery of their precious bundle of joy.

Holly H. Kalua, RN — United States
Nurse, Fertility Coach, Certified Human Behavior Consultant,
Speaker, Author, Founder and CEO of Holly Kalua, LLC
www.CoachKalua.com
www.PersonalityPerspectives.com
CoachKalua
CoachKalua
hollykalua
CoachKalua

Jenise 'Sandy' Todd

"Where do you run when what you're running from is on the inside?"

It is my desire for you to discover this — you are a living 'treasure chest' filled with countless valuables! However, sometimes the treasure appears to be hidden, not necessarily 'from' us but 'for' us (as a man of God once said), while we navigate through what may feel like an obstacle course of life. The painful memories of our past can seemingly take the steering wheel of our lives, driving us to bury our treasure underneath an inaccurate appraisal of our true value. In contrast, if money maintains its value regardless of frequent handling and mishandling, so do YOU — a more precious commodity indeed! Let's embrace the fact that despite your past, you are STILL a treasure chest, and the multitudes are waiting to discover your worth! As Les Brown says, "That which you've been sitting on, somebody's waiting on, and it's your time!" Ignite the world with what's in YOUR treasure chest!

Deliver Me from Myself

I came from humble beginnings. My twin sister and I were born in Warren, Arkansas, and when we were 4 years old my mother relocated our family to Pine Bluff about 45 miles away. Our father passed away in a traffic accident before we were born. However, my mother remarried giving us a bonus dad and a bonus older sister who lived with our paternal grandparents. To this marital union my baby sister was born.

We grew up in a community on the northside of the city near the campus of the University of Arkansas at Pine Bluff (UAPB). We initially lived in a three-room shotgun house, which was approximately 12-feet wide with a living room, bedroom, and kitchen. The term 'shotgun' house is said to be derived from the straight-line layout of the rooms — as if a bullet could be shot from the front door, pass through the house, and exit through the back door without hitting anything. There was no hallway, so we had to walk through each room to get to the next. When we first moved in, we did not have indoor plumbing, so in the daytime we had to use the outhouse in the backyard and slop jars at night. Eventually though, my dad purchased an additional lot (approximately 50 feet) to remodel the house. He had it expanded to accommodate indoor plumbing, adding a bathroom behind the kitchen. Later, he changed the bedroom into a dining room and added three bedrooms on the opposite side of the house creating a long hallway in the middle. The hallway would prove to be extremely vital during one of the most transitional phases of my life.

I enjoyed many days filled with loads of fun, laughter, and excitement growing up with my sisters in the '70s and '80s. Nostalgic moments take me back to some of the most delightful experiences. Kickball, dodgeball, and hide-and-seek were a few of the games we played in the big yard beside our house with our friends and schoolmates. Other outdoor childhood games included red rover, Simon says, and red light/green light — all thanks to my dad's purchase of that extra lot, a worthy investment in the quality of our lives. Inside, we enjoyed playing jacks in the hallway, while at the dining room table, old maid, checkers, and I-declare-war, to name a few. It was also a time in which my mom taught us to cook even as early as 6 years old, beginning with cornbread. As we grew older and started school, our responsibilities grew to doing homework, cleaning, assisting with cooking, and setting the table during the week. We would eat at the dinner table daily as a family unit. Our meals usually ended with light conversations ranging from school to work to home, often peaking with gut-wrenching laughter about things like 'soap opera cornbread.' This was an inside joke about cornbread that was inadvertently burned while mom was watching soap operas. These were some of the times I can recall when my family bonded most.

Then came the weekend family trips in which we would drive along the countryside to the homes of maternal and paternal family members. Dad (from Rison, Arkansas) came from a family of approximately 10 children, and mom (from Banks, Arkansas) was the baby of approximately 15 children — huge families on both sides! Having twins herself, mom came from a strong family line of twins — from aunts to uncles to cousins. There were no seat belt requirements back then, so we rode along playing in the back seat, sleeping, and snacking all the way. We enjoyed watching the sky and observing breathtaking scenes of nature; we cringed at the smell of chicken houses, skunks, and cattle manure violating our air space in the car. These times were priceless! They documented M and Ms (moments and memories) in our history where we bonded with our very first best friends — yes, our cousins! Visitations were *always* like celebrations involving food, fun, and fellowship — *staples of life!* We were very close-knit and always wholeheartedly enjoyed each other.

We knew we were expected to attend college after completing high school. Therefore, we began preparing immediately following graduation. This included researching information about UAPB, as well as completing paperwork for admission, financial aid, and ultimately, registration. As teenagers, we participated in the National Youth Sports Program at UAPB every summer, so we were familiar with the campus but not campus life. I was equally unaware that this period of my life would precede one of the most transformational experiences I had ever known.

At the tender age of 18, during the fall semester of college, I became pregnant out of wedlock. At the beginning of the spring semester, the pregnancy was detected as I began having symptoms. The term 'morning sickness' was a misrepresentation of my experience; it went far beyond mornings. Every waking moment, I was terribly sick and couldn't keep food or water down. I was always nauseous and violently vomiting even though there was nothing more to bring up. The sickness was so severe I literally wanted to sleep just to avoid feeling miserable. My nose became my enemy as things which normally smelled good began to nauseate me tremendously. This was followed by insomnia, fatigue, appetite changes, and unusual food cravings. *Forget the stereotypical sour pickles! I wanted sugary Froot Loops™!* Due to the intensity and frequency of the symptoms, I was not able to attend class the first few months of the spring semester. However, I wrote a note to each instructor explaining my situation and they agreed to send me weekly homework assignments by my cousin who was also in college.

My plight was so severe I finally stopped going outside. I only interacted with those in my household. The extreme emotional pressure was taking a toll on me and, ultimately, prompted a nervous breakdown. I was 19 and was experiencing overwhelming mental anguish, depression, embarrassment, humiliation, and shame. I replayed devastating thoughts of having disappointed my parents, who were considered pillars of the church and devout members in the community. My dad was a deacon, and my mother was a strong intercessory prayer warrior in the church. I was convinced I had single-handedly brought undue reproach upon my family.

This was during a time when single women, at least in my experience, had to stand before the church congregation on Sunday and apologize for getting pregnant out of wedlock.

That dreadful Sunday arrived when it was time for me to make my apology. I was anxious on the way to church in anticipation of this disgraceful moment. Riding by houses observing neighbors in the community, I wondered how the apology scene would unfold in the church. I waited throughout the service, on pins and needles, not really able to appreciate the singing, praying, and preaching. The time had come. It seemed like all eyes were on me as I made my way to the front. My 19-year-old brain was confused, and my heart torn. "Was my confession for fornication? And if so, why was I the only person out of the two involved required to publicly confess?" As I stood there looking into the faces of the people, it felt like a courtroom — or a crowd ready to stone me — instead of a church sanctuary. My heart was pounding as I struggled to find the appropriate words to say. My level of distress deepened. Feeling grossly devalued and rejected, my self-worth began to quickly diminish. Though some church members continued to show love and support, I was convinced I was being judged by others.

As I matured into adulthood and reflected on this phase of my life, I discovered I had no idea I was a living treasure chest during that time. I was blinded to this fact by the self-condemnation of my own wrongdoing. Nor did I consider the only difference in my situation and theirs was the 'visible' evidence which could not be denied. Clearly, my transgression was no greater than the 'unexposed' indiscretions of those before whom I stood. In fact, if this was the standard, everyone — men *and* women — should have been required at some point to confess before the congregation. Though my offense was not adultery, I was reminded of the principle reflected in the Bible when the woman was caught in the act of adultery. Jesus made a piercing statement to the accusers who brought her to him, "He that is without sin among you, let him first cast a stone at her," (John 8:7). Forcing them to reflect on their own lives, one-by-one, they dropped their stones and walked away. They may not have been guilty of adultery but apparently, they were guilty of something. Likewise, had it been possible for Jesus to be at the church in the flesh that day, He would have cleared the onlookers once again. Thankfully, new church leadership eventually changed this practice.

My heart and mind were consumed with unspoken condemnations about myself. I was a Christian, avid churchgoer, and confidant; a girl affectionately known as Miss Nice, Miss Sweet, and Miss Innocent. I had been a cheerleader, honor student, homecoming queen, and even lieutenant commander of Naval

Junior Reserve Officers Training Corps my senior year. Responsibility and self-accountability were not foreign to me. I was even the first among my siblings and friends to get my driver's license — a huge responsibility! I drove us everywhere — to school, stores, malls, parks, the skating rink, and the movies. Sometimes, I would drive us around just for the sake of riding with the windows down; music playing. Despite incidents like getting stuck in the mud, forcing passengers to get out and push while barking dogs ran closer, we had a blast!

Subsequently, I was gravely concerned about the kind of influence my pregnancy would have on these same friends and family members.

The more I tried exiting the busy expressway of my congested mind, the more I kept pressing 'replay.' I was clearly in a battle internally for my emotional and mental well-being — in a place my family and friends could not see or touch. How could I break out of this mental prison? Where would I go and what would I say? Who could rescue me? As the Apostle Paul asked in Romans 7:24, "Who shall deliver me from the body of this death?" Better yet, somebody! Anybody! Deliver me from *myself!* As I had this private interrogation with myself, I ultimately concluded, "Where do I run when what I'm running from is on the inside?" Frankly, I could have booked a flight to another country to get away; regardless, it was obvious that *my* baggage would be boarding the flight with me — *not on my shoulder — in my soul.* Carry-on baggage of a different sort!

A stark reality began to set in as I realized this was the first time my parents could not help me. I was disconnecting from everything and everyone — family, friends, college, and church. I couldn't bear to socialize. My feelings of utter helplessness and hopelessness caused me to run further and further away to what I perceived was the safest place at the time — INSIDE! The irony was that my hiding place and the problem were in the same location. Eventually, this coping mechanism began to affect my physical health. I began to walk slowly and slightly stooped over, and rather than turning my neck, I would reposition my entire body to respond to anyone requesting my attention. I developed insomnia so my body's clock was off-balance as well.

When my family began to constantly question my behavior, it was a rude awakening for me. Although I had slowly declined into a 'new norm,' I recognized that it was not normal at all. After several months of misery and no longer recognizing my fun-loving, responsible, independent self, one day I woke up with a desperate longing for change. Since teen pregnancy programs and support groups were not readily available then, this thrusted me into making a resolve to posture myself for total transformation. I did the only thing I *knew* I could, which was what my mother had always taught us: to pray and read the

Bible. I had never given proper weight to those words until that solemn moment.

Standing face-to-face with these truths forced me to see that only God, through Jesus Christ, could help me. I was aware of the God of Abraham, Isaac, and Jacob, even the God of my grandparents and parents. Yet, though I was saved and baptized, I didn't have a personal relationship with Him to know Him as MY God — the God of Jenise. However, this was my turning point. It was time to put into practice what mom had taught me. This was a scary place because I didn't believe God would hear me, especially since I had 'sinned' against Him. However, I repented and prayed, asking God to help me through this situation. Additionally, I promised if He would help me, I would exercise my faith by doing my part to help regain my body strength. I began reading the Bible to build my faith and forcing myself to walk upright down that long hallway every day, while talking to God every step of the way. I had to push *through* — *through* the hallway, *through* the shame, *through* the physical limitations. I kept pushing until I was able to stand totally upright and turn my head and neck normally again.

Eventually, I realized that God, who I thought wouldn't hear me, had miraculously answered my prayer. Out of all the people in the world, He took the time to listen to l'il ol' me. This was an incredibly amazing experience. I began to think wholesomely again, smile again, interact socially again, and even write again. In fact, He restored my handwriting to a better penmanship. I was grateful that despite my immediate past, He STILL brought me out of a dark place mentally, emotionally, and physically. For the first time in my life, it was evident just how much God loved me personally. Upon repentance, I had been forgiven, and He brought restoration above and beyond my former state. At last, I could say He was not only the God of others, but I could proudly and boldly proclaim, "He's MY God also."

I understand now, as stated in 1 John 5:14-15, that God always hears and answers prayers which are consistent with His will. Further, because love is an action word (as demonstrated in John 3:16) the greatest lesson I learned was that God's love is greater than my parents' love. The love of my parents was tremendous yet limited to meeting only my 'natural' needs. On the other hand, God's love is unlimited and capable of meeting my 'supernatural' needs. In other words, as my Heavenly Father, He could do what my earthly parents could not do.

After several months, I was able to return to college and attend classes again. By the grace of God, all assignments were caught up, and I finished with a GPA of 3.9 for the semester. At that pivotal moment, I discovered something in my treasure chest — **the God-given ability to bounce back and excel**! Everything had been restored, including my peace. Life looked and felt differently on the other side of *through*. Moving forward, no one could convince me that God was not real. My test had literally become my testimony, and now, I had at least one story to tell (the story of labor and delivery coming later).

Generally, when we purchase products or appliances, they come with a manufacturer's manual. Thus, when something goes awry with the product, we refer to the manual or contact the manufacturer. This also applies to our personal lives. According to Psalm 100:3, "It is he that hath made us, and not we ourselves." Therefore, He is our manufacturer. Whenever something goes awry in our lives, we can always refer to the manual (the Holy Bible) or take the product (ourselves) back to Him. So, **"Where do you run when what you're running from is on the inside?"** We run to our Creator. He alone has our blueprints, as He is the only man-making God. Since He shaped us inside and out (according to Psalm 139:14), He knows what we need, even if it means deliverance from ourselves.

Bad decisions and wrong choices made in the past do not define our destiny. Sometimes we are our own worst critic and hide our true value under self-imposed judgments. We are sometimes blinded by our negativity versus seeing the truth of what we have to give. As Paul stated in 2 Corinthians 4:7, that "we have this treasure in earthen vessels," know that you have gifts, talents, and abilities yet to be discovered. You are special and have so much to offer the world. God has bestowed upon you so many treasures. Open YOUR treasure chest and Ignite the world!

Ignite Action Steps

1. Be intentional. Faith without works is dead, so believe God, but also do whatever corresponds with your faith.
2. Seek medical attention when necessary.
3. Seek spiritual and professional counseling if needed.
4. Above all else, seek God concerning ALL issues. He can go where scalpels and medicine cannot go.

Jenise 'Sandy' Todd — United States
Minister, Author, CEO of OMG Xpressions & More LLC,
Founder of Feed My Sheep eMinistries
www.omgxpressions.org
omgxpressions omgxpressions

Ashley Montgomery

ASHLEY MONTGOMERY

"Never let the challenges or obstacles you face
paralyze you from pursuing the dreams you chase."

**Throughout life, we often experience moments that were intended for us
to stop pursuing our dreams. My goal is to encourage you to pivot and
flourish into the successful woman or man God created you to be. I want
to support you in healing from past failures, setbacks, disappointments,
tribulations, and obstacles. If we stay the course and focus on our *what*,
instead of our *why*, we will see a victory. We will see that our trials and
tribulations were not meant to prevent us, but to show us who it is we are
to become.**

GIRL... YOU WERE CREATED FOR THIS

I always knew I was different since I was a child. I have been hungry to
speak since I was a little girl in elementary school. At 9, I was speaking to my
stuffed animals. My younger cousins did not want to listen to me, so I created
my own audience. I would sit the stuffed animals in chairs and cheerfully
provide them with my own version of inspirational messages. I was excited
because I was doing what I love best — speaking — but I never received a
response, so it wasn't as fun as I wanted it to be. As I grew up, I realized that I
was planting seeds for the future by using my voice at 9 years old. I knew there
was greatness in me, that I was created for something exceptional.

My spiritual life was always the core to my sense of fulfillment. It guided me as I grew and helped me to overcome obstacles and trials that arose in my personal and financial life. At 17, in my last year of high school, I became pregnant with my son. Immediately, I felt like my life was over and I had no future. I did not know what I was going to do. I was so embarrassed to go to school. I felt like I had humiliated my mother and father, and the shame, guilt, and sense of failure were overwhelming. I shut down for a while, until one night I had a dream. In this dream I saw myself back in school then working as a nurse, making my child proud. I realized that I wasn't willing to give up, to drop out like some people expected me to. I was going to build a good life for my son. I knew that God would never leave or forsake me. I decided at that point that I was going to graduate from high school because my goals depended on it.

After graduating, I started working in multiple industries such as fast-food restaurants, casinos, chemical refineries, and call centers (just to name a few). I was busy trying to earn money to support my child, but all these distractions were delaying me from my purpose. I knew I was supposed to be doing more; remembering my dream of being a nurse. Nearly three years later, married and with the arrival of my second child, I decided to pursue my education in nursing. I was going to make my children proud and be a positive example they could model from. I did not allow the results of being a teenage mom to become my only reality. I wanted to make a difference in *many* people's lives.

After graduating from nursing school, I started working for a behavioral health agency as a nurse. I really loved my job, and my goal was to retire from there. The medical director allowed me to take on additional responsibilities, and I never once refused to perform these tasks. I was eager to learn, grow, and expand, and wanted to excel within the company. I learned everything with confidence and dedication to excellence. I was hungry for greatness. I was always the first one at work and the last one to leave, and within a few months I was promoted to the Nursing Administrator. The legendary Les Brown states that, "Life is more meaningful when you are always looking to grow and working toward a goal." That became my focus.

According to Colossians 3:23, my favorite book, you should "work willingly at whatever you do, as though you work for the Lord, rather than for people." After taking this into consideration, I invested a significant amount of my time and talents into the company. I worked obediently, with the quiet whispers of something greater on the horizon rising in my soul. But all that work came at a cost. As I kept giving all my hours to the career path I was on, my family lost my presence. My kids' events, my husband's needs, they all sat on the backburner. In time my marriage was suffering so greatly I was on the verge of divorce. "God, how can this be right?" I wondered.

My search for clarity brought me to a vision board event. I placed my vision of entrepreneurship on the board along with many more ideas I believed in. I kept faith that if I mapped out my dreams, God would notice them, and bring them to pass.

Eight months later, the Holy Spirit led me to start a three-day spiritual fast. I did not know why I was fasting but through my obedience, I did not have anything to eat or drink for three days. I starved my flesh and fed my spirit. I never told anyone (including my family) when I fasted, but they always knew because the food I'd cook for them would suddenly lack proper seasoning. My sons would often say, "Mama, you must be fasting because this food is nasty." During my first day of fasting, I felt weak and fatigued. I did not know how I was going to make it through the next few days, but I was hungry to hear from God. It was not easy, but I remained committed. As the next few days went by, fasting became easier because I was feeding my spirit with the word of God. I knew I was supposed to be doing more. I knew God was calling me to a higher purpose and I was faithful to stay the course.

As I spent time in God's presence, I became more and more aware of his guidance. I heard a spiritual leader that I follow on television say that it was time to elevate your purpose, and if needed, leave an unfulfilling job. It was as if she was speaking directly to me! I knew that was a word from God because I'd never verbally said I wanted to leave my employment. I responded in obedience to God over man and left my job, after six years of making a six-figure salary. I remember going home and telling my husband and my two sons that I was quitting my job. My oldest son asked me, "Mom, what are we going to do?" I did not know that answer. I looked strong and confident on the outside, but I was afraid and confused on the inside. I was scared of the unknown, but I did not let them see me nervous. I immediately told them, "God will take care of us. We will be alright." I needed them to know I was determined to make it work.

Plenty of nights I would wake up in tears and try to figure out what I had just done. God would constantly remind me to be still, but I was desperately trying to keep my family from going without and was determined to do everything on my own. Three weeks after leaving my job, I applied at a plasma center and started working there as the lead nurse. It took just two weeks for me to know that that was not what I was supposed to be doing. God wanted me to sit still and wait on Him, but like we often do, I responded with fear. I was afraid of living in poverty, so I was relying on being an employee instead of getting prepared to become an employer.

Les Brown says that if you put yourself in a position where you must stretch outside your comfort zone, then you are forced to expand your consciousness and to strive and achieve more. My husband and I did just that. We had to move out of our home and move into one of our family's rental homes. My husband's business was not bringing in enough income to cover the bills. Our bank account started getting low and ended up in the red, and I went from stressed to terrified, trembling at the possibility that my choice to leave a six-figure job had just sunk our family's future. At that moment, I felt like I let my family down. I was contemplating getting a job on one hand and sitting still on the other hand. I did not know what God was up to. Still, I remember looking back at my vision board and believing that those dreams I had envisioned were going to come to pass.

Three months after moving out of our home, I applied to go back to nursing school to get a higher degree. This was my dream. I studied hard for my entrance examination and passed it with an outstanding score. I remember it like it was yesterday. I called the school to see when the acceptance letters would be mailed out. The receptionist informed me that the letters were sent two days ago. I immediately went to check my mailbox and saw that my letter from the university was in there. I sat in my car rocking back and forward contemplating opening up that letter. I was afraid of the results. I knew my future was dependent on that letter. A few minutes later, I decided to open it and discovered that I did *not* get accepted into the program. I cried and became so emotional. I felt like my dreams were crumbling in my face. I felt hopeless. I had been preparing for months by studying and placing our financial security on getting accepted. I was emotionally drained for a few weeks afterward and did not have energy to do anything.

Two weeks later, I decided that I was *not* going to let the results I received become my reality. I knew it was time to get back up and do something different. I had to realize that I was created for this!

A month later, I attended the End Your Year Strong empowerment conference hosted by Dr. Cindy Trimm in Atlanta, Georgia with 15 other women from my church. I was excited for the conference and looking forward to hearing from Dr. Trimm and Les Brown. I knew that something great was going to come from that conference because I did a 10-day fast prior to it. I remember telling one of the women at the conference that I was not going to miss one session. I was determined to hear from every speaker. We laughed and cried throughout the experience, and many lives were impacted by the powerful speakers.

Dr. Trimm started speaking about the different businesses that are destined to thrive in the upcoming years. She mentioned a staffing agency and I immediately received that word for me. My body started shaking and I started crying — hearing these words moved me. I knew it was confirmation from God because this had always been my desire. I always wanted to head my own healthcare staffing agency but had always tried to give it to someone else to start. I felt like I did not have the resources or the capital to get it going; hitting roadblock after roadblock every time I made a call trying to get the paperwork started.

At that moment, I realized God never allowed the business deal to go through in the past because he did not intend for the business to be someone else's vision. The obstacles and the struggles were put there to lead me to truly strike out on my own. I knew I had faith to receive the business idea that was spoken over me, but I also knew that I needed to do the work for the company to manifest. A month later, I opened my business account with $25. I did not have any money and I was relying on God every step of the way.

In February 2020, I passed my competence examination to hold a healthcare staffing license. I was excited and eager to get going. I knew this was the beginning of becoming a successful entrepreneur and I wanted my business to be debt free. I started the recruitment process for my employees and many healthcare professionals came in and applied with my company. I had over 40 employees at the time but no work. In March 2020, I started reaching out to facilities, doing presentations to gain the contracts I needed. Then the COVID-19 pandemic hit and overnight the facilities did not want to meet with anyone. Everything was on hold. I felt like nothing was going right; like this business was a bad idea. Thoughts buzzed through my head telling me to give up, but I tried to focus on my *what*. I remember the words from a wise woman I'd once met, "For every *no*, there will be a *yes*. Do not give up. You were created for this."

A week later, I received a phone call to take an assignment in Florida, which was 17 hours from my home. Even though I did not want to leave my family, I decided to go because COVID-19 put everything on hold for my business. I did not know what I was getting myself into and I remember my mother asking me why I was going out there in the middle of a pandemic. I knew God had His hand around me and I knew I was going to be protected. I went to Florida and assisted in helping the country during this difficult time.

As I focused on responding in service to others in Florida, facilities started sending signed contracts via email to my agency. Companies needed my employees. Facilities required the services of my trained personnel. Suddenly my business took off. God started opening doors for me through my obedience and patience.

My husband raised my boys while I spent the next six months in Florida working and giving everything to my business. That was the most stressful time of my life because I was never away from my sons that long. Plenty of nights I would cry myself to sleep; I was an emotional wreck. The only times I would see my husband and sons were through FaceTime™ which made it harder for me to cope. I was trying to stay strong during that difficult time for myself and my family. I had to also focus on staying healthy when other coworkers and patients were becoming ill. It was very challenging at times. A part of me wanted to give up but I knew I was sent on a mission to care for the sick. I had to constantly remind myself, "Girl… you were created for this," which caused me to stay strong and not give up.

Every time I received money from my temporary work, I paid my employees. I was leveraging my income. I went months without seeing a paycheck of my own. I was not only a blessing to my employees, but we were also a blessing to the facilities. We were able to provide supplemental staffing to multiple hospitals, nursing homes, psychiatric facilities, FEMA, and more during the pandemic and Hurricanes Laura and Delta in Louisiana. I started my business with just $25 and my revenue jumped to six figures within a three-month span: all within the first year. It all began with a seed that I sowed into my vision, and my belief that I was created for this. I knew that it might have taken years to build, but with my faith and trust, God catapulted my dream within months. There is power in obeying God.

In life we often go through seasons where we are tempted to give up. Maybe you received a bad report from the physician, a loan did not go through, a business deal failed, or your marriage is falling apart. There might be a situation where your child is acting up or you are not able to conceive. Whatever the circumstances might be, you need to ask yourself this question: Will you let your results be your reality? Do not give up when it looks like situations are impossible. Do not quit when it looks tough and difficult to push through. You must always remember that the results you are receiving are only temporary. Focus on your reality which is the truth. Focus on your desired outcome. Focus on your goals and dreams.

I encourage you to let your light shine and continue to walk in obedience! You are an overcomer and in a few more months, you will laugh at the fiery darts of circumstance that were thrown at you. Continue to smile through your struggles and disappointments because you know God is faithful. Continue to push through the wilderness even though it's unfamiliar. You are always saying yes, that's why God's promise toward you will always be yes and amen! This new walk may be unfamiliar to you, but the glow on your life is unexplainable and the anointing on your life is untouchable. The favor in your life is unimaginable, so expect the rest of your life to be unbelievable. YOU WERE CREATED FOR THIS!

"Let us not become weary in doing good, for at the proper time we will reap a harvest if we do not give up." — Galatians 6:9

Ignite Action Steps

Create an authentic and exceptional life.

Step 1: Create a vision board. Be sure to make it visual with the things you want in your future, and use a lot of words. This world was formed by words, and your words will form your world. I recommend completing this step on a yearly basis.

Step 2: Take action now. Listen and do everything that your higher power instructs you to do. My favorite book states that faith without works is dead. Do not put it off until tomorrow, next week, next month, or next year. Take a step of faith and do it now!

Step 3: Create a spiritual fast. Your fast can last for 24 hours, three days, 10 days, 21 days, or 40 days. There are plenty of things you can fast from during this time of consecration: food, television, people, social media, internet, etc. Whatever the Lord may lead you to do, be consistent and determined to complete it. Something amazing will come from it.

Step 4: NEVER GIVE UP. Remember that for every no, there will be a yes. You were created for this. Do not let someone's opinion dictate the decisions of your future. I remember someone told me that everyone was not made to be a business owner. I took those words as a torch. Every time there was a roadblock, every time the enemy wanted me to give up, I would say, "I *am* a successful business owner." What has someone spoken over you that you can use as a torch to push into greatness?

Ashley Montgomery — United States
Speaker, Author, Mentor, CEO of Exceptional Healthcare Staffing,
Founder of Vision Ranch
www.ashleykeyspeaks.com
www.exceptionalhs.com   www.visionranch.org
ⓞ *ashleykeyspeaks* ✋ *nurseashleykey*

Pearlette Cassells

Pearlette Cassells

"Stop waiting to start. Now is the time because the life
you desire is on the other side of action."

By sharing my experience, I hope it stirs you to draw on your strength and courage to create the life you desire. Do not allow fear and procrastination to derail your plans, steal your dreams, and rob you of an enriching and purposeful life. My wish is that you be intentional in your planning and ensure that you take consistent action to make things happen and achieve your goals.

The Patient in Room D4-303

I felt a strange sensation in my throat and I wondered what it was. It persisted and I tried to inhale but there was NOTHING… no oxygen went in. I remember seeing the nurse's call button with the red tip, hanging behind my pillow on the bed rail, and I tried to reach for it but it was too far away. I was weak and tried to yell but my voice was faint: "I can't breathe. I can't breathe." Sharon, my cousin, instantly got up and ran to get help. I heard mumbling on the PA system and within minutes my room was filled with medical personnel. I saw the panic on their faces and a couple of them were fixated on the blood pressure monitor, watching the numbers quickly changing like a spin from the *Wheel of Fortune™* show. The last thing I remembered was that the reading was 175/100. "Turn off the morphine pump! Turn off the morphine pump!" shouted one nurse as another fitted me with an oxygen mask. By now I was surrounded by nurses, doctors, and respiratory therapists yelling and scurrying around as the PA system announced, "Code Blue in Room D4-303."

I wasn't prepared for what was happening. And, if you knew me, I was *always* prepared.

I wrote lists from as far back as I can remember having chores and responsibilities. Lists helped me feel organized and I took great pleasure in crossing things off. All except when it came to my dreams. They seemed so audacious and huge that I didn't know where to start and how to make them happen so they sat there on the growing list of, "Someday, I'll do it." I created a vision board by cutting out beautiful pictures from *O, The Oprah Magazine*™. They seemed so glossy and perfect for what I wanted to achieve. My cousins gifted me with a yearlong subscription and what a treat it was! I read those magazines from cover to cover the moment they arrived in my mailbox. My vision board was divided into sections: Successful Entrepreneur, *The New York Times*™ Best-Selling Author, and Philanthropist. I even wrote a check for $50 million and glued it to the Successful Entrepreneur section. They were all dreams, and I thought, "Oh well I'm young." I believed there was no need to rush; that it would simply happen someday if it was on my list.

I spent hours at the local book store looking through non-fiction books, checking out the spines of books on the shelf and envisioning my book there with my name. "Oh, when I'm successful," I thought, "my books will be at the front of the store as I walk in!" I pictured them stacked like a mountain, similar to other well-known authors like Les Brown, Brendon Burchard, and Brene Brown's books. "That's what the other successful authors do and I will definitely be one… someday!"

I'd been dreaming about this since I arrived in Canada as an immigrant from Jamaica. I left the Caribbean because I wanted a change and my Canadian family encouraged me to come for a holiday. What started as a two-week vacation turned into me applying for permanent residency. In Canada, I thought perhaps I would find my path to great success.

I had worked hard to overcome obstacles along my way; a life that early on put me in touch with tragedy. My daughter, who I'd had in my early 20s, passed away at the age of 3. In the aftermath of that devastating moment, I found one of my passions: volunteering. As I donated my child's clothes to a local orphanage, I realized it was filled with children who needed care and comfort so I began to visit them every Saturday, helping to bathe, feed, dress, and care for them. It felt like I was making a contribution and I *needed* to make a contribution for the loss of my child.

Volunteering allowed me to be involved in several opportunities within my community. One of them was to be a part of the Community Connections Program with the Cross Cultural Learner Centre welcoming refugees and new immigrants and helping them integrate and feel included in the Canadian society. I loved seeing people try to make the best of their life despite the obstacles. I admired their resilience after experiencing such traumas in their lives. They were so hopeful and held such great promise! They were oftentimes afraid and I would help calm their fears and told them to call me even if it was late at night. I know all too well about uprooting one's life and moving to a new country just to restart again. I had walked in their shoes. Their stories were my stories.

I was so fulfilled, but gradually, it became harder to work. While my heart was still in it, my body had other plans. For a few months I was experiencing abdominal pain and discomfort on a regular basis, but I was willing to dismiss it and my doctor didn't seem very concerned. Yet, I knew something had to be done when the pain became unbearable. Eventually a doctor decided it would be best to operate. After getting a referral for surgery and a scheduled date, I called my reliable cousin Sharon. She lovingly offered to accompany me even though she lived over two hours away. Just as she had been there to pick me up from the airport when I first arrived in Canada, she was there for me again in my hour of need.

At 6 AM in the morning, we arrived at the hospital. I had never been to the hospital that early before. The parking garage was so quiet and eerie. We talked about her being my power of attorney and joked that this might turn into an opportunity for her to wield her power. I was relaxed — we both were. Death did not even cross my mind for a nanosecond. The surgery was routine and there was no cause for concern.

The surgery was a success! As I was on the gurney being wheeled to an available private room, I could see Sharon and a couple of my friends sitting a few seats away from the elevator. Once the staff left, they came in. Sharon came closer to the bedside and jokingly said, "Girl, you made it." She was always cheerful and left me feeling hopeful.

Then it all changed. In the middle of our lighthearted conversation, the weird sensation started and quickly escalated to me gasping. Within minutes, there I was, hearing the sounds and seeing the chaos as my life was slipping away.

Hearing the call of 'Code Blue' was surreal. It was as if it wasn't happening to me! I must have been in shock because I was looking at everything like an observer. That's when the awareness swept in, and I thought, "This is it. OMG, all those dreams I have… they are no longer possible. THIS IS IT. Today is the day I die with all that unfinished business."

I wondered if this was what happens when you are about to die, as my mind started to race and I remembered all the things I had written on my to-do list; those things I had convinced myself I'd do 'someday.' I had been so sure I was young and had lots of time to get around to achieving my goals. Now, my life was about to be over and I didn't do any of them. I couldn't take the thought of it anymore and I said a *prayer* and *promised*: "God, if I ever make it, I am going to make sure I live the life I am destined to live and stop waiting to start."

Then, God decided to let me prove it.

As I slowly gathered strength and recovered, I was determined to get all that unfinished business done. It was the birth of my mission, the next stage of my being bold and just going for it with all that I have. I remembered the dream that was a burning desire: to become *The New York Times* best-selling author. So, on a Sunday afternoon, five months after I returned home from the hospital, I decided to just start by taking small steps to map out the week ahead. I called it *The Week Ahead Intentional Productivity Planning Session*.

I mapped out the daily tasks and then scheduled them in my planner. I tracked my morning routine and water intake to ensure that I remained focused on the task. This quickly became a habit and I realized that when things become a habit, they get done. I became relentless in creating the habit and the results were that I had two books written and self-published with a third in draft within a year. I realized that you can't wait for the right time; you have to make it so, challenges and all.

Doing this opened up so many opportunities for me. I joined the local Writing Society and got to be a part of book signings at the local library and bookstores. At one of my book signings, I noticed a woman waiting to speak to me. She always allowed others to come forward and she would hang back until no one else was waiting. She came up and spoke to me almost in a whisper about her dream of writing a book but the one thing that was holding her back was that she was procrastinating. She was curious to find out how I remained consistent enough to finish my book. My response was, "It is all in my habits."

I came to understand that things don't just happen, you have to be intentional and develop positive habits. I looked that lady in the eyes and shared with an open heart that it will not be easy, but if you are committed and keep taking a step forward every day, your goal can be accomplished. I saw how much passion she had but she needed direction and a system that would support her. It was her interest that inspired me to start a Facebook™ group. I felt that if I could help one person realize their dream using the tools I created, it would be very rewarding and the birth of a friendship.

I discovered that good habits are the steering wheel of my life and are a snapshot of my actions. I don't remember paying close attention to them before, but they became essential to my life going forward. I realized that when something becomes a habit, it has a huge impact and ripples out into everything else.

As a result, I called my Facebook group *The Impact of Good Habits* and it is now my mission to help others to be intentional in creating a lifestyle of good habits so they can live a life they desire and are proud of. I am in the process of becoming a productivity and empowerment coach.

I think one of the most overlooked steps to achieving success is scheduling tasks that are actionable, measurable, and manageable. I now fully understood the importance of the quote from Tony Robbins, "If you talk about it, it's a dream. If you envision it, it's possible. But if you schedule it, it's REAL." Many people including myself had always jumped from decision to action, but I realized that creating a schedule to get tasks done is a very crucial step in the process with a higher likelihood of a successful conclusion.

Les Brown always said, "You don't have to be great to get started, but you have to get started to be great." That motivated me to get started and create my 4-Step System called **P.R.E.P**. where I intentionally **P**ause, **R**eflect, **E**valuate, and **P**lan ahead every week. I would *pause,* take a deep breath to ground myself and recite three positive affirmations before starting big projects. I started writing a gratitude note every Sunday and dropping it in my gratitude jar. I want to soak in every bit of my life and experience it fully. I keep my WHY in full focus at all times. Even when the obstacles and challenges come, I remain committed and keep going!

By doing this I feel more prepared and organized and that makes me unstoppable. I have become more intentional about my life. I schedule things, do them, and get results. **P**ause, **R**eflect, **E**valuate, and **P**lan has helped me so much in my personal life as well. I see things from a different perspective and this totally enhances my life. I seize the day; I live a more full and vibrant life.

I have noticed that since my near-death experience in the hospital, a few people have said to me, "You have such great energy!" I agree with them. I have a newfound boldness to go after what I want. I stop waiting to start. I will course correct as necessary but I refuse to allow fear or lack of clarity to keep me from taking the next step toward achieving my goals.

I continue my volunteer efforts. After my traumatic experience, I called the hospital and asked to speak with the Patient Experience department. I told them I was grateful for the work they are doing and I also had a few recommendations to improve things based on my experience. They were willing to listen and invited me to a meeting. I am now a Patient Advisor and have shared my experience in a forum addressing new nurses and doctors. My hope is that by sharing my complications while in the hospital, another patient's life can be saved.

All this makes me quite reflective and I couldn't get this thought out of my mind: "I am here for a reason, I was given a second chance, a rebirth." My sister who preceded me passed away at 18 months old so I never met her. My only child and daughter died at just over 3 years old. At times, I feel those angels on my shoulders. I know it… I feel it and I am so incredibly grateful. I am determined to live out my purpose and to help others… Let this be a promise kept!

IGNITE ACTION STEPS

The 4-Step System **P.R.E.P** helps us to be intentional and develop the *Habit of Week Ahead Planning*. Every Sunday, **P**ause, **R**eflect, **E**valuate, and **P**lan ahead. Remember, as Michael Hyatt said, "What gets scheduled gets done."

P — Pause. Once a week, take the time to write at least one thing you're grateful for. You can write in your gratitude journal or drop a note in a gratitude jar.

R — Reflect. It's so important to reflect and be in touch with what makes your soul sing. Ask yourself reflective questions such as:
What am I grateful for? What has brought joy and laughter in my life? How was I intentional in attending to my self-care? What good lifestyle habits should I work on developing?

E — Evaluate. In order to keep evolving and growing, evaluation is key to measure what is working with the strategies and actions being taken. Are you getting the results you desire? Ask yourself evaluative questions such as:
What was a win for me? What was a challenge? What did I learn from the challenge? How will I use this lesson to improve my life?

P — Plan Ahead

"It takes both a plan and a schedule to get things done."
— Peter Turla

A plan is what. A schedule is when. Schedule it... Do it... Get results. I have found that creating a schedule is one of the most overlooked but critical steps toward achieving success. Before you plan ahead, do the following:

1. Reconnect with your WHY. Ask yourself, why is this important to me? Having a compelling WHY will fuel your progress when you face obstacles.

2. Prioritize by asking, will these actions move me closer to achieving my goals?

3. Have targets that you want to hit each week. Break down each target into an actionable, measurable, and manageable task. Schedule it in your calendar.

4. Have a morning routine that sets the tone for the day and positions you to be your very best.

5. As part of your evening routine, do a calendar sneak peek to look ahead at what your schedule is for the next day.

6. Take S-T-R-E-T-C-H breaks if you are sitting for a long period of time. Set your timer for 90 minutes, when it goes off — get up, stretch, and move around for five minutes. When you return to sitting, set the timer for another 90 minutes.

Pearlette Cassells — Canada
Author, Speaker, Coach
Pearlettecassells.com
Pearlette Cassells
Pearlette Cassells - Author
The Impact of Good Habits

Erasmo Rivera

ERASMO RIVERA

"Desire is the vehicle of life, you are the driver."

¡Hola! Are you going through a tough time? Know that you're not alone. I want my story to inspire you to believe in yourself. Just by taking the time to read this book you are already taking the first step. By growing your mindset and investing in personal development, you will be shown a whole new world. I struggled to believe in my potential for a long time. If you are struggling, this only means the life that you have right now is not the life that you're meant to be living. There's more to it; more for the taking. There's hope. Have courage. Build your confidence to find your true purpose. I hope my story will help you overcome your limiting beliefs and Ignite the way you see the world.

SPEAKING CONFIDENCE

I carry the name of a man I never met; a man who changed the course of my childhood and my life. The passing of my abuelo (grandfather), Erasmo, would set into motion a chain of events that shaped who I am and who I was meant to become. It just took a very long time before I understood the impact of it all.

The Windy City is the place I was born. Chicago, Illinois: home of the Cubs™, the Bears™, and of course the Chicago Bulls™. My parents lived in Chicago for 13 years. In that thirteenth year my father made a decision that put our life on a very interesting path. I remember my father telling my mom,

"Oye mujer nos vamos a México!" meaning "Listen, woman, we are moving to Mexico!" My mother was shocked. She couldn't believe what my father had just said.

At first she thought that he was playing around, but very soon she realized that he was serious, more serious than an unexpected heart attack. "Why do you want to leave? We have built an amazing life here. This is where our children were born, their friends are here, their school is here, and financially speaking we are doing great. Why leave?" My mother asked, concerned with his decision.

My father did not reply. Instead he walked away and came to us, his children. He asked, "Guys, do you want to go to Mexico?" My older brothers, just 11 and 12, said, "No, we don't want to leave, Dad." But my curiosity and my hunger to learn made me say yes; "Yes, Dad! I want to go to Mexico." At 6 years old, all I could visualize was me playing in sunny Mexico. I imagined the hills, the horses, my toys all laid out in the dirt; having fun (of course, I didn't picture the huge mosquitoes; those caught me by surprise.)

I don't know if my father was really interested in our opinion about moving to Mexico, or maybe he was just trying to justify his bold move. My abuelo, who lived in Mexico, had passed recently and my dad knew that it wouldn't take long for my grandmother to follow. When my abuelo died, my father was devastated because he never got to say goodbye to him due to us living in Chicago. He told us it would be different with his mother and shared, "We are moving to Mexico."

Five days after my father's announcement, we arrived at Los Sabinos Guerrero, Mexico; a small village in the deep south with a population of no more than 80 people. Modern life was very limited. There was no live TV, no buildings, no malls, no theaters, poverty was your constant companion, and wealth was nowhere to be found. The change was exciting but I was also scared. To go from one of the biggest cities in the United States to one of the smallest villages in all of Mexico was about as big as transitions come.

I got to learn a lot about Mexican culture and I adapted very well. I learned to live with limited resources and work however I could. To earn money, I collected sand from a river to sell to a construction company. I learned how to ride horses to get around, as there were no paved streets and purchasing a car was almost impossible due to poverty. Working the land was a big part of life there, so I helped grow and harvest corn. Being creative to survive was so important, and no resources could go to waste.

Once, we found a dead armadillo and decided to use its shell to hold the corn as we sowed it in the fields. It taught me to work hard and use everything around me, and within me, to live the best life I could.

A few years later, when I was 11, it was time to come back home to the United States, but not Chicago. This time it was Texas. Before moving to Texas, my parents gave me a choice. I remember my mother standing in front of me with a serious face and telling me, "If you promise to be good, you can stay here in Mexico with your grandparents, and finish your last year of elementary school. I will come pick you up next year during the summer." That was a melody to my ears: no more parents' rules, no more 'do this do that.' All I could think of was playing with my friends all the time, staying up late… I'd be free. I immediately answered, "Sure Mom, I will behave, I promise that you won't have any trouble out of me."

The following year my mother came back as she said she would. My mom returned for two reasons: the first was to pick me up and take me back to Texas with her, and the second was to bury my father. He had gotten very ill during the year that I was in Mexico, and on June 7, 1992, my father died. History was repeating itself. This time it was me who never got to say goodbye. "What have I done?" I thought, feeling sadness and confusion; the same things my father must have felt years before losing his own father.

When my father died, my confidence died with him, and not just because he was the provider. The hero. My hero! My confidence died because of the decision I made. When I decided to stay in Mexico, I saw the easy way out. I saw small obstacles to jump through and a life with no restrictions. I denied myself enjoying the last year of my father's life because I wanted comfort.

Making that decision burdened me with guilt and crushed my confidence. I believed that every decision I was going to make would be the wrong one. I became a quiet kid and antisocial. In school I used to sit all the way in the back. I hated reading, and whenever the teacher called on me, I struggled through it. I felt incompetent.

Being in Mexico for most of my elementary years meant that I developed a strong Spanish accent and when I returned to the USA, it stayed with me. I felt like a stranger and didn't belong. I went through middle school and high school without a voice; I became a follower instead of a leader.

Being shy became comfortable for me and I settled into the mindset, "This is just how life is. Life is hard." I became a people pleaser because I feared judgment from others if I made the wrong decision. The experience with my father taught me that making bold decisions for yourself can have devastating consequences.

Yet, this wasn't who I wanted to be. I always tried to improve myself and enjoyed personal development but I needed certainty before I would follow through. Phil McGraw said, "Sometimes you make the right decision, sometimes you make the decision right." I wanted to make the decision right and I wanted to be a leader, not a follower.

For the next decade I was just living an average life, stuck in a bubble of settling for whatever came up. I didn't try, I didn't know what I could accomplish. I was simply accepting the crumbs that were offered in my 'so-called' great life.

One day, while I was working in the same job I'd been doing for about 19 years, I was scrolling through my phone looking for some music to play and I came across a thumbnail. In the thumbnail was a man wearing a suit. I have always been attracted to suits so it caught my interest. I clicked on the video to see what it was all about. His name was Jim Rohn and he was giving a motivational speech. I laughed, thinking, "This is nonsense, this guy doesn't know what he's talking about." But then he said something that made me keep listening, "If you don't like how things are, change it!" He followed by saying, "Don't wish it was easier, wish it was better." Wow! Those were some strong words but I still wasn't convinced that I had that kind of control over my life.

When Jim's video ended, it automatically started another one. This time it was the motivational speaker, Les Brown. I was intrigued already, so I let the video play while I was listening. His words made an impact on me as he said, "Other people's opinion of you does not have to become your reality." Wow! That quote gave me a green light to change my life.

I started watching more videos, learned how to read better, and began to love it. I learned about goal setting. I poured myself into personal development, and I changed! I discovered I loved to speak and to use my voice to serve others; to help them believe in themselves and build their own personal confidence.

Thinking differently and expanding my mindset was a new challenge. Once again I was excited but scared of the unknown; reliving the feelings I had as a preteen of making a life-changing choice. I had a new adventure, of going to the next level in personal growth, and I was willing to crush it. But I couldn't do it without the secret ingredient: Confidence.

I discovered that confidence is a muscle that can be built every day. If we put in the commitment, the time, and the effort, confidence will grow on us and if we stay consistent, confidence will never leave.

Change is good, but for every action there is a reaction. When I decided to change and become 'the better self,' the best version of me, I started meeting new people, learning new habits, and discovering mentorship. Believe me when I say this, a mentor is the express route to success. A mentor will save you a lot of headaches, a lot of money, and a lot of time.

One day, one of my mentors said, "Everything has a price. If you decide to change, be ready because you will sacrifice your time, your friends, your family, and your God! Are you ready?" I laughed and disagreed, convinced that it was nonsense, and that this man was exaggerating. I naively believed I would make it work, moving forward and growing without sacrificing that much.

I was wrong! I slowly started trading Netflix™ for books, went from watching the news to watching a webinar, and started spending a lot of time feeding my brain with knowledge. My circle changed. I was hanging around very successful growth mindset individuals, and my old friends started to slowly fade away. At first they would call me everyday, then that reduced to three days a week, until they stopped calling as we had less and less in common. I missed special occasions and important dates because I wanted to go to self-development seminars out of town. And guess what day most of the seminars were on? Sundays. So I had to miss church. My mentor was right, success comes with sacrifice.

One day, watching Les Brown delivering a speech called, "It's Not Over Until I Win," I decided that I wanted to do what Les was doing: to be a motivational speaker. I started looking for ways to learn how to develop my public speaking skills. I found a club named Toastmasters International ™, and joined.

To my surprise I discovered that speaking and sharing knowledge was my passion. I found out that I was worthy and I was willing to invest in myself. Today I am mentored by John C. Maxwell and his team, and am experiencing something that had never crossed my mind and I never saw as possible: being mentored by Mr. Les Brown himself. I am honored to be his mentee and to continue his legacy of helping others find their voice.

Ladies and gentlemen, it *has* been a difficult journey. But it's okay, it's called life. One of the major mistakes I made was to allow my life events to shut me down. I was nowhere near reaching my potential. I couldn't find my voice, I couldn't speak with confidence. I didn't trust my reason for being here. But as Wayne Dyer said, "If you change the way you look at things, the things you look at change."

Now I know that each one of us has unlimited potential. Life allows us to never stop growing and when we grow in ourselves, in turn we help others grow in themselves. You can have whatever life you want, you just have to constantly keep growing, moving forward, and going after your goals. Confidence is the secret ingredient to moving forward. You have all the confidence you need inside of you; you just have to discover it by taking action. Let go of limiting beliefs and trust yourself. You can overcome anything that stops you from having that life you want.

Ask yourself, what things would you like to change in your life? Take the first step, read a book, take a course, learn a new skill, find a mentor. Investing in yourself will bring great returns to you, your family, and the world. Follow your passion and your dreams, discover the better version of yourself. There will be times when you will want to throw in the towel but stand your ground. Be willing to grow constantly and never forget that success comes with sacrifice, but that sacrifice will be paid with interest.

You got this!

Ignite Action Steps

I learned this strategy throughout my personal development journey and I want to share it with you. It was passed on to me by one of my mentors. I adopted his knowledge and named it, "The DDT Strategy." DO DIFFICULT THINGS!

In the beginning it is uncomfortable, but once you apply it over and over, it is super easy and a very powerful way to build confidence.

Do difficult things. When you feel your face getting hot, when you feel the sweat on your forehead starting to emerge, when your heart starts going a thousand miles an hour, do difficult things. As long as it is ethical and you are not hurting anyone (including yourself), apply it.

The DDT Strategy doesn't have to be hard. It could be speaking to the stranger next to you, reaching out to other entrepreneurs for business advice, speaking to the girl or guy that you always admired, or waking up 20 minutes earlier than usual.

How about challenging yourself harder, taking it a step further? Take out your phone right now and go live on social media or YouTube™, or speak live on Clubhouse. Create a YouTube channel, and if you know two languages, then create two! I speak English and Spanish, so I created two channels: Teachable Mindset and Empresarios 1.0.

I even have a website where you will find some products that will help you be more confident (see the resources page.)

Do not settle for crumbs; instead tell yourself these words, "Because I don't want to do it, I am going to do it," and immediately take action. Don't let the momentum escape you because it might never come back. When you start doing small challenges out of your comfort zone, you will start growing.

Happy journey!

Erasmo Rivera — United States
Motivational Speaker, Confidence Coach, Author
www.erasmorivera.net
www.erasmoacademy.com
Erasmo Rivera
erasmo_100

Katherine Vrastak

KATHERINE VRASTAK

"When you listen to your inner voice and speak the message of self-love, LISTEN, for it will be how you spread love to the world."

This chapter is dedicated to the souls yearning to truly and deeply fall in love with themselves. I wish that you, the reader, will be inspired to create a sacred vow to love yourself truly and deeply; to open up the many doors of unlimited possibilities you have. To truly love yourself, you must forgive yourself for not having all the answers and accept asking for help. Love rewires you to see the pure, light, and innocence that you are. Let the light in you remove the darkness. Throw your ego aside by showing love which will soften it; you are worth it. Love your life with much gratitude because the Universe always has your back! Be who you came here to be, and radiate LOVE.

SCREAMING SILENTLY

On a very cold, crisp winter day, I was awakened out of a deep sleep just four days after my 13th birthday. The early morning began with a huge sense of fear that raged within my gut but totally could not be voiced. In fact, that fear trembled in my belly so fiercely, it paralyzed me, leaving me unable to even speak. Overwhelmed by the intense uncertainty inside of me — like a volcano ready to erupt — I could not help myself and began to uncontrollably sob. As I sat in my grandmother's favorite La-Z-boy(™) chair, listening to the activity in the house, while everyone was getting ready to depart, I could not stop crying.

I had a huge sense within me that this trip had to be stopped. I tried to delay the departure. Some deep intuition, my sixth sense, was screaming that something tragic was going to happen. However, everything proceeded anyway; I was unsuccessful. Everyone — my mother, my brother, my two best friends, and their parents — did end up leaving, going out into the storm. Just my grandmother and I were left sitting drinking tea, praying for their safe return home.

A few hours later, both my grandmother and I were horrified by hearing the heart-shattering news on the radio that four adults had been killed in a vehicle accident taking out an entire bridge. My gut feeling was confirmed a few hours later by the police who arrived at our door to notify us that both my mother, brother, and the other two parents were dead, and my grandmother had to go and identify their bodies. The horrific accident was caused by a transport driver who fell asleep behind the wheel and killed all of them instantly. My two best friends, spared by the grace of God, survived. It was a sad and terrible way to discover that my premonitions were indeed accurate. It was a devastating way to discover that my inner knowing was aware that that would be the last day I saw my mother and brother alive.

Growing up as a child with a sixth sense, living with the guilt that I could not prevent that horrific tragedy, was a huge responsibility that cost me much happiness over the years. I suffered senseless unresolved forgiveness not only for not speaking up, but for failing to listen to my inner intuition.

In hindsight, it is no surprise they did not listen to me. I was always being silenced, especially by my single mother. A survivor of childhood trauma herself, she would take out her frustrations on me (often physically) telling me I was 'in the wrong place at the wrong time.' If she discovered I had spoken up in school, she would hide me away; likewise keeping me hidden from social gatherings to 'protect me.' There were no birthday parties, no sleepovers at friends' houses. Any socialization I could muster would take the form of playing guidance counselor to my friends; a means of proving my value, since I was constantly left to question whether I had any. My outer voice was soon so quiet, people would have to lean in to hear it. My inner voice, the whispers from God within my soul, were still loud as ever, but instead, I let it manifest in the form of being a keen listener who put others' sorrows before her own.

I settled into the role of caretaker and supporter, focusing all my energies on being a source of strength for those around me, even if it was to my own detriment. There was NO choice but to be resilient, grow up quickly, and be the adult in the home at only age 13. I took on many roles and responsibilities while caring for my very fragile grandmother with a weak heart and diabetes.

In taking care of her I had to be empathetic and constantly resourceful; helping to save her life when she had heart attacks and learning to do the banking, cooking, cleaning, and work to support the needs in the home all while still getting an education. I was also caring for a disabled border while working three part-time jobs and attending high school. I remained a straight A student, always striving to be my best. Yet, I was also my worst critic, refusing to see my best as 'good enough,' no matter what my efforts were.

Nothing could have prepared me for the moment that I knew I was going to be orphaned five days before Christmas when my grandmother died. Unfortunately, I had a sixth sense about this death too but could not prevent it, as she was in the hospital and died suddenly of a brain aneurysm. This time I was feeling more empowered and instrumental in assisting my grandmother in getting her affairs in order before she passed, which gave me some confidence. Listening to the inner voice, the sixth sense, had allowed me to do good things for her in those final days. But that confidence could only scratch the surface of how I carried myself. The deep pain from losing my last family member, my lifeline, left my heart shattered in pieces and kept me from getting close to anyone.

My solution at the time was throwing myself into my studies, using time others may have been socializing, to complete three years' worth of high school studies in one year at a private school. As a youth who had grown up very fast, I took a landslide into bulimia and depression after completing high school as I went off to Bible College immediately following high school to follow what I felt was my mother's wish. I realized I wasn't treating my life like it was mine to live. I had been trying to get the love and approval from everyone which I didn't get from my own mother while she was alive. I even ran off chasing my mother's dream of becoming a missionary, but it came to an abrupt halt. I was enrolled in a one-year missionary program to work with the Billy Graham crusade in England. When out of the blue, while acting in a role as an abused mother in a drama, I experienced a trigger that shook me to my core. I realized at that moment, I could not continue being on autopilot, just pretending that I was okay anymore. I came to the realization that I was acting out my own life and could not separate my emotions but rather was caught in the thrust of them. Immediately it became transparent that I required time to heal from my traumatic childhood experiences. The Bible College dean was the first person that heard my screams for help and realized I had to take time to heal. A close friend came to help me return back home. I left my dream behind of being a missionary to follow in my mother's footsteps, so I could begin doing my own grief and deep trauma healing work.

My personal self-discovery healing journey motivated me to move out of my hometown, to start a new beginning. I realized I did not want to continue in my mother's footsteps after all. Indeed, it was up to me to STOP the cycle from repeating. I actually stopped being silenced and instead surrendered and continued to reach out for resources and specialized help. For the first time, I used my VOICE and asked for help, never looking back only forward to find inner peace. Giving myself permission to focus on myself showed genuine self-compassion which involved finding self-forgiveness for NOT listening to my intuition before.

I had been so numb to my past and by playing a role that portrayed a mother of a child who had been badly abused, I realized I was *that* child. I had to take time to heal. I couldn't do it any longer; stay and pretend everything was okay when it just wasn't. So, I took a stand and made a conscious choice to do my OWN healing journey to let go and heal from the inside out.

Taking responsibility and choosing not to project my pain from my childhood was my first priority. It took me on a journey first to get a broken nose repaired, which had been done to me as a child by my own mother. This started my self-love journey where I learned that I must forgive myself first for not having all the answers and accept asking for help. This was an Ignite Moment and where I finally took time to heal my physical appearance. I then began loving the person I looked at in the mirror. My personal healing journey evolved where I began to speak my TRUTH. It brought me to my life purpose of helping other trauma survivors too. It was a deep self-love journey, in fact, it began to open many doors of Ignite Moments.

Choosing to not dwell on the past, instead to let go and learn to embrace my innocence and forgive myself for only doing the best I could with what I knew, brought forth deep forgiveness and a better understanding for others. Making a conscious choice to continue to be passionate about giving back brought me to complete my postsecondary studies in social services. Later I became certified in energy healing modalities, shamanism, and then neuro linguistic programming.

Devoting many years to first saving my own life from the entrapment of the darkness from grief and trauma, I chose consciously to become diligent in helping end the mental health stigma for others. Using my own life as a catalyst to be the change in the world, as once living in the legacy of my mother, who had always silenced me, meant the voice that could speak my truth remained quiet, hidden under unceasing efforts to prove I could be of value to everyone else. I ended up doing several jobs from a place of service but only on autopilot, not fully present, as my cup was empty, and my heart had a huge void. I realized I was always trying to fill the deep longing to feel love but always came up feeling empty, as I fell into all my old habits. As I got older, I abandoned my own needs, aiming to serve and please everyone. I worked so hard all the time; I never took time to look within. Whether I was in desperate need of surgery, pregnant with a child, dangerously ill, or emotionally devastated, I refused to allow attention to be placed on my own well-being. I was always taking care of others, convinced I either didn't deserve or wouldn't get the support or love of those around me: my husband, my family, my colleagues, or the friends for whom I was always 'the rock.' I numbed my emotions by just being in perpetual motion, however my body kept the score and it caught up to me, nearly killing me several times. I decided to take back my life and choose to LIVE.

Two of my favorite quotes by Les Brown are: "You have to be willing to allow the person you are today to DIE so that you can give birth to the person you are meant to become." The second is, "Forgive yourself for your faults and your mistakes and move on." These two profound messages have shown me that healing is a journey: a process that takes many tries and much effort. They also remind me to let go and surrender to vulnerability and transparency which has been the path to my own journey of self-love.

The Bible College incident was my first step onto the path of healing, but it would take much longer and much more effort, before I could really begin to give my inner voice an outer voice. Once I began to give myself love and compassion, where there was very little as a child growing up, then I was able to open my heart to invite love all around me and stop pushing it away. Discovering this deep love for myself made me realize I am rare, unique, and I matter; choosing to never give up. I now choose to value myself enough to step into my greatness! Like Les always says, "You must remain focused on your journey to greatness."

Thankfully, after forgiving myself, my healing has also allowed me to forgive my mother as she truly did the best she could with all that she had. I know that she loved me in her own way. I am here in this world because of the love my mother had for me, and she even gave me my life.

Today, I live constantly in Ignite Moments as I allow for self-love and self-forgiveness to rule my perspective. It has opened me to both love and forgiveness. When you listen to your inner voice and speak the message of self-love, LISTEN, for it will be how you spread love to the world. I have incrementally learned to trust using my own voice, entrusting my friends to appreciate the value they place in me. I am continually asking for help, reaching out for resources, and learning to stand in my own empowerment with both my heart and head in alignment. I desire to help others reach the profound power of forgiveness in themselves. I want them to let go finally of all the anger, sadness, fear, guilt, and shame that has taken up resonance in their body. Les shares, "Ask for help not because you are weak, but because you want to remain strong."

I have always been a soul desiring to make an impact on the world and to be a positive mentor for many; it was my life purpose since I was 10 years of age. However, throughout the years, limiting beliefs and an unresolved need for self-forgiveness kept me shackled in fear of NOT using my voice, resulting in me not living up to my fullest potential. Once I decided to make the conscious choice to forgive myself for holding onto all the stories of my past, I then could embrace telling my stories with love in my heart. I choose, over and over again, to reject being a hostage to my mind and instead return home to my heart, fostering the most healing love possible. As I reflect on the messages of my past, I realize that my inner voice and powerful intuition had been putting me in the right place at the right time, all along.

I encourage you to commit to a sacred vow of loving yourself from the inside out. Let go of attachments to what others think of you. Love yourself by showing self-compassion so your self-confidence will skyrocket. We seek what we love the most so learn to listen to your inner voice. Asking for help is also a commitment to loving yourself. When you become empowered to make a commitment to love yourself, life always loves you back. Life then becomes magical. Trust yourself to follow your intuition, as it is always your best guide to making the healthiest choices for you. Rescue yourself first as you are the only one that can. Create a new routine that creates peace, love, and growth with healthy boundaries. When we truly love ourselves, we shine and bring love to those around us too. One of my favorite quotes from Les is, "Accept responsibility for your life. Know that it is you who will get you where you want to go, no one else."

The quote that I now choose to live by, which is my own is: When you listen to your inner voice and speak the message of self-love, LISTEN, for it will be how you spread love to the world.

IGNITE ACTION STEPS

- Write a sacred vow to yourself that you will love yourself truly and deeply and repeat it daily twice.

- Sit daily for 10 minutes with your hands on your heart, breathing in for four counts, holding for seven, and exhaling for eight. Let the emotions have a voice by letting them just be what they are, not getting attached to the story. As the emotions move through you like a wave, state the ho'oponopono prayer: **"I'm sorry, please forgive me, I love you, thank you,"** several times. This will help shift your energy and even release emotion that was perhaps stuck and needs to come up for healing. Every tear shed is releasing 72 toxins, so welcome the release as it washes like a wave through you while you keep repeating the prayer.
- If you have a past with trauma and loss, do inner child healing work by writing letters to your inner child with your less dominant hand, then burning them. This can really release the stuck emotions in your cells and free you. It helps to have a picture of you as a child in front of you as you do this.
- Give yourself self-compassion by listing five things every day about yourself that you are grateful for. Stand in front of the mirror and state "I am" statements that are empowering even if you are working on believing them, these words, thoughts, and consistent behavior patterns have power! Any habit takes a minimum of 21 days, so stick with it.
- Doing a daily grounding exercise first thing in the morning such as Tai Chi, walking outdoors in nature, or doing Qigong are all very healing and nurturing and shift the stuck energy so your heart can remain open to unlimited possibilities.

Healing past trauma is a journey not a destination. Love you as Perfectly Imperfect.

Katherine Vrastak — Canada
Speaker, Author, eNLP Certified Practitioner
www.sacredrootscoaching.com
4Sacred_Roots
chatty37718-701-3820
Kate Vrastak

PATRICIA BARNES

"Your voice is powerful. Speak up and you can change the world."

This chapter is dedicated to everyone who has silenced their voice: anyone who doesn't like the sound of their voice, runs from public speaking, or doesn't feel qualified to speak to elite audiences. Whether you're a first-generation college graduate, a professional who feels their speech doesn't match up to other colleagues, or someone who believes their speech isn't eloquent enough to change the world or add value to important conversations, today is the day we say, "No more!" Together we will find empowerment, so you know your voice matters. Be encouraged to speak up and allow yourself to break free from insecurities and fears. Activate your voice and Ignite the hunger within you. Shine bright like the star you were born to be and let the world hear your unique voice.

'SPEAKING FRENCH' AND BEING HEARD

"Before I formed you in the womb I knew you, before
you were born I set you apart."
— Jeremiah 1:5.

No one said the journey to being set apart would be easy. I was born to stand out. My grand entrance to the world came with a rare medical emergency when my mother's placenta detached from her womb. The doctor told her that her baby may not get enough oxygen or nutrients and wouldn't thrive academically. Defiantly, I proved the opposite was true because I have academically excelled by being an honor roll student, making the dean's list in college, graduating at the top of my class, winning several academic awards, and graduating successfully from nursing school, one of the most challenging college programs available.

An interesting part of my background is that my grandparents were sharecroppers from North Carolina. Education wasn't a big factor. My grandfather has a fifth-grade education and my mom didn't finish high school. My family speaks broken English. My dad speaks 'French,' a southern accent mixed with Baltimorean slang. If someone tries to correct him, he just smiles and says, "It's not my fault if you don't understand French." Naturally, I speak like my family, the phenomenal people who raised me with a southern charm and Baltimorean flare.

My loving family paved the way for me to have the opportunity to excel in school. Until I was about 14 years old, I was raised in a predominantly white neighborhood peppered with other cultural groups. One of my teachers in elementary school noticed the way I spoke was 'different,' so after my 'normal class' I would spend time with a tutor for English and reading. That was the first time I became aware that my family's style of speaking wasn't easily understood.

I was naturally shy in school. My family could sit in the same room for hours without saying a word so speaking up in groups was hard to adjust to. Throughout the years I became even more afraid to say certain words because I recognized I didn't speak 'proper enough.' I learned that my family members aren't great spellers, have limited vocabulary, and find it hard to pronounce several words. Sometimes our sentences are choppy and it's hard to follow what we're saying. We mumble our words or try to say a word and stutter until we can say the word right. Because of this, I never raised my hand to ask questions, vocalized my thoughts, shared my viewpoints, or answered my teachers' questions. I avoided saying certain words I knew I couldn't pronounce correctly. I let my voice stay silent.

I was never ashamed of my roots. I appreciate who I am and where I come from. I was the first person in my immediate family to go to college. However, I felt unconfident, had a fear of public speaking, and avoided being social due to anxiety when meeting new people. I was embarrassed to open my mouth because some words I pronounced 'sounded funny' and seemed to overshadow my accomplishments and how hard I have worked.

Some people would ask me, "Why do you talk like that?" "What are you saying?" "Why do you pronounce words funny?" Over time, that led to even more insecurities like resenting the sound of my voice and feeling like I couldn't express myself well. Truth is, if you continue to hide from sharing in a way that scares you, and run from your fears and insecurities around your voice, you will never become a confident or well-spoken individual. You must speak up and speak more to improve your speaking skills.

I always admired both my mom and my grandmother. My mom is a nursing assistant who advocates for her patients to get the best care; my grandmother was a caregiver and had a loving touch. I was inspired by them to pursue nursing as I remember watching them taking care of others so kindly. I enjoyed helping people, but at the same time I was soul-searching and realizing I wanted to live my life's purpose. Even if I didn't want to speak up, I still had the desire to serve others somehow.

I wanted to obtain a higher education in nursing, so I explored different nursing options and wondered if I should go into nursing education to become a college professor or a nurse practitioner. The only problem was that I truly believed that I was born to stand apart. I had to be honest with myself about what I was born to do. The more I thought about it, the more I realized I wanted to help people in some other way. That meant I had to learn to find my voice from within and discover my true purpose.

I found that unexpected calling when I went on a mission trip to South Africa. I pushed past my comfort zone by flying and traveling alone then living in a hostel with 10 women I'd never met before. Taking a mission trip was something I had always wanted to do and mastering those risks allowed me to accomplish the goal to serve and help the less fortunate, struggling populations. I wasn't sure what was ahead, but I just had this feeling that something great was going to happen.

We went hiking over 2,000 feet. I'm afraid of heights. I had no idea what was transpiring but the women around me were ready to quit, so I ended up encouraging them. I told them, "We are going to make it to the mountaintop." WE DID IT! I didn't realize my voice was being *heard* as I was encouraging my fellow hikers to not quit or give in to their fears.

As I was taking in the views, I overheard a videographer tell one of the ladies, "Patricia is a motivational speaker." I thought I was overcoming my fear of heights, but instead was conquering my greatest fear of all. I was using my gift, my unique voice, to bring empowerment to others. When I was serving people who needed me, I was no longer afraid to speak.

I accepted my gift as a motivational speaker, which is when I started to understand the power of speaking up and using your voice. I decided I no longer wanted to be the little girl from elementary school, the girl I carried inside me all the way through college and even as a career woman, who ran from public speaking!

The next step was acknowledging the fears and insecurities associated with why I ran from public speaking. I evaluated myself; went deep to figure out where those fears started and why they had taken control for so long. Then, I asked myself what steps I was willing to take to move toward my purpose.

I joined Toastmasters International™ and committed to presenting 10 speeches. Each topic was something I'm passionate about. I discussed overcoming pain, fears, and insecurities. I talked about healthy living including nutrition and fitness. I even spoke about self-actualization: controlling your emotions, thinking outside the box, loving yourself, and finding financial freedom.

I was voted the best speaker for five out of 10 speeches. Not bad for a girl who was afraid each time. Fear caused me to tremble and stutter, gave me bubble guts, and revealed every symptom of nervousness. But I love a challenge, so I allowed fear to motivate me to embrace public speaking.

Moving forward in my speaking career became intentional. It was about embracing my identity and personality by loving my voice and speaking slang to connect with people who can relate to me. At the same time, it was about having confidence to speak with people who are well-spoken. I wanted to be comfortable with who I am and how I share my message, both properly and in *my* own unique way.

After watching the reality TV show *Love and Marriage Huntsville*, cast member Latisha inspired me to seek a speech pathologist to see if I had any speech impediments. Latisha shared a similar insecurity as a southern woman from Alabama who is college educated but doesn't feel well-spoken like her colleagues. Education wasn't a major factor in her family. She is quiet because she doesn't want to sound unintelligent, has issues articulating her thoughts, and doesn't feel smart enough. Watching her sometimes felt like seeing myself on the screen. When she went to see a speech pathologist, the therapist told Latisha, "Speech is not intelligence." Instantly, I felt that in my spirit. The way we speak doesn't determine how smart we are. In fact, we are so smart when we are born that we automatically pick up the language nuances of the people that raise us and the people we spend the most time with.

On New Year's Eve, I visited a speech pathologist. On the edge of a brand-new year, I was excited to make progress and move toward my purpose. I held my breath and my shoulders were tense as the therapist read me my results. That stress became relief when it was determined I didn't have any intellectual issues.

Yet, I still had work to do; work I keep up to this day. I have to retrain my language to code-switching when appropriate to standard English from slang. I was shown how to breathe better (talk on the exhale) and clearly articulate certain words by slowing down. I use a metro timer app to help while reading out loud and collect my thoughts before speaking.

After my six sessions I had an epiphany moment: I am way too hard on myself! I was stuck focusing on the past and not who I am becoming from personal development; reliving embarrassing moments when I mispronounced a word instead of being realistic that I am a work in progress. It's normal to mess up or say words incorrectly especially if I'm tired. I give myself grace when I need to start a sentence over, reminding myself, "At least you're putting yourself out there." This resilience is something I have actually always had. Even when I was younger and more afraid, I never allowed my own insecurities, fears, negativity, or constructive criticism from others stop me from excelling in life. I would stutter my way through a presentation if that meant I passed the class. I was willing to look like a fool to win and grow through the process.

I can't help thinking of my dad and the 'French' that he taught me to speak. I can smile and respect the pride he had in who he was. But the truth is, to be heard I needed to learn to speak my language better. Sometimes, the truth hurts, but if you can listen to the truth to develop and filter out the negativity, you will evolve and become better. If you allow good people to help you, you can grow and develop real confidence.

Today, I'm committed to becoming the best version of myself. I am working toward being well-spoken and improving my communication skills. I have promised myself I am going to speak up! My voice defends the helpless, encourages the hopeless, and blazes trails never walked before! I am currently speaking, coaching, blogging, co-authoring books, and inspiring others one-on-one. My goals are to bring everything into alignment, work on a solo book, and show people that every single voice matters.

Les Brown said, "You don't have to be great to get started, but you have to start to be great." Tell yourself you will become better! Shout louder over those negative thoughts because that's how you turn insecure thoughts into confidence.

I believe we all have the capacity to create positive change with our voice. A divine message exists in every one of us. Use your powerful voice, and you will discover that like mine, your voice is extraordinary! The ability to share and use your voice will set the captives free and move mountains. Owning who you are, sharing authentically, and inspiring others is something we all *can* do. I encourage you to step forth, speak out, and Ignite the hunger in you!!

Ignite Action Steps

A goal without a plan won't work. Actively work on articulating better, owning your voice, and speaking with confidence.

Here are a few helpful tips to articulate better:

- Study great orators to learn from them.
- Record yourself talking to critique and improve your speech.
- Allow people to correct your speech without being offended.
- Don't feel embarrassed to ask people how to pronounce words you don't know how to pronounce. Challenge yourself to learn how to say the word even if it's difficult. Say it out loud until you pronounce it correctly.
- When someone says a word you don't know the meaning of, take a mental note to look up the word and/or ask the person what it means. This will help to expand your vocabulary.
- Be honest about what you don't know. If you don't understand what someone is saying, ask them. There is no shame in it. It's how we learn and grow.
- Learn new words on dictionary.com.
- Read one to three books per month.
- Speak consistently. Listen to what you're saying and afterward take time to reflect on how you could have articulated better.
- Pay attention to when people seem confused about what you are saying. Find ways to change so people understand. If you use slang, make sure you can explain what you mean.

Own your unique voice:

- Speak from your heart. Figure out your uniqueness that makes you stand out from others. People will love you for you and what you bring differently to the conversation.

Speak with confidence:

- Practice makes you feel less anxious. Remember, when you speak it's not about us but the sincere desire to help others. When you think like that, it can be easier to release nervousness and perfectionism.

- Don't apologize if you mess up, just correct your thoughts, and keep going.
- Everything you need to be successful is already inside of you, but you must decide that no matter how hard it gets or no matter how embarrassed you may feel, you WILL NEVER QUIT!
- You must speak up even if your voice shakes or you stutter; even if no one will listen or if you don't feel qualified, ready, or secure.
- Don't allow yourself or anyone else to make you feel inadequate. When you start something new, the old insecure you will try to creep into your mind. You may start thinking, "Maybe I'm not good enough. Maybe what people say about me is true. Maybe I'm not well-spoken, maybe I can't do this?" But being a winner is about your mindset so set yours to win!

Loving your voice:

- We all have our own unique style; find yours.
- Turn your insecurities into confidence. Accept your unique accent and voice. Fall in love with how you speak.

Patricia Barnes — United States
Speaker, Blogger, Founder of Go Patty LLC
gopatty.com
🛈 gopattybrand

Felecia Froe

FELECIA FROE, M.D.

"In this life filled with options, choose responsibly — your life depends on it."

I would like to inspire you to recognize your true desires; to move toward what you want. Positive and negative events and relationships in our lives propel us. You always have a choice. My goal is for you to improve your sense of personal responsibility, in all aspects of your life, empowering you to reach for all that you desire.

DOING WELL AND DOING GOOD

My mother was the kind of woman who knew how to take care of things. I am who I am today because of her. One of my earliest memories of my mother was in our two-bedroom brick house in an all Black neighborhood in Tuskegee, Alabama. It was the late 1960s. My sister and I were playing in our bedroom, jumping from the top of the bunk bed to the floor, climbing back up and doing it again, laughing and making a lot of noise. It was dark outside. We were probably supposed to be getting ready for bed, but...

I went to the bathroom and ran back to play with my sister without turning off the light. Mom, sitting in the living room with its mint green walls, could see the bathroom from her chair. She yelled to me to turn off the light. I hurried back, turned it off, and went back to play. Mom yelled again, "I told you to turn off that light!" I *had* turned off the light. What did I do wrong? I was all of 6, but clearly recall my confusion. She then called me into the living room and apologized for yelling at me. She further explained, quietly and somewhat shakily, that she was upset with my father. Back then, at such a young age, I didn't put all the pieces together, but it was a pivotal moment in my future to come.

I was in the third grade when my father graduated from veterinary school and moved us to Terre Haute, Indiana in the Midwest. We bought a house in a White neighborhood, and for the first time in my life I was confronted with the fact I was Black. People moved out when we moved in. Dad told me it was because they didn't want to live near Black people. It wasn't just White people we had problems with though; Black children at school didn't like me because we didn't live on 'their side' of town. It was the first time I learned I was 'different' from others and the beginning of feeling that I didn't belong and wasn't enough.

In the sixth grade, while running on the playground, I ran into a boy. We both fell. He got up and said that he was going to 'get me' after school. My sister and I walked home from school, afraid. Nothing happened. I told my mother about it, and she said that if a fight happened to make sure I got the first hit. She told me to hit him in the head. It was her way of making sure I would always protect myself.

Several weeks later, on the Friday before Christmas break, my sister and I were walking home, in the opposite direction of most of the Black kids in our school. A group of kids ran up behind us and I saw him. He was no bigger than me, coming out of the crowd with his brown jacket and medium afro. My sister was beside me and I handed her my books. There were about 20 kids around, my sister later told me, laughing, that she had counted them. He started taking off his jacket and all of a sudden Mom's words came back to me: "Get the first hit." While he was taking his jacket off, I swung at his head and struck him in the left temple. He fell, then jumped up and tried to hit me. He missed. He turned and ran back in the direction of his home. The crowd dispersed, I took my books from my sister, and we walked the remaining two and a half blocks home. I was shaky and still scared but I also had a feeling of accomplishment and triumph. By the time Christmas break was over and school restarted, the incident had been forgotten by everyone else, but it left me feeling proud and with a new sense of confidence.

Growing up, I loved hearing my dad's stories about animals he cared for and loved all of the animals we had had as children. I loved going to the pig farms to give the baby pigs their medicine; Dad even let me hold them while he put the medicine in their mouths. One day, early in my senior year of high school, I tentatively went into his bedroom where he was sitting on the side of the bed, but something told me he had not had a good day. After I blurted out that I wanted to be a veterinarian, he looked at me calmly and said, "If you're going to go to school for that long, you are going to be a doctor." From that day forward, I was convinced I was going to medical school.

I had the same group of friends from seventh grade through junior year of high school. I was on the tennis team, volleyball team, had a boyfriend — all the things that go with high school. But the summer before senior year Dad was transferred to another state. I was upset that right before the funnest year, when I could be one of the top dogs with all of my friends, they wanted me in a new school where I knew no one. I talked to my best friend and her parents, who said they'd let me live with them for my senior year. When I suggested it to my parents, you would have thought I wanted to divorce them. They were not having it. My mother was especially vehement, with her finger in my face telling me that I was going to move. We moved. I started at my new high school, taking the classes that I needed to be premed in college, while also working outside of school and having it count for academic credit. I tried to like the school; I joined the tennis team and made some friends. But I was not happy. All I could think about was leaving and the day I could make my own decisions.

For graduation, my parents gave me a trip to Europe with the People to People Ambassador program. With about 20 other high school graduates, I traveled to Moscow, Poland, The Netherlands, France, and England, having the chance to live for several days at a time with local families. I learned about different customs, cultures, and diversity, and this is where my love of traveling and freedom started.

When I got back to the US, it was time to get ready for college. I was accepted into Northwestern University in Chicago and the University of Missouri in Columbia. I really wanted to go to Northwestern, excited I'd been accepted to such a prestigious school. Dad decided the cost was too high, so off I headed, disappointed, to Columbia. I had been a relatively 'good' girl throughout high school. That changed in college. I partied a lot. My major was biology, so I had a heavy schedule of tough classes. My mother warned against taking all these classes at once, but I didn't listen; it was what my advisor had recommended. Only with the help of tutors was I able to make it through my first two years. The struggle had taken its toll. I was now in my early 20s thinking about the rest of my life. It seemed medicine would be all consuming. Could I get married, have a family and the life that I imagined I wanted, *and* be a doctor? I had my doubts and people around me supported the idea that having a family and being a doctor were not compatible. Ultimately, I decided to leave the university and go to pharmacy school. Being a pharmacist seemed much more aligned with the life that I envisioned.

I spent the first year of pharmacy school at the St. Louis College of Pharmacy. I traveled 250 miles to St. Louis alone by bus with what I needed to furnish my dormitory. My parents were in the midst of a divorce, so my needs and wants were not a priority for them. I was on my own finally, but I was also disappointed that my parents left me to handle everything on my own. I was afraid of being solely on my own and responsible for my decisions. It was the first time I realized that as hard as it was, you can do this!

Pharmacy school bored me. Medical school was calling again. I had a decision to make: finish another year of pharmacy, or leave to get a general undergraduate degree. If I finished pharmacy school, I could make money to help support me through medical school. Mom encouraged me to take the risk while Dad advised against it, concerned I would not get into medical school. Ultimately, I chose to leave pharmacy and get a BA in Chemistry. I set about enrolling in the program and figured out what I needed to do to apply to medical school.

About nine months later, I was in my evening chemistry lab when I saw my family in the hallway. What had happened? Who had died? I walked out nervously as my dad handed me a sealed envelope. It was from the University of Missouri School of Medicine. For 10 seconds my head spun. What if I was rejected? What would I do, how would I act? Would a rejection letter be so thick? I opened the envelope. "CONGRATULATIONS" was all I saw. There were hugs all around. I felt huge; there was a permanent smile on my face. I knew then and there that I could take a chance and win.

Of course, medical school had its challenges. I made it through the first two years with help from the friends I made. I had decided before starting that I was going into family medicine or pediatrics. The third and fourth year we did rotations with different specialties. My first rotation was pediatrics — I hated it. I loved the kids, but I couldn't stand seeing them sick, nor did I like dealing with the parents of sick children. Okay, I would do family medicine — I hated that too. Too much sickness with no cure; the same patients with the same problems that didn't get better. What if I had made a mistake and I really did not like medicine? I was scared.

My next rotation was general surgery — I liked it! Then I went on to OB/GYN — I loved it! Then I did urology — I *really* loved it. The doctors that were teaching were happy and rested. They liked mentoring and seemed to want us to do well. I was going to be a urologist. A perfect combination of surgery and medical management.

Urology is mostly about treating men, and at the time there were less than 100 female urologists in the country. I was told by several people that I was not likely to be accepted into a urology program; that it would be very difficult to be accepted as a woman. Again, I had a choice to make: go for what I want or accept something else. I went for it! I was accepted on my first try and became one of two female urologists working at the program. At 26 years old, I became the first Black chief resident in the history of the University of Missouri Columbia. AND, during my residency, I defied the odds by getting married and having my first child. All those years of wondering if it was possible; I had made it possible.

My first job was in St Paul, Minnesota. It was there that I learned a lot more about female urologic problems. I also realized that I would not be a physician for my entire life. It took a while for me to understand why. I thought that it was the place and the people that I was working with, so I changed that. When I was in practice by myself, I realized I did not like the 'business' of medicine. I was forced to look at patients as income, whereas I preferred spending time with my patients, getting to know them. The business of medicine did not allow that. I could not spend the time I wanted and still cover my expenses. I ultimately decided that there was no way to practice the way that I wanted, so I closed my business.

My husband and I had learned about real estate investing and had bought several rental properties before I closed my practice. I thought it was just a matter of time before the real estate would cover our expenses and support us. While he was working on our real estate portfolio, we still needed income. I left my husband and two girls in Kansas City and went to work temporarily in El Paso, Texas, 940 miles away. Over the year and a half, I spoke to my girls twice a day and flew home as often as I could. Things didn't go as planned with our real estate investments and I soon realized that I would need to continue working as a urologist to support us. I had recently visited Kauai, part of the Hawaiian Islands, and found it to be very beautiful and inspiring. If I was going to continue practicing medicine, I was going to do it in Hawaii. I set about looking for a practice to join there.

Within about six months we moved to Honolulu. Medicine was still unfulfilling, but the scenery was beautiful, and I felt good. My children were doing well in school. My husband stayed on the mainland for several months getting our properties rent-ready. He joined us in early 2007 when the global financial crisis was just starting, before it became full-fledged in 2008 and took us down. We worked hard to keep our 19 properties afloat, but ultimately, I decided I could not keep throwing money at them and keep our family safe financially. Another hard choice needed to be made. I have never purposefully let something fail and the consequences were painful. We had been struggling in our marriage for quite a while and this was the last nail in the coffin. We were able to complete the divorce without attorneys or obvious scarring to our children. I took a big financial hit. Still, I felt real estate was the vehicle to get me out of medicine and we just had not done it properly. I had to dig deep and find that part of me that could turn things around. I had heard a quote by Les Brown that said, "Wanting something is not enough. You must be hungry for it. Your motivation must be absolutely compelling in order to overcome the obstacles that will invariably come your way."

I was not making enough money to continue living in Hawaii while recovering financially, so I found a job in California that paid enough AND had a handsome signing bonus! I bought two cars, one for me and one for my daughters, who were now teenagers, and three single family houses for rentals in Kansas City, Missouri. I hired a management team and still had some cash for the surprises that can come with owning rental properties. The team got the properties rehabbed and rented in good time. I was back. But not quite satisfied with just buying and renting single family houses. It was going to be a long haul to financial freedom. I started listening to podcasts and reading a ton. I learned about syndication and ultimately joined an inner circle where I was mentored on raising funds to help average folks own big real estate. It was fun, but not fulfilling, just the way I felt when I first recognized that I would not practice medicine forever. I could do it and be good at it, but still had a nagging feeling — this isn't it.

Les Brown also says, "If you don't program yourself, life will program you." That propelled me toward what I do now, helping others more holistically. I found a way to create my own fulfillment by fusing together the two worlds I had known. I focus on empowering medical professionals, especially women, to understand that getting their money to work for them is absolutely necessary to having financial and time freedom. I teach how to accomplish passive income through investments outside of Wall Street and their 401K. At the same time, I use what I loved about practicing medicine; building relationships and creating helpful solutions. It is amazing to see the lights come on when they realize the possibilities. And they deserve it!

One of the best things about hanging out with people doing the same thing you do is learning things you didn't know you didn't know. At one meeting I met Gene Guarino. Gene built and ran residential assisted living homes, teaching others how to do the same. I attended his three-day course where we visited several of his properties. I knew that this was what I wanted to do — do well and do good. These family style homes were much better than the institutional facilities I knew of. They felt like home, they smelled like home. There were happy elderly who seemed well cared for. I felt like I had found what I wanted: a way to do well financially and make a difference. My first assisted living home was opened in 2018 in Kansas City. Later that year, I was asked to help with an indoor controlled farm project and grocery stores in food deserts in Tulsa, Oklahoma. Yes! Doing well and doing good! The grocery store project is so important to me that I moved to Tulsa to be closer and more involved.

I have dedicated my life to creating a sense of security for others: boosting their health, increasing their financial stability, and creating safe, happy spaces in which they could live. If 'home is where the heart is,' then the key to my happiness was traveling that long, winding path to find my heart. With the help of a very good friend and businesswoman, my company, *Money with Mission,* was born. At Money with Mission, we leverage every dollar invested to improve communities and our investor's bottom line. We are doing well and doing good. It feels like home; I am where I'm supposed to be.

We all know where we are supposed to be. I believe you know what you want. Have the courage to go out and do it. Take a chance on you and know that when you do, *you will win*!

IGNITE ACTION STEPS

- Take a good look at where you are today. Your work, your relationships, where you live.
- Now think about how you got here. Why are things as they currently are? What do you want to change? What would your perfect life look like?
- Take the time to write a list, a story, or a prescription even, as to what you want your future to be.
- Then, do the work and make the changes needed to get closer to that perfect life. Find who can help you get there.
- Actions produce results.

Felecia Froe, M.D. — United States
Founder, Money with Mission, 18 Seconds for Health, Author, Social
Impact Real Estate Investor and Syndicator, Urologic Surgeon
www.moneywithmission.com
 moneywithmission
 moneywithmission

Shashonee L. Sales

SHASHONEE L. SALES

"Find your purpose; then you will be able to persevere despite your fears."

My intentions are to encourage all mankind to find and pursue their God given purpose for being on this planet. I stand as a symbol of hope, as a living testimony to those who may have lost hope along the way. I encourage you to tap into your natural gifts, talents, and abilities, nurture them, and manifest them into the world. Find your purpose. Find what it is you were born to do rather than what or who you've conformed to. If you find your purpose, only then will you be able to persevere in spite of life's inevitable circumstances.

THE 48 HOUR MIRACLE

Every day my alarm clock goes off, and I roll over to see that it's 5 AM. My feet hit the floor, and I'm headed out the door and feel the cool crisp morning air that causes me to shiver. I make it to the barn where my 'show calf' meets me at the barn door anxiously waiting for me to halter him and lead him on. I measure out his morning ration, smelling the sweet molasses with each scoop. I spend hours air-drying and treating his coat, my fingers numb from the cold temperatures and the morning air, but rinse, brush, treat, air-dry, and repeat. By 7 AM, it's time for me to head back into the house, grab a bite to eat, get ready, and then head to school. All day in classes, then on to sports, just to head home to tend to more chores and do it all over again.

I established a hard work ethic very early in life. As most Southerners might say, "It was born and bred into me." Growing up on a farm and ranch allowed me to gain a sense of responsibility and appreciation for life's blessings at a very early age, although at times I hated getting up before dawn and having to pitch in on my assigned chores. I learned so many priceless and valuable lessons growing up on the farm that I now have such an appreciation for. When other kids were gathering for a weekend excursion, I was working in some way, shape, or fashion on the farm and ranch. I'd work and doctor sick cattle, help deliver calves, and attend to any other loose ends that needed to be addressed. I would plow the ground, help sow the wheat crop, build barbed wire fences, then during the appropriate season, cut and bale hay in the summer so we could feed cattle in the winter.

It's crazy to look back on my adolescent and teen years knowing all of the challenges and struggles that I was able to make it through. Nonetheless, the biggest contributing factor that has led me to live the life that I live now dates back to the day I was born. I was born in Fort Worth, Texas, through complications, and my mother had to undergo a C-section. I was born with half the amount of blood in my body due to the fact my mother and I were both hemorrhaging. I had to receive an immediate blood transfusion in order to sustain life at birth, and at just 17 months old, I was diagnosed with Large Cell Lymphoma Cancer. My sister and I were raised by a single mother who worked as a clerk at the downtown Fort Worth USPS™. She was holding down a full-time job, recovering from a previously physically abusive marriage, and fighting to gain full custody of my older sister, all while taking me to my chemotherapy treatment sessions. There were two instances when I completely lost my hair, and at one point I was a walking skeleton with a swollen abdomen. After a year and a half of treatments, nothing was working. Cancer was in my bloodstream, and it was eating my kidneys and bones. The physician who was responsible for my care told my mother, "I hate to be the bearer of bad news, but your baby boy only has **48 hours to live."** My mother immediately began to beg and cry out to God, "Lord, if you would just give my babies back to me, I would give my babies back to You." My mother's prayers miraculously were answered. Thanks be to God's healing hand, 28 years later I am cancer FREE, and I have been cancer FREE ever since the day God healed me from the inside out. My mother received full custody of my older sister, and I recovered fully without having any further complications.

I have to agree with Abraham Lincoln who once said, "All that I am or hope to be, I owe to my angel mother." Growing up in a single-parent home, I was always loved and supported, but I struggled with my identity for years and battled with insecurities about my self-worth; confused as to why my biological father chose not to be involved in my upbringing. Later in life, a close relative who I looked up to as a father figure, disowned me at a point when I most felt the need for his presence. During that phase I was dealing with a state of confusion as to who I was as a man, and why the men that I had looked up to my entire life had chosen to remain absent or abandon me after my grandfather had passed away. Had I done something wrong? I felt unwanted. I searched for who I was; looking for happiness and a place I belonged. Over time I was drinking to fit in with the crowd, which led to me meeting my first wife (at a bar that I frequently went to at the time). Falling head over heels I found myself saying, "I do," committing to a toxic relationship that left me in a more devastating position and ultimately led to my first divorce. I found myself spiraling down this long road of heartache, dazed and confused as to why I was this way.

Trying to find my place in this world, I went down the road of mass destruction. I obtained my four-year degree with the intention of pursuing a job with the Oklahoma Highway Patrol only to flush it down the drain after getting pulled over under the influence. I spent seven years of my life chasing the neon lights and drinking to numb the pain I was battling within. I found myself pursuing the sport of rodeo, where I rode bulls unprofessionally for seven years. That lifestyle led me to drinking excessively, bar fights, doing cocaine, weed, and pain pills. In addition to this destructive lifestyle, over the course of 10 years, I pursued nine different career fields in search of my place in this world. Although my life was a mess, I've always had a burning desire to excel. At the time I didn't know exactly how I would achieve my desired level of success, but I've always felt that I could become more than what I had recently been limiting myself to being.

Despite my lessons learned, setbacks, and confusion, I have always been a very determined and genuine individual. What you see is what you get, love me, or hate me. I was determined to find a better way for myself and for my family. I felt that there had to be more to life than what I had experienced. We know scripture that says, "Seek, and you shall find." So, I set out seeking in a way that was constructive rather than destructive.

In late March of 2020, at 28 years old, I secured a loan to purchase the necessary equipment to kickstart my custom farming business. Determined to keep the family farm from going under, I was eager to expand the business through custom farming. The cattle operation I had begun five years earlier was turning full circle and things were beginning to look up. I had also been working full-time for the past two years as a delivery truck driver. I had built up some tenure and a good reputation with the company. This extra income allowed me to cover my living expenses and accrue savings, as well as secure loose ends in regard to expenses for the operation. After securing my equipment loan to start my new business, I couldn't have been more excited! Then, just three days later, I received a telephone call from the Vice President and the HR Director regretfully informing me that my position as a delivery driver had been terminated due to a lack of work caused by the COVID-19 pandemic. The VP told me that they appreciated my service and hard work, but there was nothing they could do. Devastated and shocked, I could not believe what I had just heard. My heart sank! Filled with frustration and shocked with the news, my mind immediately went to the equipment loan I had just secured three days prior. How could this be!? I had just received a loan to start my custom farming business, and now I'd been fired! I had never been fired or terminated from a job in the 10 years I had been in the workforce. As the great Les Brown would say, "Life is a fight for territory, and once you stop fighting for what you want, what you don't want will automatically take over." That very moment changed my life forever! I was forced to realize that no matter how hard I worked, having a four-year degree, along with a list of credentials stacked up on a resume, did not ensure that I would have a steady job from one day to the next. I knew right then in that very moment something had to drastically change!

The COVID-19 pandemic struck our country and world like a plague. What we knew to be the norm drastically changed over the course of 2020. Knowing that I still had 30 years plus in the workforce, Lord willing, I questioned where I needed to focus my energy, time, and resources. The biggest question I posed to myself was, "What are highly successful people doing that I'm not doing?" I began researching people who I felt were achieving success, such as Tony Robbins, Jim Rohn, Bill Gates, Elon Musk, and the list goes on. One of the wealthiest men on the planet, Warren Buffet, once stated, "The best investment a person can make is in themselves." That quote in particular struck a chord with me, and I began to further my research. I began reading every personal development book I could get my hands on. I started practicing meditation to enhance the transformation process of my mind, because I knew that in order to have a better life, I had to change from the *inside out*.

I also opened my eyes to the inspiration within the life I already had led. Many of life's lessons can relate to the farming and ranching industry. For instance, when a farmer plants his seed in the ground, he is forced to practice patience by giving that seed time to grow. The 'law of the farm' is a common practice applied in business, regardless of the industry. This law refers to the fact that in order to become successful, one has to respect and nurture the process. Once I began investing in myself by expanding my knowledge, skills, and my level of consciousness, drastic change happened for me. My life began to make a major shift from confusion to clarity. Life and business are similar to that of the changing seasons. It is inevitable that the winter times will come our way, but instead of ducking or trying to run from those hard times like I had previously done, I learned that I had to face those difficulties and persevere in spite of them. Every single time I would push through life's inevitable circumstances, I found myself becoming more confident in myself, and I would come out of those situations a better man having gone through those hard times head-on.

We've heard it said that faith not tested can't be trusted, so I encourage you to keep moving forward and simply ask for what you desire and believe you will receive it. I asked God to open doors that needed to be opened and close those that needed to be closed. It just so happened that hay season, *harvest* time, was right around the corner after I was terminated from my job. Even though I couldn't see the blessing in disguise, it unfolded in the perfect way. In the first year of doing business, I acquired enough revenue to pay my loans and set enough money aside to cover the next year's annual operating expenses. I've learned to give credit where credit is due, and I assure you that the good Lord provided a way when I could not see one.

I have learned that there is no security beyond the security I create for myself. As a result of choosing to invest in and become the best version of myself, I have discovered a sense of inner clarity that I never dreamed I would have discovered. I feel that the primary reason God has spared me 28 years now, post cancer, is so that I can instill hope in others; encourage and help people to find their purpose in life and to manifest their God given gifts, talents, and abilities into this world. I have gone on to start a life and business coaching program, called Legendary Freedom, and I continue to share my message and story with the world as an inspirational speaker.

My journey thus far has taught me to focus primarily on two things: One is working on myself so that I can better serve others, and the second is being quick to lend a helping hand. Giving initiates the receiving process, and by fulfilling my purpose, I can rest assured that I will have left this world in a much better place. Looking back on my life, to where I am to this day, some of the hardest challenges or setbacks ended up being some of the biggest blessings in disguise.

I think it's safe to say that life will present itself through various setbacks, disappointments, failures, lessons learned, and bad doctor's reports. But I encourage you with everything I have to keep fighting the good fight and NEVER give up! Regardless of the doctor's predictions, or the odds that may be stacked against you, don't quit, because you have power within you and God's divine promise set for you. Science only goes so far, and then comes the grace of God.

I will never forget those days growing up on the farm and ranch being so hard and challenging. The times where I couldn't understand the importance of the many lessons, and would ask, "Why me?" Those extremely hot days when I would be assigned to haul hay out of the fields with no air conditioner, knowing that my friends were all at the lake having a good time. Or the many times I would doctor an animal and care for them while they were sick but still could not prevent them from passing away. There were so many valuable lessons I learned on the farm and ranch that at one point in my life I was eager to leave far behind... But now it is the very place I have spent the past seven years trying to save. It's funny how life pans out, but I am forever grateful for all of those close calls, restless nights, losses, mistakes, and hardships. It is precisely because of *those* experiences that I have been led to becoming the man I am today.

In closing I would like to share with you a unique poem that I wrote.

"Get Out Of Your Own Way"

Standing in the middle of the road having no true direction on which way to go is sadly the sum of most people's lives. If you would only get out of your own way, you would notice that thing you seek to find has been within you this whole time. You may say it's really not that simple, but I say to you yes it really is. Enlighten me for a minute… When was the last time you had a good day? That day where everything within you and around you just made all your doubts and fears go away... Tell me... What happened on that day? Let's go back to the moment you woke up and your feet hit the floor. Let me guess, you just felt like today was going to be a good day? If I'm close, let me go on to say, that following that feeling of anticipation that good things were soon coming your way, you felt much lighter on your feet. You felt strong rather than weak, and in spite of all of the negative energy within and about you, you didn't see it. How could this be? *Truth is, you are what you* ***T.H.I.N.K.***

Trouble, Hate, Insignificant, Naysayer, Killer
versus
Thought leader, High achiever, Innovator, No matter what, Knowledge seeker
Get out of your own way.

I encourage you to get out of your own way and know that you are more than capable of achieving anything you set your mind to. Your purpose will come *in time;* he who 'seeks' will 'find.' Allow the 'law of the farm' to apply to your life; be patient and respect the process because life's a journey and not a sprint. Or as we like to say on the farm, you reap what you sow.

Ignite Action Steps

I encourage you to do the following things if you are HUNGRY to be the best version of yourself and you have decided to be a POSITIVE wrecking force in life…

1. **DON'T put your life on hold**! Pursue your heart-centered passions and dreams. Find your purpose! Do the inner work and gain clarity on who you are and what you feel called to do. Start meditating.
2. **Regardless of where you are in your life**, you can make changes today! Begin the sowing process by planting the seeds of what brings you joy. Make a list.
3. **Strap on your seat belt** and hang on tight because the best version of yourself is on its way! Remember the answer to all you are meant to be is at the end of this question: **"If you had 48 hours to live, how would you live it?"** Answer this.

Shashonee L. Sales — United States
Life and Business Coach, Author, and Speaker
legendaryfreedom.com
f *Shashonee L. Sales*
in *Shashonee Sales*

Marcy Cody

MARCY CODY, RN

"It's easy to be SPRY way past 65."

Unless you die young, you will get old. It is possible to be independent, impactful, and in shape well beyond age 65! I want to prove old Benjamin Franklin wrong when he said, "Old too soon, and wise too late." I encourage you to be wise NOW, break self-sabotaging habits, and nurture habits that powerfully catapult you into your destiny, fulfilling your God ordained purpose for your life. It is necessary to plan to age vibrantly, not just gracefully, so establish a strategic aging plan — it is the start of being SPRY past 65. You are worth it, you can do it, and your destiny is waiting!

WALK NOW, OR USE A WALKER LATER

Do you plan to live past 70? Well, honestly most of us don't really plan to get old, we just keep waking up every day and old age creeps up on us whether we want it to or not. My mentor Les Brown says, "To be successful in life, you must be willing to do the things today that others won't do, in order to have the things tomorrow that others won't have." For me, health is one of those things.

As a child, my grandparents' house was the family's gathering place. It was a huge mansion on the corner of a very nice part of town in Chicago, Illinois. Chicago is the third largest city in the United States, designed like a waffle, so each house is equidistant apart. The houses were so close together that you could hear the neighbors next door if they raised their voices.

Every Sunday my siblings and I would walk to church and then walk to our grandparents' place from church. It was about a mile walk. We passed a candy store on the way, and would occasionally stop at the candy store if we had extra money. That was when candy was a penny! My dad worked nights and my mom went to a different church, so they would meet us over there later.

It was actually my great aunt's seven-bedroom, two-bathroom mansion. My great aunt and uncle lived on the main floor and my grandparents lived upstairs. My grandma cared for my aunt and uncle, who were very old and didn't have any children. Neither of my parents had siblings. So, we were the only children there and would have to sit at the 'kids table' in the living room. There was a huge chandelier above the long dining room table. I remember a platter in the middle of the table with every kind of breakfast meat imaginable. Bacon, several different types of sausage, and ham. There was also homemade applesauce and biscuits. I watched as my brothers loaded up their plates and then went for seconds, but not me! All I wanted was a little 'eggs' and half of a sausage. My grandpa said that I ate like a bird. He used to brag that he only ate meat and potatoes and that he didn't eat 'rabbit food.' He had a dedicated refrigerator in the basement for beer. He ended up dying from a heart attack after a 15-year fight with colon cancer, living with a colostomy bag. Sometimes I dreaded going there when the focus was all about my aging relatives.

I loved my grandparents because they didn't act like old people. My great aunt had a habit of taking her teeth out after she ate and putting them on her plate! This was so repulsive to me. Eventually, after my aunt and uncle passed away, my grandparents inherited the house, and I started loving going there. I would invite friends over also. We would play board games or card games after dinner. We were very competitive.

As a child I really disliked food. My mother didn't cook, because she worked evenings and went to school during the day. She would leave a note for my older sister, Mary, to 'make dinner.' "Put roast in the oven at 350 degrees for 90 minutes," was usually how it read, and whatever came out was what we ate. I was the salad maker. I made a different salad every day. My favorite was the Waldorf salad, because it not only tasted delicious, it looked delicious. The lush and crunchy greens of the lettuce, apples, and celery, the thick cold mayonnaise, and the sprinkling of walnuts was a match made in heaven. To this day I love salad and have made a habit of eating salad every day. But, now my salads are a complete meal.

I was also very active as a dancer from age 4. Creative modern dance, ballet, liturgical, gospel, ballroom, disco, and Latin dancing. Dancing has always been a stress reliever and kept my weight healthy. It wasn't until I stopped dancing that my weight became a problem.

I was a teen mom and got married and had three children before I turned 28. I was focused on working and caring for them, and although I missed dancing, I never had time for it. It was difficult working full-time, caring for children. My own desires and dreams got placed on the back burner. Suddenly, getting them to school and keeping them fed and in clean clothes became my priority. Dancing was not reintroduced until they were all grown up and I started taking Zumba™ classes, which led me to becoming a Zumba instructor and starting a nonprofit called Highest Praise Dance Fitness.

Although my dancing was dormant for several years, my interest in health never wavered; it led me to become a registered nurse. During college I was taught about disease processes and conventional therapies and treatments. I learned that **every** year over 600,000 people die from heart disease, which is the number one cause of death in America. Research shows that making healthy lifestyle and diet choices could prevent most cases of heart disease, stroke, diabetes, and many cancers. When my husband was diagnosed with a life-threatening disease, my focus shifted. I was extremely interested in length and quality of life. I was able to research and coach my husband, and others with life-threatening diseases, to replace self-sabotaging habits with life-sustaining habits. This included me helping my dad, who had remained independent, driving and caring for his new wife, despite his life-threatening disease, all the way to age 87.

On my dad's 89th birthday, we had to make the arduous decision to place my parents in a nursing home. I had never been inside a state-funded nursing home before. We scheduled a tour, and I'll never forget when my sister and I walked into that dingy place, the sights, smells, and sounds broke my heart into pieces. How could I put my parents, who I loved so dearly, in such a gloomy and yucky place? The staff seemed nice, but the place looked like it hadn't been renovated since the 1980s! I was shocked, sad, and totally surprised at how unkept this place was. The lobby was tiny with a single couch and armchair with mismatched cushions.

We were taken past residents sitting around the nurses' station in wheelchairs staring at us and smiling. They were not happy smiles, they were more like fake smiles. They made me nervous. I was thinking, "Why are they sitting out here?" I didn't realize until after my parents had been there a while that the common areas for the residents had been closed over a year due to COVID-19 restrictions.

We were taken way down to the end of the hall, through a plastic hallway divider closed with a zipper. I remember thinking to myself, "What is this?"

It turns out that the area past the plastic was not being used due to COVID-19. We were shown a very large room with a beautiful view of a grassy lawn. This room looked bright and cheery, had lots of windows, and made me feel more at ease. There were no beds because 'the room wasn't set up yet.' My sister and I decided that it wasn't too bad and initiated the admission process; not fully understanding what we were in for. Feeling sad and guilty about having to send my parents there, I rationalized that even though the facility had a two-star overall rating, they had a five-star rating in patient care. I was hopeful that the stellar care would make up for the lackluster appearance.

There is a scripture that is written in red letters: "Very truly I tell you, when you were younger you dressed yourself and went where you wanted; but when you are old you will stretch out your hands, and someone else will dress you and lead you where you do not want to go." *(John 21:18 NIV)* I had taken my parents to a place that they did not want to go. Many times, as a child, my dad had taken me places that I didn't want to go. But, he didn't leave me there.

Dad had been so independent up until age 87. He had his own school bus company. He and his lovely wife made sure that the children got to and from school safely. He created route maps and kept both of their medication lists updated on the computer. He ordered supplements online and played solitaire on his phone to keep his brain sharp. But as Denis Waitley said about health, "One day it's there and then it's gone."

Was there something that we could have done to prepare for this? Now the tables were suddenly turned. This is a tremendous weight on my shoulders, as I am the designated decision maker for my parents' health. I am a professional Registered Nurse. I know all about end-of-life care. But, this is my daddy!

Once we had moved them in, it hit me. I couldn't imagine living in a place where I had no choice of meals; where I couldn't go outside on my own or even down the hall; couldn't change the TV channel because the remote didn't work. I couldn't imagine being dependent on others to bathe me on their schedule. This was, in my eyes, worse than prison. It reminded me of the reality TV show *Scared Straight,* where troubled teens were taken to visit a prison to try to scare them away from a life of crime.

Visiting my parents at that nursing home made me super scared. It forced me to look at my own health and ramp up my own longevity coaching efforts. I wondered what would happen if I was unable to care for myself and who would take care of me. That's how I feel every time I visit the nursing home. What I realized is, no one would want to live like this or subject a loved one to this.

Some say that knowledge is power. I say knowledge plus action is power!

Knowing all the right things to do is totally different than doing them. Witnessing the decline of my parents' health opened my eyes to how fragile life is. Everything was fine and we were able to manage at home with extra help, then one day we couldn't handle them at home anymore. It was too late for them to put into practice the knowledge that I wrote in my book, *90 Ways to Age Vibrantly: A Baby Boomers Devotional Journal,* in which I share 90 nuggets of wisdom and practical strategies people can take to age vibrantly. I wrote this book before their quick decline and they even had a copy of it. My own health journey inspired me to write the book, and seeing their health challenges pushed me to share my knowledge more vigilantly. I know I can help others avoid a similar journey by applying the knowledge in my book. I researched how other cultures and philosophies lived a long vibrant life. One of the most interesting tips is 'earthing,' also known as grounding. This method states that connecting to the earth's surface by allowing your bare feet to touch the bare ground, grass, sand, or natural body of water, or even hugging a tree, just a few minutes a day, has physical and mental healing benefits. People are often shocked and skeptical to hear the benefits of cold showers, but once they try it, they are so happy they did. There are so many things that you can incorporate into your daily routine that don't cost you anything, but will add so much value to your quality of life as you age; like deep breathing, Kegel exercises, legs up the wall, and heel drops.

When my husband received a cancer diagnosis in 1999, we immediately did research and started making healthier choices, like eating a more alkaline diet. This was huge. Since we have a 15-year age difference, our date nights were usually spent going to fancy restaurants. Suddenly, we only went to vegan restaurants. We learned about 'detoxing' our bodies and lots of other alternative health practices. A few years after my husband got his diagnosis, my dad was also diagnosed with cancer.

Now I had accumulated quite an arsenal of cancer-fighting strategies, which I was able to share with my dad as well, mostly diet related. Dad liked his fast food, but did use supplements, health shakes, and smoothies. What I must say here may seem cliche, but an ounce of prevention weighs more than a pound of cure. The absolute best cure is to *prevent* disease. Western medicine isn't big on prevention. They want to 'treat' illness instead of preventing it. It's business. Doctors admit to practicing medicine. A medicine by definition is a toxic substance. If it's not toxic, then it is a supplement. This realization opened my eyes to a more Eastern, holistic approach.

It's really a whole new world once you decide to make healthy choices.

Some people may call you a 'health nut' when you say you don't eat cheese or sugar because they can't imagine a life without cheese or sugar. You have to bring your own food to family gatherings. I'll never forget when we went down South to visit my husband's family. Days before we were due to go, we told them that we were now 'vegan.' However, they made a 'special' seven-layer salad for him that had three kinds of cheese and chicken in it. We had to try to pick the lettuce out of it! They just didn't understand. He had lost quite a bit of weight, so they were scared that he was super sick, when he was actually the healthiest that he had ever been.

That was over 20 years ago, and my husband is still alive and well, independent, and impactful at age 78! He has been stage IV for almost 10 years, but feels no pain and is super active. To look at him, you would have no idea that he has that diagnosis. When you ask him how he's doing, he says, "I'm doing great for the rest of my life!" He believes in living life to the fullest, because tomorrow isn't promised.

I know that I am not at my ideal weight. I know exactly what to do to reach my ideal weight, but until I consistently do those things, I will not reach my goal. It's all about habits. You become what you repeatedly do. Practice makes permanent. We make choices hundreds of times a day. It's absolutely a mindset and decision that has to be made. It's like flipping a switch in your head. Like a switch on train tracks will divert you to a different set of tracks. Like reaching a fork in the road and taking the road less traveled. Two scriptures that confirm this mindset shift are:

The mind governed by the flesh is death, but the mind governed by the Spirit is life and peace. — Romans 8:6 (NIV)

Therefore, I urge you, brothers and sisters, in view of God's mercy, to offer your bodies as a living sacrifice, holy and pleasing to God — this is your true and proper worship. Do not conform to the pattern of this world, but be transformed by the renewing of your mind. Then you will be able to test and approve what God's will is — his good, pleasing and perfect will. — Romans 12:1-2 (NIV)

Success happens when you consistently avoid the self-sabotaging habits and repeat the healthier habits until it's ingrained in your subconscious mind. The power of the subconscious mind, galvanized by the power of community and accountability, assures awesome results. Choose the things that lead to an optimal life and repeat that.

Having a great quality of life as you age is not that labor intensive, but you must be willing to maintain it. What are you willing to do today, so your future self will be independent, impactful, and in shape for decades to come?

What legacy are you leaving for generations to come? What example are you leading by? Yes, you are leading by example. Will you be independent or require a nursing home?

Everything looks different through those 'my health is my priority' colored glasses, and it is worth making the sacrifice! As Maya Angelou said, "Surviving is important. Thriving is elegant. My mission in life is not to merely survive, but to thrive; and to do so with some passion, some compassion, some humor, and some style."

You are worth it, you can do it, and your destiny is waiting!

IGNITE ACTION STEPS

I believe that you can be spry way past 65. Develop a sustainable and enjoyable daily routine, tweak, and repeat! Your future self will thank you later.

- Exercise the muscles that you want to continue to use, or plan to use a walker, wheelchair, or scooter.
- Brush the teeth that you want to save, or plan on wearing dentures.
- Pay attention to the relationships that you want to last, or plan on being alone.
- Save the money that you want to spend, or plan to work indefinitely.
- **S — Sustainable Habits: "To thine own self be true."—Shakespeare**
  Do a habit inventory. Identify habits that aren't serving and find ways to improve.
- **P — Pleasurable and Satisfying: "Just a spoonful of sugar helps the medicine go down in the most delightful way."—Mary Poppins**
  Find a way to sweeten up that habit to a point where you look forward to it.
- **R — Repeat until it's automatic. "We are what we repeatedly do. Excellence then, is not an act, but a habit."—Will Durant**
  Keep tweaking and repeating until that healthier habit becomes ingrained in your subconscious mind.
- **Y — Yes you can! "If you think you can or think you can't do a thing, you are right!" —Henry Ford**

Marcy Cody, RN — United States
Faith Based Holistic Longevity Coach, Author, Motivational Speaker
www.MarcyCodyRN.com
mhcody   MarcyCodyRN

Maynard Neal

MAYNARD NEAL

"We all leave footprints. Will yours be in sand or cement?"

I hope to touch your heart and help you open your mind to believe that you can erase the mental blocks and chains that hold you back. No matter what challenges you have, you can overcome them and allow the true YOU to come out. You have a purpose for being here. I wish for you to go beyond those challenges and become who you were born to be. They don't define who you are.

BROKERING FOR MY FREEDOM

"Can I carry your bags for you?"

As a young preteen in Highland Park, Michigan, this is how I was keeping food on my family's table. I grew up very poor, and when I was about 11, my dad was laid off. That meant...

There was no food in the refrigerator, so I would walk up to the local grocery store each day and hang around outside the entrance. When the doors would open, I would ask people if I could help them carry their bags and put them in the car for them, in hopes of making 50 cents to a dollar or whatever they would give me. After doing that for sometimes two or three hours, I would make six to eight dollars, then I'd go inside the store and buy some pork chops, hamburger, or chicken. I'd take it home so my mother could cook it for dinner.

There were lots of challenges growing up in 'the hood'! There were several different gangs, and at times I would hear gunshots; I'd look down the street to see people running and later learn that someone had been shot. There were lots of drug dealers in the neighborhood as well. I had to be careful what clothes I wore walking to school. I remember there was a coat with a fur-trimmed collar. It was called a 'Max Julian jacket,' and if you wore that jacket, you stood to be robbed or 'checked in.' If you had on nice gym shoes, jeans, or a shirt, you were at risk of walking home in just your underwear. The clothes that you were wearing would be stolen right off of your body along with you getting a physical 'beat down.'

I remember getting into so many different fights in high school. If something was said and it could be interpreted positively or negatively, I would take it in a negative way. Conflict was such a regular part of my life that it eventually landed me in prison. I wasn't with my classmates walking across a stage for graduation; I was with my cellmate stuck behind bars and standing still.

My first offense was worth one and a half years to the judge. When I got out, I was totally relieved, but the sad thing was that I also knew my stint in prison came with 'bars,' which meant credibility to the people I grew up with in the hood. It had me wondering what was next for me. I was determined to stay out of trouble if I could.

I managed to do exactly that for over 10 years. I worked for a check verification company but was let go when they downsized after Y2K. So I went into real estate and got licensed. I met a girl in Canada who I dated for several years. Life was going alright, but an unscrupulous broker put a bad taste in my mouth for real estate, and eventually I fell back in with some questionable people. Trying to choose the 'quick money' route ultimately sent me back to prison, this time for nearly four years.

When I got back out, I was in good shape for a few years until I violated my probation. My new girlfriend at the time was seven months pregnant with my daughter. The federal judge allowed me to stay home until my daughter was born, and then informed me I would receive a letter telling me when and which prison to turn myself in to. My feelings were a mix of relief that the judge was gracious enough to let me see my baby girl enter the world, and fear about going to prison soon after.

The experience of my daughter being born and holding her was magical. Hearing her cry took my breath away. I was able to cut her umbilical cord. These were stolen moments for me because based on all the things I'd done, I should not have been there. Leaving her when she'd been on this earth less than two months hurt me to my soul; to my core. So much so that I started hating myself.

The day I turned myself in to the federal prison, they didn't have any bed space available so they *kindly* put me into 'the hole' — solitary confinement for the first three months. I was missing my daughter, my family, and my life, and I didn't realize how important those things were until I got completely quiet. There were many nights I cried facing the wall quietly because I didn't want the other guys to hear me and be looked upon as weak. Almost three years later, when I came home, I knew I had to do something different because my precious little girl who had gotten to know her father from the visiting room, now had her father with her every day. It caused me to look at life differently. After finally understanding a different kind of love, and knowing I'd caused it to be ripped away from me, it left a hole in my heart and made me want to change. There was another life that was counting on me — a life that I helped bring into this world. She didn't ask to be here yet here she was, and she needed a father. Realizing I never wanted to be away from my child ever again gave me the sense of responsibility to be more careful about the choices I made.

My daughter's mother and I rekindled our relationship and had another child, a little boy. I got back into real estate, determined to take it seriously and become successful for my family. But after two and a half years, the relationship eventually ended. I became a single dad and went from *wanting* to be a success to *needing* to be a success.

An opportunity came for me to leave the real estate company and open up my own market center to be an associate broker for another firm. As I made plans to leave the current company, the broker and his team became aware of my decision before I could share my plans with them. I was called into the office conference room. When I got there, the head administrator, the associate broker, and the brokerage's corporate lawyer were sitting there waiting for me. They shared that they knew I was planning on leaving and told me they were severing things immediately. They threatened me, saying I'd better not try to steal agents or they would make it bad for me. After three years of truly applying myself, being a top producer for them, and becoming one of the top 10 real estate agents out of 380 at the brokerage, I was shocked to hear this. I expressed that my desire was to do the best for me and my family and I had no intention of calling other agents.

However, other agents reached out to me over the next few weeks asking me why I left and wondering whether or not they were missing out on something. They were asking if they could come by to see my office and talk to me about the possibilities of teaming up. Within two months of me leaving, I had accumulated over a dozen agents to join my brokerage company. Things were going wonderfully.

That is, until the broker from my past office revealed publicly to hundreds of realtors, including the agents that were working at my brokerage firm, that I was a felon; that I had been to prison. As my past was revealed and my integrity questioned, it became one of the hardest moments in my life. Everything I had worked to resolve was being used against me and my past was threatening my future. I suddenly saw how my actions, my behavior, and the choices I made were caging me in and holding me back from becoming who I was meant to be. Sadly, their tactics cost me all of my agents, and caused me loss of money, embarrassment, and shame. But it also made me want to show the world that I am not that person that they were describing. I no longer lived that way! That life is dead to me, and I have worked hard with blood, sweat, and tears to build what I had.

Their actions hurt me in so many ways, consciously and subconsciously. But more importantly, they made me dig deep within my soul and realize that the bad decisions I made in my past didn't represent me now. I was not going to allow that to define me! I wasn't going to sit around and wallow or let them paint a picture of me that was no longer true! I listened to my mother's wisdom about having more in me and not sitting there saying I'm worthless. She'd taught me not to let the past define me, but to move forward and share the understanding that anything is possible when I set my mind and my heart to it.

When this defaming and shaming happened, I reached out to Mr Hatchett, a top-ranking attorney that I'd hired to represent me for past cases. He became a mentor to me and a supporter. I'll never forget the gesture and belief in me that he had before I recognized the power within. One day in his office years prior, he told me he was erasing the debt of $3,500 that I owed him because he believed in me and he wanted me to keep that money to take care of my family and follow my dreams. When I shared what was happening, he advised me to keep doing what I was doing and not let what they were saying stop me because I was very good and that's what they feared. His advice and act of kindness brought tears to my eyes and courage to my spirit. It reminded me to hold my head up and to keep moving.

My greatest support in my darkest moments was speaking to my father, who's now a retired pastor. He shared with me a story out of the Bible about how God puts an armor plate on the front of us, not on our back. It resonated with me and meant so much to know God covers the front of me only because I was not meant to turn around and go backwards. I was meant to keep moving forward toward my dreams and goals no matter what, whether it's by an inch, a step, or a mile.

As hard as it was with the embarrassment, the shame, the ridicule, and even more importantly the unconscious effect that it had on my mind, I kept working and moving forward. I drew on the wisdom shared with me that touched my heart and a strength in me that I previously didn't know I had. I kept fighting and going as I felt I had no other choice but to keep pushing. At first, I felt numb, but then I became more and more motivated to not allow other people to determine my destiny. That's what they wanted: for me to give up, to stop trying, to quit. They wanted me to succumb to the pressure they had created; their efforts to discredit me and shove me in a box. But I'd already been in a worse box, and was stronger and more debilitating than they could ever know. Their actions only motivated me to become better and to try harder. Plus I had my reason — the most important reason — to keep going: Looking at my son and my daughter, they became the wind beneath my wings.

Things started happening. Doors started opening. The energetic force of positiveness drew me to opportunities that were unreal; opportunities I would not have ever imagined could happen for me. I started to understand more and more about the law of attraction and the power of my mind; the power of belief and the words in our head that aren't spoken. Even more importantly I understood the power of the words that come out of my mouth. Once spoken, it is committed to the Universe. I had to be careful what I was thinking and saying. The impressions I left could be temporary like footprints in sand, or left in cement to stick around forever. I knew whether those impressions became good ones or bad ones was up to me.

I've had many chances since to make new impressions. I have been recognized in magazines, interviewed by a local news station, and described as "a local real estate broker that has overcome many challenges in life to build a successful brokerage and give back to the community." All of this shows that perseverance, belief, changing the mental chains in our mind, and doing the right thing pays off.

It makes me want to share my story as a voice of encouragement; to be a living example of coming from a negative mindset and having a poor mentality to believing and achieving more than my mind could ever conceive. Many of us have mental chains that hold us back from being the highest and best expression of ourselves. Many of us struggle to move forward, to take the steps and to make the positive footprints that we can.

I want you to be inspired to feel and believe that no matter what experiences and choices you may have made before today, they don't define you or make you who you are created to be! You CAN take responsibility for your life and choose your future knowing your past has only created you to be who you are today, and who you will become tomorrow. The past is exactly that… the past.

Today is called the present for a reason. It's the gift of a new day with blessings and opportunities to conquer your dreams, your goals, and become who and what you decide. It's a new day and it's up to you to live 'your life' and to have an impact on others to leave a positive legacy. It's a new day to get beyond the mental barriers of the mind and the naysayers — to know and understand that God is not done with you yet! It's a new day to see that you have greatness in you; to realize that the hurts, pains, and challenges that come to us in life are there to be used and built upon, not to lock you in place and allow that to define who you are. Your struggles show you who you are and mold you into the direction of the highest and best expression of what God designed you to be.

There have been words spoken for centuries: what you believe, you can achieve. Yet it goes so much deeper. The thoughts in our mind cause the Universe to react. The beliefs in our heart allow visions to become realities. The energy and actions we combine shape the impressions we leave on the souls we touch. We breed each new reality, each new character, each new life experience. And it is our choices, and our choices alone, that ultimately bring us closer to our true purpose.

Today I have a new purpose to help others achieve their greatest dreams. I want to inspire them to think beyond their circumstances and create those powerful, new impressions that will bring them success. Les Brown has said numerous times, "Don't let the negativity given to you by the world disempower you. Instead, give to yourself that which empowers you." He also says, "Act the way you want to be and soon you'll be the way you act." These words remind me that we have the ability to define our future and become who we were meant to be. That means break free from anything that binds you, holds you back, or cages you in. Step into the true version of you and create the footprints in your life filled with all joy and blessing you dream of. You get to choose your future so choose who you want to be.

Ignite Action Steps

Feed your mind daily with positive videos, quotes, and people.

Tap into the internet to find an unlimited supply of motivational videos that you can listen to at the start of the morning or put yourself to sleep with at the end of a day. Visit your local library as they also have great material you can borrow at no cost. Watching motivational videos has the power to open the mind and spark new learning in a fun and visual way.

Download a positive quotes 'app' to send inspirational quotes directly to your phone and give you a perfect pick-me-up at any time of the day. Get a quotes calendar that you can tear off a new page each day or find a book filled to the brim with quotes designed to motivate you. Post your favorite quotes on your computer, fridge, or bathroom mirror. Memorize the ones you like the best and share them with friends in conversations and interactions with others. Always have an uplifting quote to bring joy to the day.

The most important thing you can do is surround yourself with positive people. Find others who encourage you and support your ideas. Learn from those who are a few steps ahead of you and gain insight and knowledge from them. Eliminate the naysayers and spend less time with those that don't support your dreams. We all need cheerleaders and mentors, find yours.

Wake up early for 'you' time: To pray, meditate, and/or plan your day.

Take time in the morning to pray to your Higher Power and give thanks for all that you have. An attitude of gratitude and humility go a long way and bring forth something bigger for yourself by using your great gifts.

Meditation allows you to connect with and hear the deep desires of your inner self. Find a sylte of meditation that works for you and commit to it. Even 15 minutes a day makes a huge difference. Anyone can find 15 minutes in their day to give themselves this gift.

Set daily habits and constant routines and see how much more you accomplish. A planned out day yields a productive one.

Measure your growth and always celebrate your accomplishments.

Maynard Neal — United States
Speaker, Author, Real Estate Broker, CEO of NERG Global inc.
www.MaynardNeal.com
www.NergRealEstate.com
 MaynardNealMentor
 MaynardNealMentor

IGNITING THE
HUNGER IN ME

Find a quiet space when you do this inner work and turn off your phone! Eliminating distractions and creating space for your awareness is vitally important. You will discover more and hear your deepest desire when you set the stage to truly listen and go within. All of the work you are about to do is meant to show you what that hunger is that lies in you. Every person has their own unique recipe and ingredients that defines their hunger. There are no two alike, and in fact, your passions and aspirations are yours and yours alone. Like the thumbprint you have, your hunger and the many facets that you bring into being are truly special to only you. When we compare, or want to be like someone else, we dim that urge. When we covet or envy, we darken the path before us and look in the wrong direction. Taking the time to find our uniquely divine way reveals a much greater and more meaningful adventure; one filled with the greatest richness of life that we personally desire.

Embark on the questions below in a kind and loving manner with yourself and your inner voice. Be patient, relaxed, and curious to see what transpires for you. When you take the time to ask the right questions and become intrigued to hear the answers, you will be amazed at what unfolds.

"It isn't in watching that makes us feel complete,
it is in doing it ourselves that makes us feel transformed."
~ JB Owen

What were the three top lessons or ideas that I learned from reading the stories that had the most impact on me?

1. _____

_____

_____

_____

2. _____

_____

_____

_____

3. _____

_____

_____

_____

List five things that 'Being Hungry' or 'Having a Hunger Inside' means to you:

1. _____

_____

2. _____

_____

3. _____

_____

4. _____

_____

5. _____

_____

Write out what you really loved doing when you were a kid. When life was simpler and your heart desired something that meant the world to you, what was it? What did you just enjoy doing that no one had to tell you to do?

_____

_____

_____

_____

_____

_____

_____

_____

_____

Do you remember a time or incident when that desire was squashed or diminished? Do you recall how or when that passion was turned off and forgotten? Write out what we call an 'Ignite Moment' that impacted you to let go of the thing you truly wanted to obtain.

_____

_____

_____

_____

_____

_____

_____

_____

You are not a kid anymore, but it is valuable to ask yourself how much of that childhood 'hunger' (that feeling you had as a kid) is still within you. Do you feel it like a tiny whisper inside or is it like a corked volcano wanting to erupt? Many times the desires from our childhood do not go away, but instead lie dormant inside us; buried beneath the practicalities of life. Sometimes, when we are given permission to reawaken those desires, we remember how much they mean to us and the importance they had. We feel inspired to re-ignite them in our current lives when we take the time to listen to them once again.

Take a few moments to revisit the wishes and desires from your childhood and ask yourself how much the hunger for them is still alive.

_____

_____

_____

_____

_____

_____

_____

_____

_____

_____

_____

_____

_____

_____

_____

_____

_____

_____

Knowing if you have residual hunger from the past is vitally important so that you can move on to the Hunger that wants to come forth in you today. Revisiting old desires to see if they still exist makes room for them to either be reawakened or for a new one to take their place. Often we don't have what we desire because we are not clear on what it is. The following exercises are designed to help you gain the clarity you need to truly IGNITE THE HUNGER IN YOU!

What do you LOVE doing?

_____

_____

What would you do even if you were never paid to do it?

_____

_____

What makes you feel complete?

_____

_____

What talents are you innately good at?

_____

_____

What gifts do you long to bring forth to the world?

_____

_____

When do you most feel as though you are deeply contributing to others?

_____

_____

What do you want to be known for?

_____

_____

What dreams do you most want to achieve?

_____

_____

If you could do anything without limitations and you knew you would be a success, what would it be?

_____

_____

If you were to be magnificently obsessed with something, willing to go full-out, knowing it wants you as much as you want it, what would that be?

_____

_____

_____

_____

_____

_____

_____

_____

_____

As soon as we declare what we deeply desire, the Universe hears us. Then, it works magically and devotedly to give us exactly what we want. Knowing that what we focus on we create, what would YOU like to focus on right now in your life? What positive, winning, enjoyable, fun, and fabulous experience would you like to create in your life that you can get ferociously passionate about achieving?

_____

_____

_____

_____

_____

_____

_____

_____

Nothing comes to us without work, effort, and conviction. What new things, skills, knowledge, and training can you acquire that will help you achieve your goals?

_____

_____

_____

_____

_____

_____

_____

_____

What new habits and consistent behaviors can you implement into your life TODAY that will systematically and consistently bring you closer to that which you desire? (Hint: Use the many Action Steps in this book.)

_____

_____

_____

_____

_____

_____

_____

_____

_____

_____

Who do you need to get close to, meet, connect with, and bring into your life to gain wisdom, knowledge, and support from? Imagine people like Les Brown and the top motivational leaders on the planet being in your corner. Think big, bold, and with the knowingness that those people are out there and *want* to help you. List the people that you feel would support you on the path to your dreams. Be it friends, colleagues, teachers, mentors, or even celebrities, no one is off limits to you. Make a dream list of the people you want on your support team and then trust that when the time is right, and you are ready, each and every one of them will appear.

1. _____

2. _____

3. _____

4. _____

5. _____

6. _____

7. _____

8. _____

9. _____

10. _____

This powerful introspection and honest sharing is now the framework you need to go after your dreams and use the hunger inside of you to manifest the life you have always wanted. Read over your answers often and update them as much as you need to keep fueling the fire and rekindling the flames that lie within you. Your greatness is right there ready to come out and Ignite the brilliance in you.

My Commitment To Myself

To achieve anything, including listening to the hunger within you, you need to commit. Creating a commitment contract with yourself will be the make-or-break action you take to follow through and stay with it. Honoring your inner hunger and the fortitude you have within to reach your ambitions will undoubtedly be the key to ensuring you do it. Only you must commit to you! Your actions will reflect your promise to yourself. Staying committed to the Self is an inside job, and in signing a commitment contract with you, you are declaring that no one can take away that impassioned hunger you have except yourself!

I commit to doing everything in my power to Ignite the Hunger in Me each and every day. I listen to my inner voice and connect with the part of me that is devoted to fueling my hunger and feeding it with powerful and inspiring messages, support, and influences. I devote time daily and consistently to fostering my hunger and fuel it with everything it needs. I let go of old ideas and limitations to faithfully discover new ways to Ignite the greatness in me.

I do this wholeheartedly and with love, conviction, caringness, and a deep reverence for who I am, where I am, and what I have at my disposal right now. I work diligently to gain all the knowledge, learning, and training I need to empower myself. I ONLY surround myself with people who support my dream.

This is my promise to myself, and I know in doing this, I will IGNITE THE HUNGER IN ME to achieve ALL my dreams!!!!!

I, (name) _____commit to this promise to Ignite

The Hunger in Me on this day _____, of _____.

_____

Signature

BOOKS AND RESOURCES MEANINGFUL TO THE AUTHORS OF IGNITE THE HUNGER IN YOU

Ashley Patterson
- Tasha Cobbs Leonard - You Know My Name (Live) - YouTube

Chad E. Foster
- ChadEFoster.com/Videos

Erasmo Rivera
- My English Youtube channel Teachable Mindset: https://www.youtube.com/channel/UCuBleAefDils0Qlg6rtR2PA
- My Spanish Youtube channel Empresarios 1.0: https://www.youtube.com/channel/UC1PwyZkWT-0-mMBqf2ufbIg
- My website: www.erasmorivera.net
- Links to my programs: www.erasmoacademy.com
- Tola Faminu Media Productions: www.tolafaminu.com
- Juwealth Digitable Hub: https://juwealth.com.ng/

Ermos Erotocritou
- Yourunleashedpotential.com

Jacki Semerau Tait
- www.StrongSingleMoms.com
- Coaching Program for real estate professionals: RealEstatebyRelationship.com

Jameela Allen
- YouTube: Jameela Allen — On Hiring the Right Staff

Jenise 'Sandy' Todd
- The Holy Bible: King James Bible
- Bowlby, Katie 2019. *So, What Exactly Is a Shotgun House?* Country Living, accessed July 11, 2021, <https://www.countryliving.com/home-design/a29858240/shotgun-house/#

Jessica T. Moore
- *Embracing Imperfections* by Jessica T. Moore

- jessicatmoore.com
- YouTube: The Jessica Moore Show
- Apple and Spotify: The Jessica Moore Show

Jo Dee Baer

- *21 Days to Your Best You* is the first edition of my book and available on Amazon.com
- *The BLean: Lasting Weight Loss* is a second edition of my book and available for purchase from my website: www.healthcoachjodee.com and Amazon.com
- *Green Miracle Drink* can be found under the blog section of my website or by downloading from my homepage: www.healthcoachjodee.com
- *10 Daily Rituals for your AM Routine* eBook: https://www.healthcoach-jodee.com/10-daily-am-rituals-the-ebook-by-health-coach-jo-dee/

Katherine Vrastak

- *The Life You Were Born to Live A Guide to Finding Your Life Purpose* by Dan Millman
- *You Can Heal Your Life* by Louise Hay
- *How to Do the Work: Recognize Your Patterns, Heal from Your Past, and Create Yourself* by Dr. Nicole Lepera, The Holistic Psychologist
- *Rebuilding When Your Relationship Ends* by Bruce Fisher, EDD Robert Alberti, PHD
- Morrnah Simeona - Founder of Ho'oponopono (hooponoponomiracle.com)
- https://youtu.be/QQTtoOBaypw
- https://youtu.be/1JaBnaFfaLo

Marcy Cody, RN

- *90 Ways to Age Vibrantly: A Baby Boomers Devotional Journal* - **www.90WaysToAgeVibrantly.com**
- *Atomic Habits* by James Clear
- *The Longevity Solution* by Dr. James Dinicolantonio and Dr. Jason Fung
- *The Longevity Paradox* by Dr. Steven Gundry
- Roman 8:6, Romans 12: 1-2 and John 21:18 NIV

Maynard Neal

- Late Attorney Elbert Hatchett (The Law Firm of Hatchett, DeWalt, & Hatchett)
- Pastor Elder Robert N Neal (Father)

- Channel 7 WXYZ Detroit 7 Upfront (Planning Editor - Dan Zacharek)
- Toronto Caribbean Newspaper (Chief Reporter, Operations Manager - Simone Jennifer Smith)

Nik Reyno
- YouTube: bit.ly/YourDreamIsPossible_LesBrown
- *What's So Amazing About Grace* by Philip Yancey
- *The 5 Love Languages: The Secret to Love That Lasts* by Gary Chapman
- *The Road Back to You: An Enneagram Journey to Self-Discovery* by Ian Morgan Cron and Suzanne Stabile
- *Hey Babe: What I Wish I Knew Then* by Meghan Robinson
- *Boundaries: When to Say Yes, How to Say No to take Control of Your Life* by Dr. Henry Cloud and Dr. John Townsend
- YouTube: bit.ly/theCallToCourage_BreneBrown

Pat Labez
- *The Dash - Making a Difference with Your Life* by Linda Ellis & Mac Anderson

Patricia Barnes
- Launch your speaking career and improve your public speaking skills with my coach Les Brown at www.hungrytospeak.com
- Personal Development Coach. Sign up at https://gopatty.com/coach/

Rachel Harvey
- *The Prosperity Paradigm* by Steve D'Annunzio
- *Daring Greatly* by Brené Brown
- *Braving the Wilderness* by Brené Brown
- *You Learn by Living* by Eleanor Roosevelt
- *Chasing Excellence* by Ben Bergeron
- *Choosing your Future* Audio Series by Les Brown
- *You've Got to be Hungry* by Les Brown
- *The Power of Purpose* by Les Brown

Dr. Raolee
- DrRao10k.com

Renee L. Cunningham
- The King James Bible

- Les Brown

Shashonee L. Sales
- **Regardless of where you are in your life**, myself, and my team will meet you **EXACTLY** where you are. We are here to transform your level of success!
- Email us at support@shashoneesales.com or go to legendaryfreedom.com
- Enjoy a 7-day Self-Development Program that will help you gain clarity about your purpose, who you are as an individual, and the direction you desire to go in life. https://urlgeni.us/kajabi/selfdevelop

Susan Welton
- "You Are Loved" by Stars Go Dim

Suzanne A. Nakano
- Daily Bible Reading Plans: bible.org, bible.com
- www.suzannenakano.com

Dr. Tyra Good
- Practicing Culturally Sustaining Engagement: https://remakelearning.org/blog/2019/12/12/practicing-culturally-sustaining-engagement/
- Passionate Social Justice Educator: https://www.elms.edu/ceue-director-is-a-passionate-social-justice-educator/
- Teaching Teachers in Haiti: https://www.pulse.chatham.edu/blog-stories/2018/6/20/teaching-teachers-in-haiti?rq=teaching%20teachers
- Deeper Learning Equity Story: https://www.equityfellows.org/apps/pages/index.jsp?uREC_ID=1239631&type=u&pREC_ID=1716141

Dr. Yasmine Saad
- https://madisonparkpsych.com

PHOTOGRAPHY CREDITS

Ashley Montgomery - *Angela Mitchell, Founder of Revelation ALM Studios*
Atul Bhatara - *Nigel Alfred of Nigel Alfred Photography*
Chad Foster - *Roya Ann Miller Photography*

Curtis Ghee - *Floyd Shade of NightShade Images*
Diana Lockett - *Ian Coll*
Erasmo Rivera - *Tola Faminu*
Ermos Erotocritou - *Christina Ghannoum*
Felecia Froe, MD - *Nichole Newton*
Glenn Lundy - *Brandon Randolph, Chief Production Officer*
Holly H. Kalua, RN - *Ronald Vincent Porter*
Jacki Semerau Tait - *Melissa Dunstan*
Jameela Allen - *Jin Kim Studios*
Jo Dee Baer - *Marv Broadrick*
Jenise 'Sandy' Todd - *Nikita Seahorn*
Jessica T. Moore - *Aaron D. Moore*
Katherine Vrastak - *Hailey Kelly*
Marcy Cody, RN - *Yavonka Muhammad*
Pamela Bishop - *Rebecca McGregor Photography*
Patricia Barnes - *Keith Garner Jr*
Pearlette Cassells - *Craig Richards*
Dr. Raolee - *TaraOla*
Renee L. Cunningham - *Arthur Braud*
Rachel Harvey - *Keech Photography*
Shashonee L. Sales - *Shapauni S. Budler*
Stacie Shifflett - *Arianna J. Photography*
Steph Elliott - *Herring Photography*
Susan Welton - *Gravity Photo Company*
Suzanne A. Nakano - *Dwight Okumoto of Studio 3 Photographics*
Dr. Tyra Good - *Leonard Underwood*

AUTHOR DIRECTORY

At Ignite we always want you, the reader, to have the best experience possible, that is why we have made sure you have access to our authors and an easy way to connect.

Using the technology of QR codes you now can immediately find an author using your phone. Just scan the corresponding QR code and instantly be transported to their website or landing page. Find out what they are doing, how to work with them, and how to reach them.

Our authors are here to support you so have fun connecting with them.

Curtis Ghee

Police Officer, Non-Profit President, Speaker, Author, and Life Coach

Helping people unlock their potential and live purposefully

Diana Lockett

Founder of Re-Align to Thrive™ Transformational Coach

I empower individuals to Re-Align to Thrive™ in all areas of their lives

Dr. Raolee

Author, Speaker, Educator and Sickle Cell Gladiator

Inspiring people to change their limiting narrative.

Dr. Yasmine Saad

Top 3 rated NYC Psychologist

I offer holistic psychological services tailored to you

Erasmo Rivera

Motivational Speaker

Motivational Speaker. Themes: Leadership & Personal Growth

Ermos Erotocritou

Performance Coach and Author

Personal and Group Coaching - Unleashing Greatness

Felecia Froe

Founder

We help women learn to invest for multiple streams of income

Holly H. Kalua, BSHA, BSM, RN, CHBC

CoachKalua™ - Relationship Enhancer, Fertility Strategist and Coach

Guides and empowers couples through their fertility journey

Jacki Semerau Tait

Founder/CEO, Strong Single Mom Network

Community, connecting, and coaching for single moms worldwide

Jameela Allen

Childcare Strategic Business Coach, CEO of Themba Creative Learning Center LLC

I teach childcare owners how to operate a profitable center

JB Owen

CEO of Ignite Publishing, JBO Global and Lotus Liners

Publishing, author, and brand managing, book printing, coaching

Jessica T. Moore

Author, Entrepreneur, Transformational Coaching and Women's Empowerment

I help women who have experienced trauma to own their story.

Jo Dee Baer

Certified Health Coach and Holistic Nutritionist A.B.D.

Alternative Health and Nutritional Consulting

Jocelyn McClure

Counselor

Christian Counseling

Katherine Vrastak

CEO Sacred Roots Coaching

One-on-one and group sessions on how to reach forgiveness

Marcy Cody, RN

Holistic Longevity Coach

One-on-one and group longevity coaching with accountability group

Maynard Neal

Author, Real Estate Broker, Coach, Motivational Speaker

Helping Individuals Overcome Mental Barriers in the Mind.

Nik Reyno

Artist, Speaker, Author, Coach

Interpersonal Intelligence Training and Motivational Speaking

Pat Labez

Third Act Encore

I help seniors amplify their joy in their Third Act of life.

Patricia Barnes

Personal Development Coach

One-on-one coaching and strategy/consult calls for goal setting

Pearlette Cassells

Author, Speaker, Productivity Coach

I help busy people save time and get things done.

Renee L Cunningham

CEO of the Polished Experience

I specialize in personal leadership development

Shashonee L. Sales

Life and Business Coach

Digital marketing and coaching is what I do.

Stacie Shifflett

Founder and CEO Modern Consciousness

Helping you live consciously and joyfully in a modern world

Steph Elliott

Coach

Intuitive coach that offers one-on-one and group coaching sessions

Susan Welton

Founder of Warrior of Light Healing

After betrayal and traumas I teach people how to Trust.

Suzanne A. Nakano

President, Suzanne Nakano Realty, Inc.

Encourager, Real Estate Investment Advisor, Dream-Releaser

Rachel Harvey
Fearless Progress
Relationship coaching, organizational coaching, and retreats

Ashley Montgomery
International Motivational Speaker, Public Figure
Leadership Corporate Training, Business Consulting

Chad Foster
President
Motivational Speaking, Resilience/Leadership Coaching

Jenise Todd
CEO of OMG Xpressions & More LLC
Greeting cards, journals, t-shirts, canvases, mugs, pillows

Dr. Tyra Good
University Professor and Education Consultant
Curriculum & Professional Learning Design; Speaker

Pamela Bishop
On Purpose with Pam
Take that first step to discover your purpose! On purpose!

Ashley Patterson
Founder and CEO
Business Consulting

Atul Bhatara
AtulSkincare
Founder and CEO

THANK YOU

A tremendous thank you goes to all those on the IGNITE team who have been working tirelessly in the background teaching, editing, supporting, and encouraging the authors. They are some of the most genuine and heart-centered people I know. Their dedication to the vision of IGNITE, along with their integrity and the message they convey, is of the highest caliber possible. They each want you to find your Ignite Moment and flourish. They all believe in you, and that's what makes them so outstanding. Their dream is for your dreams to come true.

Production Team: JB Owen, Dania Zafar, Peter Giesin, Katie Smetherman, and Liana Khabibullina

Editing Team: Alex Blake, Chloe Holewinski, and Michiko Couchman

Project Leader: Diana Lockett

A special thanks and gratitude to the entire team for their support behind the scenes and for going 'above and beyond' to make this a wonderful experience. Their dedication made sure that everything ran smoothly and with elegance.

A deep appreciation also goes to each and every author who made *Ignite The Hunger in You* possible. It is your powerful and inspiring stories, along with your passion and desire to help others that will Ignite a hunger within each and every one of us.

To all our readers, we thank you for reading and cherishing our stories; for opening your hearts and minds to the idea of igniting your own lives. We welcome you to share your story and become a new author in one of our upcoming books. Your message and your Ignite Moment may be exactly what someone else needs to read. Readers become authors and we want to be that for you.

Thank you for being a part of the magical journey of IGNITE!

WRITE YOUR STORY
IN AN IGN TE BOOK!

THE ROAD TO SHARING YOUR MESSAGE AND BECOMING A BEST-SELLING AUTHOR BEGINS RIGHT HERE.

We make YOU a best-selling author in just four months!

If you have a story of perseverance, determination, growth, awakening, and change... and you've felt the power of your Ignite Moment, we'd love to hear from you.

We are always looking for motivating stories that will make a difference in someone's life. Our enjoyable, four-month writing process is like no other — and the best thing about IGNITE is community of outstanding, like-minded individuals dedicated to helping others.

With over 700 amazing individuals to date writing their stories and sharing their Ignite mome we are positively impacting the planet and raising the vibration of HUMANITY. Our stories ins and empower others and we want to add your story to one of our upcoming books!

Go to our website, click How To Get Started, and share a bit of your Ignite transformation

JOIN US TO IGNITE A BILLION LIVES WITH A BILLION WORDS.

Apply at: www.igniteyou.life/apply   Find out more at: www.igniteyou.li

Inquire at: info@igniteyou.life